The First Ladies

★ ★ ★ ★ ★ ★ ★ ★ ★ ★

The First Ladies

★ ★ ★ ★ ★ ★ ★ ★ ★ ★

by Sol Barzman

COWLES BOOK COMPANY, INC.
NEW YORK

For Belle

★ *Acknowledgments* ★

The writing of a book is often a lonely and frustrating venture. To my good fortune, my long months of work on this project were relieved by the fascination of the material and by the kindness and cooperation of many people, most of whom I had never met. I trust the listing of their names will indicate, in small measure, my gratitude to all of them. My thanks go, firstly, to a number of libraries and their personnel: Miss Helen Ruskell, of the New York Society Library, and her ever cheerful and helpful staff; Mrs. Walter Hoskins, of The Joint Free Public Library of Morristown and Morris Township, N.J.; Mr. Joseph Swartz, of the New York Historical Society Reference Library; to the entire staff of the Genealogy Room, New York Public Library, Main Branch. My thanks also to Laurence Gouverneur Hoes, president, The James Monroe Memorial Foundation; to Mrs. Ethel M. Wetzel, personal secretary to Mrs. Dwight D. Eisenhower; and to Mrs. Lucy Winchester, social secretary to Mrs. Richard M. Nixon.

Four people were particularly helpful, and to all of them I am especially grateful: S. D. Ehrenpreis, associate professor (History), Bronx Community College, C.U.N.Y., for his careful reading of my manuscript and his corrections and suggestions (any inaccuracies or misjudgments that remain are my sole responsibility); my good friend Bud Hollzer for the long hours of listening and clarifying; Miss Adelaide Farah of the Cowles Editorial Department for her invaluable support and help in the final and crucial phases; and

vii

ACKNOWLEDGMENTS

to my wife, Belle Barzman, for contributions that cannot be measured. She was my diligent research assistant, perceptive critic, tireless typist, and somehow, through it all, mother to our two daughters.

There is one final acknowledgment. I first met Robert Meskill some years ago, when he was an editor for the now defunct *American* magazine. But I did not really get to know him until we began working together on this project early in 1969. I was most fortunate to have him as my editor, for he was a man of gentleness, taste, and discrimination. To an author enduring the pains of his first book, Robert Meskill's tact and encouragement were essential. I think he would have been proud of the finished product, but he did not live to see the result of his patient work and guidance. After an illness of two weeks, he died on January 6, 1970, at the age of fifty-one.

S. B.

★ Contents ★

CONTENTS

★ *Preface* ★

When Franklin Delano Roosevelt was four years old, he was taken to the White House to visit Grover Cleveland. Mr. Cleveland, then serving his first term as Chief Executive, said to the boy, "I wish for you that you may never be President."

It was a curious wish, for it had already become a popular legend that any native-born American boy could grow up to be President. Perhaps few gave it serious consideration, for only an elite handful have served as Chief Executive, but there must have been those who nevertheless dreamed of it, as others dreamed of becoming a fireman, or a policeman, or a doctor.

Some Presidents reached the White House by hard work and design; others by accident. It is probable that no First Lady set out, in her girlhood, to become mistress of the Executive Mansion. It may be that a few of them realized, later in life, that the White House was indeed within their reach, and perhaps their prodding, gentle or otherwise, may have pushed their husbands along the path that eventually led to the Presidency.

The backgrounds of our thirty-six Presidents, and of their wives, are as divergent as is the geography of the United States. But as varied as are the presidential beginnings, so are the accomplishments. Many Presidents served with distinction. Others had little to offer either to their country or to history. Yet all our Presidents, good or bad, had one thing in common—they became public property the moment they were elected. The presidential families no longer had private lives; whatever they did was closely followed by the entire country and chronicled in detail while the President served, and often beyond his term.

But how much is known or remembered today about the First Ladies, particularly those who lived in the eighteenth and nineteenth centuries? The country may have known a great deal about them when they were alive; for the most part now they are forgotten, or rarely mentioned anywhere, except as a biographical footnote.

Our First Ladies have been as different from one another as our Presidents have been. Some of them had humble beginnings; others, like the original First Families, were born into wealth and prominence. Most of them had little to do with shaping the political doctrine of the country, yet all of them may have had a great deal to do with shaping their husbands' personalities and philosophies. It will be helpful, therefore, to examine the human aspects of the Presidency, for our Presidents must be subject to the same personal stresses and strains as the rest of us, although in different measure.

We think of our Presidents as being superior, as if there is a mysterious alchemy that suddenly transforms them on Inauguration Day. We expect and hope they will rise above the daily tensions that beset the ordinary citizen, and often they do. Yet they cannot entirely remove themselves from the impact of their family relationships, and it is in this context that we examine the lives of those most intimately involved with the Presidents—our First Ladies.

Who were these women? How did they respond to their husbands, to the Presidency, and to their times? What effect, if any, did they have upon the country, and upon history?

Tragedy was no stranger to the First Ladies, nor were turmoil and despair. But they knew happiness as well, and contentment. Behind the scenes, and sometimes in them, they moved, manipulated, and served their husbands and their nation. Some of them made no lasting impression on their own times, or on the times to come. Yet each First Lady, in her own way, did have something of herself to offer to her country.

NEW YORK CITY   SOL BARZMAN
MARCH, 1970

Martha Washington
1732–1802

In 1759, when George Washington married Martha Dandridge
Custis, the Western world was in turmoil. England was at war with
most of continental Europe; American Indians were ravaging the
boundaries and border settlements of the thirteen royal colonies.
The struggle for control of Canada, a bitter contest between England and France, was rapidly reaching a climax. Though no one
was aware of it at the time, the coming victory of the English in
Canada would ultimately affect the fate of the entire North American continent.

The thirteen colonies, still outwardly loyal to the Crown, were
beginning to stir. Restiveness was evident in Virginia, home of the
Washingtons, the Custises, and the Dandridges. The Virginians
had become prosperous through the cultivation of tobacco and the
importation of slaves, who made it possible for a relative handful
of plantation owners to amass their wealth with the cheapest of all

1

labor sources. But the tobacco had to be shipped directly to England and exchanged there for the staple goods the colonies were not permitted to manufacture. The aristocratic Virginians, like many of the other American colonists, preferred to have more control over their own affairs. What would later become the American Revolution was beginning to ferment in the small discontents of the 1750s.

George Washington had, by this time, become somewhat of a hero. At the age of twenty-two, he had been commissioned a major in the Virginia militia. Despite his youth, the appointment was well deserved for he had been instructed in basic military technique by a British Adjutant, and more importantly, he was a "gentleman," son of a man who had been a wealthy and prominent plantation owner.

Washington participated in two campaigns against the French, most notably with British General Edward Braddock on the Monongahela River in a section of the wilderness that is now a suburb of Pittsburgh. The Monongahela battle, in which Braddock lost his life, took place in 1755. It was a defeat for the British, but somehow George Washington managed to emerge triumphant. Racked by dysentery, weak with pain and suffering, he was barely able to stay upright on his horse. He was the only officer on Braddock's staff who had not been killed or severely wounded, so it was left to him, despondent and agonized by his illness, to lead the battered remnants of Braddock's troops back to the safety of Virginia and a hero's welcome. His fellow Virginians rewarded his resourcefulness and military know-how with an appointment as commander-in-chief of all their militia. It was a remarkable honor to bestow upon a loser.

There is some difference of opinion among Washington biographers as to the exact date and circumstances of the first meeting between George Washington and Martha Dandridge Custis. In one romanticized version, the historic encounter took place in 1758 at the home of friends, when Martha was a widow. Washington, on his way to Williamsburg for treatment of an attack of dysentery, supposedly made a long detour on horseback just to meet her. Another biographer, utilizing the same incident, tells us "the hero was charmed—nay spellbound, by the beauty of the person and the fascinating manners and good sense of the young widow." It is much more likely that Washington and Martha met while her husband was still alive, during the 1757 social season in Williamsburg, where Washington was serving as a burgess.

There is some confusion as well about Martha's actual age. Her date of birth is often given as May 2, 1732. According to the Dandridge family Bible, she was born on "June 2, 1731, between 12 and 1 o'clock." As for Washington, it has been definitely established he was born in February of 1732, thus making him eight months younger than Martha.

Little is known of Martha's early life. She was born in New Kent County, Virginia. Her mother was Frances Jones and her father Colonel John Dandridge, owner of a small plantation. In terms of the Virginia landed aristocracy, he was not a wealthy man, but he was nevertheless accepted by other plantation owners as more or less of an equal, so it was inevitable that Martha would, in time, meet and marry a rich man.

Martha had little formal schooling, as illustrated by the following excerpt from instructions she wrote to her London agents in 1758: ". . . I have sent a night gound to be dide of an fashonob Corler fitt for me to ware and beg you would have it dide better that I sent Las year that was very badly don this gound is of a good Lenght for me."

Despite her poor education, Martha was adept at "stitchery" and proficient at the spinet, so she had enough of the necessary social graces to justify her future role as mistress of a Virginia mansion.

She met Daniel Parke Custis in 1749, when he was thirty-seven and she was eighteen. He had waited a long time to take a wife; his wealthy and eccentric father, Colonel John Custis, had himself had an unhappy and disastrous marriage, and consistently refused

3

to sanction marriage for his son. Daniel, as his father's heir apparent, would do nothing to jeopardize his legacy, and patiently waited for the right moment.

That moment came when Daniel met Martha; somehow, the crusty old gentleman relented, and even though her family were far from being Custis peers, he did approve of her. Martha and Daniel married in June of 1749.

That same year, in a fit of pique, Colonel Custis made a will leaving his entire estate to a young Negro slave by the name of Jack. Fortunately for Daniel and Martha, and eventually for George Washington, the old gentleman was persuaded to write a new will in Daniel's favor. As if by prearrangement, he passed away exactly eight days later, on November 22, 1749.

Daniel and Martha moved to a plantation on the Pamunkey River, into a home they called "The White House." There, four children were born to them. Two of them, Daniel Parke, Jr., and Frances Parke, died in early childhood of unspecified causes. Death, at any age, was common in colonial times, so the deaths of the Custis babies were not unusual enough to warrant special mention in history. Of the other two children, John Parke (Jacky) Custis was born in 1754, and Martha Parke Custis (referred to by everyone as "Patsy") was born in 1756.

On July 8, 1757, Daniel Parke Custis, forty-five, died of apparent heart failure. Martha was then twenty-six.

Martha inherited all of her husband's considerable holdings—more than seventeen thousand acres of tobacco land and tenant farms, fisheries, 150 slaves, "The White House," and thirty thousand pounds sterling. By anyone's reckoning, she was a wealthy young widow—a good catch for an ambitious Virginia aristocrat, especially one with great plans but short of the necessary funds to bring his dreams to fruition.

Such a man was George Washington, who had inherited Mount Vernon from his half-brother Lawrence. Lawrence had died of tuberculosis at a young age. He had left Mount Vernon to his widow, with the stipulation that it was to pass on to George after her death, but she remarried and gladly permitted her former brother-in-law to acquire the estate by default. The house at that time had eight rooms; the land around it consisted of some two thousand acres, much of it uncultivated.

It would not be entirely correct to suggest that Washington's sole purpose in wooing the widow Custis was to gain control of her fortune. Many young men of his day did marry for exactly that reason, and such marriages were considered proper and justified. Whatever Washington's motives, it is known he came to visit her at "The White House" soon after he learned of her husband's death.

It is also known that Martha was far from being his first choice for a wife, or was ever his real love. When he was in his teens, he met and fell in love with a married woman named Sally Fairfax. She was two years older than he, but this difference in their ages did not deter him, nor did the fact that she was already married.

Many historians refuse to acknowledge that George was actually in love with Sally and stayed hopelessly in love with her for many years. Some of them go to great pains to establish that Washington felt only a great affection and friendship for Sally, not physical love or passion. Perhaps so. Yet Douglas Southall Freeman, who wrote a definitive biography of Washington, makes this admission: "That he was in love with the wife of his nearest neighbor, even after his engagement to Martha Custis, scarcely can be denied."

Martha and Sally were dissimilar in a number of ways. Sally was tall, slim, sophisticated; Martha was short, approaching plumpness, and much more interested in homemaking than in world-building. According to some sources Martha was beautiful, and she may have been, for colonial times. By modern criteria, Sally was far more attractive. Martha's nose was much too long, her mouth too small, and her round face undistinguished, except for her hazel eyes, which were warm and quite lovely.

Martha and George were married on January 6, 1759. The site of the ceremony is disputed; some authorities believe it to be St.

Peter's Church in New Kent County while others insist it took place at "The White House" on Martha's plantation. Wherever it was held, the wedding was a colorful affair, replete with scarlet and gold uniforms, white satin waistcoats, gold buckles, silver trimmings, and powdered wigs. The twenty-seven-year-old bride wore a white satin quilted petticoat, a heavy corded white silk overshirt, high-heeled shoes of white satin and diamond buckles, and various pearl ornaments. In the wedding cavalcade, she and her three bridesmaids occupied a "coach drawn by six horses, guided by liveried black postilions, while Colonel Washington, upon his magnificent horse, richly caparisoned, attended by a brilliant cortege of gay and cultured gentlemen, rode by the side of his beautiful bride." The Washingtons spent a three-month honeymoon in her Williamsburg home, "The Six Chimneys," and then moved with her children to Mount Vernon.

The early years at Mount Vernon seem to have been pleasant. With the help of Martha's fortune, which, by law, had now come under Washington's supervision, he became a wealthy tobacco planter and landowner. He was a resourceful manager, and a first-rate administrator. The mansion and the plantation were gradually enlarged; more and more guests, true to colonial custom, dropped in for a casual visit or extended stay. The Washingtons, despite his taciturnity and Martha's lack of worldliness, were apparently popular. The main house, even then, was graciously attractive, with spacious and well-tended grounds.

Martha was not a sparkling conversationalist. She had read almost no books during her lifetime, and was not the least interested in literature or world affairs. But she was an earnest and friendly woman who charmed her visitors and made them feel at home. A thorough housekeeper (she kept a bunch of keys hanging at her side), she was becoming famous throughout the Virginia plantation counties as an exemplary hostess and magnificent cook. She exhibited a fondness for collecting recipes, and other women made a point of requesting copies.

About a year after their marriage, in January, 1760, an event occurred that may have had a profound effect upon both Washingtons. As George noted in his diary: "Mrs. Washington broke out with the Meazles." It has been suggested this illness may have been responsible for her sudden barrenness. Whatever the reason, she and George never had children.

Life on the plantation was not always carefree and easy-going. Despair and sadness all too frequently visited the Washingtons with word that a relative or friend had passed away. Such a time of grief came for them in 1773, when Martha's daughter, Patsy, was seventeen. She had always been a sickly child, subject to "fitts," which must have been epilepsy. Martha had carefully shielded the child from birth, but like so many others in colonial times, she was helpless in the face of disease. On the twentieth of June, 1773, in Washington's words, Patsy "was siezed with one of her usual Fits, & expired in it, in less than two minutes without uttering a word, a groan, or scarce a sigh."

Patsy's place in the household was fortunately filled by Martha's new daughter-in-law, the former Eleanor "Nelly" Calvert, who married Martha's son, Jacky Custis, when he was eighteen. Martha, still grief-stricken at Patsy's death, did not attend the wedding, but sent a motherly greeting to the newest member of her family. "MY DEAR NELLY,—God took from Me a daughter when June Roses were blooming—He has now given me another daughter, about Her age when Winter winds are blowing, to warm my Heart again."

Through the war years of the American Revolution, Martha spent every winter with Washington, enduring the hardship of colonial travel and rigors of camp life. Beginning with the winter of 1775, and continuing into 1783, she made the long and hazardous trip by horse and carriage from Mount Vernon to her husband's various headquarters, including Valley Forge.

But Martha did not complain, despite the strain of the war and the absences of her husband. She was terrified of gunfire, yet she could cheerfully say she "preferred the sound of fifes and drums . . . to any music that was ever heard." Her presence was always a calming influence for Washington, who had his share of problems

7

and enemies. One French volunteer found her "small and fat . . . dressed very plainly and her manners simple in all respects"; to another "she well deserved to be the companion and friend of the greatest man of the age."

In the early winter of 1781, personal tragedy struck once again at Martha. Her son, Jacky, twenty-seven, died of "camp fever." A few weeks earlier, Jacky, who had done nothing constructive with his life except to marry and live on the money his father had left him, impulsively decided he must be a soldier; joining his step-father's staff, he journeyed with Washington and his troops for the showdown battle with General Cornwallis at Yorktown. During the siege of Yorktown, Jacky became ill, a victim of a disease endemic to colonial encampments, a severe dysentery often referred to as "bloody Phlux." Those who were sturdy enough managed to survive it, but Jacky had neither the physique nor the stamina to withstand the onslaught; he died in November, soon after Cornwallis surrendered.

Jacky left a wife and four children. George and Martha promptly adopted the two youngest—Eleanor Parke Custis and George Washington Parke Custis. Jacky's widow later remarried, but her two youngest continued to live with George and Martha Washington, their adoptive parents.

With the end of the war in 1783, Martha was hopeful that George's service to his country would no longer be demanded. By 1789, the fledgling republic badly needed a popular figure who could bind together the divided leaders of the new states. The only possible choice for the task was George Washington, whose years of soldiering under the most difficult of conditions had taught him to lead and create unity from disorder.

Martha had little desire to leave Mount Vernon to be the new First Lady of the land. But once again she journeyed north, as she so often had in the past, this time to New York, where the first capital of the United States was established.

Her career as First Lady was not particularly distinguished, although she did institute a series of Friday night receptions, rather stiff affairs that ended promptly at 9 P.M., when Martha and the President retired for the night. The receptions were later extended to 10 P.M., after the capital was moved to Philadelphia, but the additional hour did not add to their luster or excitement.

Washington's personal popularity unquestionably was reflected in the warmth accorded Martha's appearances in public. Plump, double-chinned, addicted to frilly lace caps and bonnets, she was neither elegant nor glamorous, nor was she the picture of a queen, as some had earlier feared she might become. Yet she was always treated as if she were in truth the Grand First Lady of the land; she was often referred to as Lady Washington. Abigail Adams, wife of the Vice President, was deeply impressed by Martha. "Her manners are modest and unassuming," wrote Mrs. Adams, "dignified and feminine, not the tincture of Ha'ture about her. . . . A most becoming pleasantness sits upon her countenance. . . ."

Martha and George had two years of privacy still left to them when he completed his second term in office. In 1797, he refused to run for a third term (a precedent which lasted until 1940), and the Washingtons retired at last to Mount Vernon. But their retirement was pitifully short. Washington died two years later, on December 14, 1799, as the result of a severe cold (diagnosed by his doctors as "quinsy," a form of tonsillitis) complicated by numerous bleedings, a popular colonial therapy. He was sixty-nine.

Martha's death followed his by two and a half years. She had lived quietly at Mount Vernon, remembered by some and forgotten by others. In a land eager for growth, Lady Washington was "an echo of a past generation." A Rev. Manasseh Cutler, visiting her early in 1802, wrote his impressions: "Mrs. Washington appears much older than when I last saw her in Philadelphia . . . [but] very little wrinkled and remarkably fair for a person of her years. . . . She spoke of the General with great affection, and observed that, though she had many favors and mercies, for which she desired to bless God, she felt as if she was become a stranger among her friends, and could welcome the time when she should be called to follow her deceased friend."

After an illness of seventeen days, during which she suffered recurring attacks of a "malignant bilious fever," Martha Washington died on May 22, 1802, at the age of seventy-one. She and Washington are buried side by side in a vault at Mount Vernon, at the foot of the Vineyard Enclosure. They had spent forty eventful and historically memorable years together.

Abigail Adams
1744–1818

The presidential years of John Adams were marked by political contrasts. Under George Washington, the Presidency and the government stabilized. When Washington declined to run again, the country's leaders separated into two parties, Alexander Hamilton's Federalists, who believed in a strong central government, and Thomas Jefferson's Democratic-Republicans, who fought for states' rights and the rights of the common man against the aristocratic vested interests represented by Alexander Hamilton's group.

In Europe, France became a republic. On July 14, 1789, the French citizenry seized control of their country, to the wild delight of their American counterparts. When Adams was inaugurated second President, the American temper changed. France, governed by an ambitious five-man Directoire, seemed anxious to rule the world, and cast covetous eyes upon the American territory still owned by Spain and upon French Canada, which they had earlier lost to the British. On the seas, French military ships waged a small, undeclared war with American vessels. The situation, fanned by the angry demands of much of the American population for a show of independence against the French encroachments, could easily have led to an all-out war with France, but Adams, by adroit statesmanship, avoided the final confrontation. By the time his term ended, the threat of war with France had dissipated.

Despite his success in averting war, John Adams was never a popular figure. He was disliked by his associates and by his own party. A devoted public servant, he was blunt, aloof, and temperamental.

During his many long years in government, Adams made more enemies than friends, but always served his country with a high sense of duty. His career and his accomplishments are the more notable because of the extraordinary woman he married in 1764, Abigail Smith. Self-taught, she was brilliant, perceptive, and, on occasion, opinionated to the point of blind prejudice. She exerted much influence upon her husband, subtly, sometimes openly, during their fifty-four years together. John Adams may have been our second President, but Abigail was indeed, as many have claimed, our first "Mrs. President."

Abigail was not yet eighteen when she decided she would marry John Adams; he was twenty-six. She lived in a parsonage in Weymouth, Massachusetts, where she had been born on November 11, 1744. Her mother was Elizabeth Quincy, and her father was the Reverend William Smith. Abigail was the second eldest of their three daughters and one son.

Like Martha Washington, Abigail had no formal education. Her later development becomes all the more remarkable when one realizes that she never went to school. Credit for Abigail's training and intellectual growth must go to her maternal grandparents, Colonel John Quincy and his wife, the former Elizabeth Norton. Abigail spent many summers with them at their home in Mount Wollaston, Massachusetts. They encouraged her to use their extensive library, and it was from them she developed her taste for intensive reading. Her spelling was not always perfect, but this was a common failing in her day.

From the beginning, Abigail's mother made it all too apparent she was not enthusiastic about John Adams. Her family and her husband's family, the Quincys and the Smiths, were among the most distinguished in Massachusetts. John Adams, a struggling lawyer, had no aristocratic ancestors. Though the first of his family had arrived in Braintree, Massachusetts, in 1638, the Adamses had become neither notable nor wealthy.

Mrs. Smith saw little of value in the prim and humorless young man. In her eyes, he was short not only in stature but in future, despite the Harvard education he had managed to acquire. But John and Abigail were in love, much in love, and were willing to outwait her. Outwait her they did, for she finally gave them her blessing, two years later, and they were married on October 25, 1764. Abigail was then twenty, and John was twenty-nine.

Abigail, like John, was short, but where he ran to plumpness (he was a round little man when he became President in 1797), she was slim. She was rightfully proud of her figure, retained, more or less, through the bearing of five children.

In John's eyes, Abigail was beautiful, but in truth, she was far from that. Yet, despite the resolute and austere character of her face, Abigail was most attractive when she smiled, for she was a warm, companionable, and friendly person. Puritanical as John in her thinking, Abigail nevertheless knew how to enjoy her life and to make the most of it.

After their wedding, which took place in Weymouth, John established his new bride in the small house at Braintree inherited from his father, next to the larger house where he had been born and raised. From the beginning, the marriage seems to have been an auspicious one; Abigail quickly became pregnant, and John's fortunes took a dramatic turn for the better. He attracted much attention with his opposition to the notorious Stamp Act of 1765, and his law practice flourished.

Their first daughter, Abigail, was born on July 14, 1765; two years later, July 11, 1767, their first son, John Quincy, was born; Susanna followed him by a year and a half, on December 28, 1768; on May 29, 1770, Charles was born; and their last child, Thomas Boylston, was born on September 15, 1772. Only four lived to maturity; Susanna, always a sickly child, died on February 4, 1770, at the age of fourteen months.

Abigail's first genuine test of loyalty to her husband came later in 1770, when Adams chose to defend eight British soldiers and their captain, accused of murdering five American citizens in the Boston Massacre of March 5, 1770. John felt the soldiers had acted properly, in line of duty, and had been provoked into firing by an unruly mob. From the beginning, sentiment against Adams was bitter and acrimonious, but Abigail supported him completely. His defense was based upon legalisms; Abigail agreed with his reasoning, for, like her husband, she preferred the intellectual solution rather than the emotional. John's defense proved correct; all nine of the men were acquitted, except for two who received minor punishment, a branding on the thumb.

During the years of the Revolution, Adams was frequently away from home and it was left to Abigail to raise and educate their four children, and to manage their farm, which had grown into sizable acreage. It was Abigail's common sense and skill in administering their funds that made it possible for them to live comfortably after John retired from public service.

Examination of Abigail's letters written in the 1770s reveals that she was a strong advocate of independence for America. In one of her more noteworthy quotes, she wrote the following to John: ". . . A people may let a king fall, yet still remain a people; but if a king let his people slip from him, he is no longer a king. And as this is most certainly our case, why not proclaim to the world, in decisive terms, your own importance?"

Adams apparently agreed with her, for he began openly to work and argue for independence. He served with the Continental Congress and urged the appointment of George Washington as commander-in-chief of the American revolutionary forces. In June,

1776, John was appointed by the Second Continental Congress to a committee of five to prepare a Declaration of Independence from the British Crown (the first draft was written by Thomas Jefferson). The final draft was voted on July 4, 1776, and John Adams became one of the fifty-six signers.

In 1778, he was sent to France on a special mission on behalf of his young and struggling country. He took with him John Quincy, who was then eleven. Separated by an ocean, Abigail's first thoughts were of her husband, rather than her son. On March 8, 1778, she wrote to John: " 'Tis a little more than three weeks since the dearest of friends and tenderest of husbands left his solitary partner, and quitted all the fond endearments of domestic felicity for the dangers of the sea. . . ."

For the next six years, John and Abigail were apart, while he served his country in the capitals of France, Holland, and England. During that time, Abigail retained her sense of stability, though she missed her husband intensely. She worked for their farm and worked on the education of their children. She even taught them Latin, which she had first to teach to herself.

Finally, in 1784, Abigail sailed to Europe to join her husband and John Quincy. She placed the younger boys, Charles and Thomas Boylston, in a school in Haverhill, Massachusetts. She took her daughter and two servants with her to London, where she met John and John Quincy after a dreary crossing that lasted a month.

Abigail spent four years in Europe, in Paris and London. As the wife of a diplomat, she met and entertained many important people in both capitals. She did her best to like the people and the cities, and she partially succeeded. But she was never completely at ease anywhere else than in her native New England. The Puritan in her disapproved of the immoralities and "indecent" clothing of the French and English.

As a diplomat, John had to entertain frequently, and Abigail was expected to wear a new gown for every occasion. Congress was none too generous with John's salary or allowance, and they lacked the private means enjoyed by other diplomats. It was a long struggle to keep up appearances.

In 1785, the Continental Congress selected John to be the first American minister to the Court of St. James in London, and he moved his family from Paris to England. His appointment was not greeted with universal acceptance by the English. A leading London newspaper editorialized: "An Ambassador from America! Good heavens what a sound!" But a complete American legation was established in London, in spite of the sneers.

One of the secretaries to the legation was a thirty-year-old American named Colonel William Smith. Twenty-year-old daughter Abigail, trying to recover from a frustrated love affair broken up by her disapproving parents, was easy prey for the gallant and handsome Colonel Smith. Her mother and father, while not overjoyed at the match, preferred him to the other man, whom they considered a wastrel and unstable. (Ironically, the man they rejected, Royall Tyler, later became a most distinguished American jurist, and Chief Justice of the Supreme Court of Vermont.) Colonel Smith and daughter Abigail were married in June, 1786. A year later, the Smiths had a son, and John and Mother Abigail were grandparents. Abigail was then forty-two years old.

In 1788, Adams resigned his position as minister to England and the family returned to the United States. Nine months later, he was elected Vice President of his country. George Washington was a unanimous choice as the first President of the United States. Of the other candidates, Adams received the largest number of votes, thirty-four out of sixty-nine, enough under the newly established regulations to make him the Vice President. Adams was never completely happy in his secondary role. He belittled the Vice-Presidency, calling it "the most insignificant office that was the invention of man," but he was probably the best Vice President our country has ever known.

Abigail frequently found herself in the position of defending her husband's good name. Whenever the occasion demanded, Abigail made the most of her literate and acid pen in defense of

John Adams and his policies. As she was to write, when her husband had become President: "I expected to be vilified and abused, with my whole Family when I came into this situation. Strickly to addhere to our duty, and keep ourselves unprejuced, is the path before us. . . ." She attacked her husband's associates as well as his foes. When Alexander Hamilton plotted, in 1797, to deprive Adams of the Presidency, Abigail wrote that Hamilton was "ambitious as Julius Caesar, a subtle intriguer. . . ."

Hamilton's plot did not succeed, and Adams was elected President by a narrow margin over Thomas Jefferson, who became Vice President. During the four years Adams served as President, from 1797 to 1801, the public abuse continued; Abigail as well as John suffered the slings and arrows of outraged citizens. It was during this period that she was often referred to as "Mrs. President," for it was a widely held belief that many of President Adams' decisions had been influenced by Abigail. One, in particular, unquestionably bore her mark. It proved to be a political blunder.

Abigail bitterly resented the newspapers of the day who were waging an editorial campaign of vilification against President Adams. She strongly supported the Alien and Sedition Acts of 1798 and urged Adams to lend his support as well. There were four acts in all—the first three aimed at aliens, and the fourth directed against political opposition to the party in control (which just happened to be John Adams' Federalists). Reaction against the acts, especially the fourth, came from all sections of the country, often in violent form. The extreme unpopularity of the acts contributed to Adams' failure to win reelection to a second term as President, and led to the downfall and eventual disappearance from the political scene of the once-powerful Federalists.

Another source of public indignation against the Adams administration was nepotism, which John and Abigail developed to a fine degree. An especial target of outrage was President Adams' appointment of their bankrupt son-in-law, Colonel William Smith, to various governmental posts.

Of their three sons, Charles was a major disappointment. He

and his two brothers had been educated at Harvard, but unlike John Quincy, who was already devoting his life to government service, Charles had no real direction. He had married Sally Smith, Colonel William Smith's sister, despite his father's disapproval and stern warnings against marriage without financial security. Though Charles was practicing law, he gave no evidence of succeeding.

Perhaps because of his inability to adjust to the rigorous Adams standards, Charles became an alcoholic. Abigail visited him in New York in November of 1800, and reported the following in a letter to her sister Mary Cranch: ". . . I found my poor unhappy son . . . laid upon a Bed of sickness, destitute of a home. A distressing cough, an affection of the liver and a dropsy will soon terminate a Life, which might have been made valuable to himself and others."

Her prognosis was sadly correct. Charles died on November 30, 1800, chiefly from cirrhosis of the liver.

Abigail herself was not well. Through the years she had suffered intermittently from rheumatic aches. Even as a child she had been subject to many colds; as an adult, she had to endure the pain and discomfort of frequent attacks of "rheumatick." When the Executive Mansion in Washington City was finally ready to receive its first occupants, in the fall of 1800, Abigail was once again ill with her "rheumatick" and President John Adams went off to Washington alone, though he desperately wanted her at his side. She herself arrived at the new capital in December.

It was a dreary sight that greeted her—the roads were mud, what buildings there were seemed scattered "over a space of ten miles," and there was unused lumber lying everywhere. As for the Executive Mansion, it was a "great castle," though she did find it well built, with a magnificent view of the Potomac River.

John and Abigail were the first occupants of the new mansion. They should never have moved in, for it wasn't actually ready for them. Many of the rooms were unfinished, and those rooms that were completed were huge and drafty, requiring many fires to keep them warm. There were not even provisions for one of the most elementary of housekeeping requirements—a place to hang the laundry. Abigail, with true New England practicality, hung her wash in the formal East Room.

They were to stay in Washington for only a few months. In his bid for reelection, Adams came in third, with sixty-five electoral votes. Thomas Jefferson and Aaron Burr tied with seventy-three votes each; Jefferson was finally selected by the House after a number of ballots, and John and Abigail left active politics forever.

The next seventeen years were comparatively peaceful, although John and Abigail had more than their share of sorrow. In 1813 their daughter Abigail died of cancer, from which she had suffered horribly for three years. Their son-in-law, Colonel William Smith, died three years later, very much a failure. He had made little of his life, and he and daughter Abigail had never really known prosperous times.

In 1816, at the age of seventy-two, Abigail saw her son John Quincy appointed Secretary of State by President James Monroe. Though she did not live to see John Quincy become the sixth President of the United States, she must have known immense pride at the appointment. Charles, who had died so tragically sixteen years before, and her youngest son, Thomas Boylston, had never given her much cause for rejoicing, but she found it in John Quincy.

In October of 1818, Abigail suffered a severe stroke. She lingered for days, unable to move or speak; finally on November 10, 1818, at the age of seventy-four, she died—surrounded by her family, her husband, her children, her grandchildren, her great-grandchildren.

She and John had known fifty-four years of happiness and companionship. Not often are two such people fated to come together, for they were perfectly matched—in intellect, temperament, and appearance.

After she died, her son John Quincy must have known what his father would have said, for he wrote this about her: "She had been fifty-four years the delight of my father's heart, the sweetener of all his toils, the comforter of all his sorrows, the sharer and heightener of all his joys."

John Adams lived eight more years without her. He died on July 4, 1826, on the fiftieth anniversary of the Declaration of Independence. He was ninety-one.

*Martha Jefferson**
1748–1782

The decline of the Federalists in the presidential election of 1800 left control of the United States securely in the hands of Thomas Jefferson and his Democratic-Republican party. His supporters now had every right to expect sweeping changes, but Jefferson confounded his followers by his moderation. Although a number of Adams' last-minute judicial appointments were eventually nullified by Jefferson, there was no wholesale purging of Federalists.

Jefferson's moderation extended to international diplomacy as well. During his first administration he was confronted, more than once, by demands from one warlike faction or another to wage immediate war against England or France, as the situation warranted. But Jefferson avoided a direct declaration of war against either of these powers, although he did conduct a small-scale war against the pirates of Tripoli, who were demanding ransom for the release of American merchantmen and their crews captured on the high seas.

As was always the case with the early American militants, Jefferson's moderation was not popular. But he survived his critics to win a second term handily. One of his most notable achievements, and perhaps one of the most spectacular in our entire history, was the Louisiana Purchase in 1802. Including interest charges, the total cost came to slightly more than $27 million, or about four cents an acre for an area of 885,000 square miles extending from the Mississippi River to the Rockies. There was some question as to whether Jefferson had the constitutional right to make such a purchase without prior authority from Congress, but his opponents were never able to prove otherwise, and the Louisiana Territory became the largest single acquisition in the entire history of the United States.

No portrait of Martha Jefferson is extant.

Patsy Jefferson Randolph

(Daughter of Martha and Thomas Jefferson)

Idealist and liberal, Thomas Jefferson was a pragmatic politician who preferred to move the country with his eloquent pen rather than with fiery oratory. His fervent and vivid credo that "all men are created equal" has served as the cornerstone of our democracy, and the foundation of democracy everywhere.

His wife, Martha Wayles Jefferson, did not live long enough to see him emerge as one of the supreme statesmen of his day. She was with him for only ten years, but played a most important part in his life. She was dead long before he reached the Executive Mansion, yet no discussion of the First Ladies (or of Thomas Jefferson) can be complete without her.

Martha Wayles was born on October 19, 1748, in Charles City County, Virginia, west of Williamsburg. Her father was John Wayles, a prominent and successful lawyer and landowner. Her mother, Martha Eppes, from a wealthy Virginia family, was married to John Wayles for a little more than two years. During the first year, she gave birth to twins, neither of whom survived. The following year she gave birth to Martha, and died soon after.

John Wayles did not remain a widower for long. He was married three times, all told. His second wife was a Miss Cocke, with whom he had four daughters. His third wife, whom he married in 1760, was the widow of Reuben Skelton. John Wayles was even less fortunate with her than he had been with his first two wives, for she died a year later, without any children.

In November, 1766, his daughter Martha, now a lovely young woman, tangled the Wayles genealogy almost beyond recognition when she married Bathurst Skelton. Bathurst was the younger brother of Reuben Skelton, who had been the first husband of John Wayles' third wife.

Martha was eighteen when she married Bathurst. Within a year, she had a son, who was named John. Not too long after, in 1768, her young husband died and she moved, with her son, back to her father's estate, "The Forest," in Charles City County.

Thomas Jefferson met her perhaps two years later, most probably during the social season at the Virginia capital, Williamsburg. He began courting her in 1771, the year he moved into "Monticello," which had not yet been completed. In 1767, while he was still living at his ancestral home in Shadwell, Virginia, he had begun building his own house on a mountain top. He originally called his new home "The Hermitage," but later changed it to "Monticello" ("little mountain," in Italian).

Although no painting of her exists, Martha Wayles Skelton was said to be beautiful. According to available records, she was short and slight, with an attractive figure, large hazel eyes, and auburn hair, richly luxuriant. It is also said she was a sprightly and amiable young woman.

She had other virtues for Jefferson besides beauty. She was wealthy, of course, or would be after her father died. Like other true Virginians, Jefferson was not one to disregard either beauty or wealth; a combination of the two was irresistible. She was an accomplished musician—her instruments were the harpsichord and pianoforte. Jefferson evidently purchased a pianoforte for her, which he ordered months before their marriage.

In June of 1771, Jefferson wrote to his London agents canceling a previous order for a clavichord. "I have since seen a fortepiano," Jefferson's letter explained, "and am charmed with it. Send me this instrument instead of the clavichord." He then went on to say he wanted the case and the workmanship to be "worthy of the acceptance of a lady for whom I intend it."

Music must have been a catalyst in their romance. Jefferson was a competent performer on the violin and cello. With Martha at the harpsichord or pianoforte to accompany him, they literally made beautiful music together.

In the summer of 1771, Martha's son died at the age of four. Jefferson was almost as disconsolate at the boy's death as was Martha. During the months he had courted her, Jefferson had come to think of her son as his own.

Jefferson and Martha were married on January 1, 1772. Even though "Monticello" was not yet the magnificent mansion Jefferson had envisioned it to be, he moved his new bride into the unfinished house. They arrived at his mountain top on horseback, during a heavy snowstorm, making their way, in the middle of the night, through snow drifts three feet deep.

There is not a great deal known about Martha. Jefferson referred to her only sparingly in his correspondence and in his diary, which he called his "account book," and if she herself had much correspondence, which is doubtful, only two of her letters survive. Neither letter gives much insight into her character or her thinking.

One fact can be stated with certainty. In her short life, Martha knew much tragedy and grief. By the time she married Thomas Jefferson at the age of twenty-three, her mother, two stepmothers, a stepsister, a husband, and a son had died. And death was to call upon her with even more frequency in the few years left to her.

Yet she must have known contentment as well. Though Jefferson was not a demonstrative man, the early years at "Monticello" were happy. Jefferson was a member of the Virginia House of Burgesses when he and Martha were married, but spent little time in political activity during the first part of their marriage. He and Martha were together constantly; from the beginning he was attentive. He was also concerned about her health, which had begun to show small signs of future danger. Their first daughter, Martha (later known as "Patsy"), was born on September 27, 1772.

In May of 1773, Martha's father, John Wayles, died at the age of fifty-eight. He had not married again. When his considerable estate was divided amongst his heirs, Martha's share (eleven thousand acres of land and 135 slaves) was more than enough to double her husband's holdings. There was also a large debt left by Mr. Wayles, and Martha and Jefferson had to assume their share of this as well. Jefferson was forced to sell about half of Martha's land, but there was still enough left to keep them wealthy.

After the birth of their second daughter, Jane Randolph, on April 3, 1774, Jefferson again took up his political duties. In 1775, the Virginia convention selected its representatives for the Continental Congress scheduled to meet in Philadelphia. The seven-man delegation included, among others, George Washington and Patrick Henry. Thomas Jefferson was chosen as an alternate, to substitute for the delegation's chairman, Peyton Randolph. As it happened, Randolph was called home after the Continental Congress had been convened, and Jefferson went to Philadelphia in his place.

When the Continental Congress recessed in the summer, Jefferson returned to "Monticello." And once again personal sorrow came to Martha, this time to be shared by Jefferson. He arrived in time to watch, with Martha, the death of their daughter, Jane Randolph. She died in September of 1775; she had lived only for eighteen months.

In 1776, Jefferson returned to Philadelphia as part of the Virginia delegation; in June of that year he was selected for the committee of five (along with John Adams and others) to draft the Declaration of Independence. He wrote the first draft, which was largely the final version, although John Adams and the others contributed their thinking and some phraseology.

Later that year, Jefferson was appointed commissioner to the Royal Court of France, but declined the appointment because of Martha's health. She had been weakened by her various pregnancies, and was not strong enough to cross the ocean; Jefferson had no desire to travel abroad without her. He accepted, instead, election to the Virginia state assembly, which was to convene in Williamsburg.

On May 28,1777, a third child was born to Martha and Thomas Jefferson. This time Martha gave him the son he had so long wanted and waited for. As always, Jefferson was restrained in demonstration of his joy. His entry in his account book was direct, and to the point: "Our son born 10 p.m." Not quite three weeks later, there was another simple entry (on June 14, 1777): "Our son died 10:20 p.m." Jefferson and Martha had not even had time to name the boy; or, if they had, Jefferson did not record the name.

Thomas and Martha Jefferson had three more children. On August 1, 1778, Mary was born (she and the first daughter, Patsy, were the only two of Martha's children to survive to maturity). On November 30, 1780, Martha's fourth daughter, Lucy Elizabeth, was born. By then, Jefferson had become governor of Virginia, and the family was living in Richmond. That winter, when British troops threatened Richmond, Jefferson sent his family to safety. But they had to travel through snow to escape. Lucy Elizabeth, like the other Jefferson children who had died, was frail and sickly. Exposure to the winter weather was no help for her; she died on April 15, 1781.

Soon after that, Martha became pregnant again, and this time it was evident her health was seriously threatened. She was never a sturdy woman. Each succeeding pregnancy weakened her, so that by the time she was carrying her seventh child, she was dangerously ill.

On May 8, 1782, her fifth daughter was born (the infant was given the name of Lucy Elizabeth, to replace the first Lucy Elizabeth who had died the previous year). Martha was now a very sick woman. Jefferson spent almost every waking moment at her side.

Four months later, without having left her bed, Martha Wayles Jefferson died, not quite thirty-four. The date was September 6, 1782. The moment of her death was recorded simply, and poignantly, in Jefferson's account book: "My dear wife died this day at 11:45 A.M."

Although he himself would never discuss it, Jefferson's grief over Martha's death was intense. The following description comes to us from his daughter Patsy:

> He kept to his room for three weeks, and I was never a moment from his side. He walked almost incessantly night and day, only lying down occasionally, when nature was completely exhausted. . . . When at last he left his room, he rode out, and from that time he was incessantly on horseback. . . . In those melancholy rambles, I was his constant companion, a solitary witness to many a violent burst of grief. . . .

There is little to be added to the story of Martha Jefferson. Any of their private letters that may have remained were deliberately destroyed by Jefferson after her death. He wanted no other eyes to witness the intimacies that had passed between them. But there is one scrap of paper that somehow survived, and while it may not tell us much of Martha Jefferson the living woman, it does reveal Martha Jefferson in the last few weeks of her life.

Shortly before she died, she copied a passage from Laurence Sterne's *Tristam Shandy*. She must have struggled on it laboriously, for any exertion, even a simple task such as putting a few words on paper, would have been almost beyond her.

These were the words she wrote:

> time wastes too fast: every letter
> I trace tells me with what rapidity
> life follows my pen. the days and
> hours of it are flying over our heads
> like clouds of windy day never to
> return—more everything presses on—

She could not continue. She stopped there, and Jefferson completed the quotation for her, without correcting some errors she had made:

. . . and every
time I kiss thy hand to bid adieu, every absence
which follows it, are preludes to that eternal separation
which we are shortly to make!

A persistent legend tells us that when Martha was dying she asked Jefferson never to remarry. He gave her his promise and remained a widower for the rest of his life.

Jefferson's official hostess during his two terms as President was his daughter Patsy (Martha) Randolph, except for those times when she was giving birth to one of her twelve children. When Patsy was confined, Dolley Madison, wife of Jefferson's Secretary of State, substituted for her.

Like John Adams, Jefferson lived to an old age—he was eighty-three when he died. But unlike John Adams, his final years were far from comfortable, for he had never been frugal. During his time as President, Jefferson spent more than he earned; when he retired to "Monticello," it was the same. Before his death, he was virtually bankrupt. Although not an extravagant man, he was too generous with family and friends. He willed "Monticello" to Patsy, but it was a romantic and futile gesture. Encumbered with debts, the estate had to be sold after his death.

Ironically, Thomas Jefferson died on the very day that John Adams died, July 4, 1826, the fiftieth anniversary of the Declaration of Independence.

Dolley Madison
1768–1849

From the beginning of the nineteenth century, the United States was constantly on the brink of war. Trouble had been brewing for years. During his two terms as President, Jefferson maintained a tenuous peace. It had been a difficult and delicate task, for there had been provocation enough both from England and Napoleonic France against American shipping to satisfy not only the militants but the average citizen. The American flag had been insulted everywhere; the only answer was revenge.

Jefferson managed to avoid conflict, but his hand-picked successor was not to be as lucky. The mess that had been simmering during Jefferson's administration suddenly came to an intense boil when James Madison was President, and spilled over into active warfare in the last year of Madison's first term.

The War of 1812, which settled no issues at all, cannot be entirely blamed on the unfortunate James Madison. He was faced by an angry and belligerent nation—two-thirds of the country insisted upon war, with anyone. In addition, Madison had a Congress that had seen many of the stalwart colonials and revolutionaries, grown old in service to their country, replaced by a fiery group of young war hawks. Madison could not resist their demands; under his wobbly leadership, the United States took up arms against England.

Throughout the two years of conflict that followed—in fact, almost up to the very moment enemy troops marched upon Washington to burn the President's House—stood the indomitable figure of Dolley Madison, wife of the fourth President. Despite the chaos of battle, despite the terror of invasion and pillage, she was the unruffled hostess of Washington and leader of fashion for the entire country.

Popular history neglects James Madison's impressive role in the drafting of the Constitution in 1787 and chooses to concentrate its attention upon the unfortunate war he could not control twenty-five years later. And it chooses instead to pay homage to Dolley, who was neither statesman nor politician, although admittedly one of the most fascinating women of her time.

Washington Irving once referred to Dolley as a "fine, portly, buxom dame," while he called James Madison a "withered little apple-john." Not entirely complimentary, the descriptions were accurate, for Dolley was taller than Madison, larger, and much younger.

Madison was forty-three at the time of their marriage; Dolley was twenty-six. Except for one brief romance when he was thirty, he had had no experience at all with women. Dolley, widowed the year before, had no lack of male admirers. While not an outstanding beauty, she was attractive enough to turn many a masculine head when she walked down the street.

Dolley was the third of nine children. Her parents were John Payne, of Goochland County, Virginia, and Mary Coles. Mr. and Mrs. Payne, of the Quaker religion, were visiting relatives at the

New Garden Quaker settlement of North Carolina where Dolley was born on May 20, 1768. (It should be noted that Dolley was her given name, although many biographers mistakenly omit the "e.")

The Paynes returned to their Virginia plantation on Little Byrd Creek in 1769. John Payne seems to have prospered, but in 1783, as many other Quakers were doing, he freed his slaves. He gave up his plantation and moved his family to Philadelphia, where he became a manufacturer of starch.

Like all young ladies of the Quaker faith, Dolley wore the plainest of gray garb. She gave no hint of the elegant lady of fashion she was destined to become. Perhaps she dreamed of a world beyond the narrow Quaker confines; whatever her dreams or her plans, Dolley was never, at heart, plain and prim. She enjoyed the company of young men, and they enjoyed hers. She had dark hair and blue eyes; she was tall, almost large, properly and distinctively proportioned. Her education was sufficient; the Friends believed both sexes must at least be taught the rudiments.

Dolley's father did rather well in the manufacture and selling of starch; but in 1789, during a general economic crisis, his business failed. He went into bankruptcy, and the Friends immediately read him out of the Pine Street Monthly Meeting, for a Quaker must, above all, pay his debts. The disgrace was too much for him; he retired to his bedroom, never to come out again until his death.

In the meantime, Dolley had met a young Quaker lawyer named John Todd. He fell in love with her almost at once. She apparently did not feel as strongly about him, but he was loyal and attentive through the troubled time of her father's bankruptcy. Though her mother converted their home to a boarding house, money was tight. John Todd's devotion and the family's need for financial help may have finally influenced Dolley's decision in his favor, for she married him on January 7, 1790. She was twenty-one and Todd was twenty-six.

The first two years of their marriage were comparatively quiet. But a great deal happened in the next two years. On February 23,

1792, their first son, John Payne Todd, was born. Not long after, Dolley's father died. In the summer of 1793, her sister Lucy, only fifteen, ran off to marry George Steptoe Washington, nineteen-year-old nephew of the President. Lucy was expelled from the Friends for marrying outside her faith.

In August of 1793, Dolley gave birth to a second son, William Temple. Suddenly a vicious and devastating yellow fever epidemic swept through Philadelphia. John Todd immediately moved Dolley and the children to the country to escape the disease. He himself returned to Philadelphia to do what he could for the sick and the dying. The epidemic claimed four thousand lives before running its course. One of the victims was John Todd, who died on October 24, 1793; shortly after, Dolley's infant son, William Temple, died of the disease, though he was in the country away from the center of infection.

Dolley too had been ill; when she recovered, she moved back to Philadelphia with John Payne Todd, not yet two. She was twenty-five, widowed, and the mother of a small boy, but she soon had her share of admirers.

One man who showed interest was James Madison, a member of Congress, meeting at the time in Philadelphia. Madison asked the help of Aaron Burr in the early stage of his courtship. Burr had met Dolley when he was living at Mrs. Payne's boarding house. When he acted as intermediary for Madison, she made no objection, as she explained in a letter to her dearest friend:

"Aaron Burr says that the great little Madison has asked to be brought to see me this evening."

"The great little Madison" had competition, but by September of 1794 he triumphed, for Dolley finally consented to marry him, after weeks of indecision. Even on the very day of their marriage, she was troubled. She wrote to a friend that "in the course of this day I give my hand to the man of all others I most admire. . . ." Her letter went on: "In this union I have everything that is soothing and grateful in prospect—and my little Payne will have a generous and tender protector. . . ."

She and Madison were married later that day, September 15,

1794; she added this revealing postscript to her letter: "Evening—Dolley Madison! Alass! Alass!"

By the end of the year, she too was expelled from the Friends for marrying a non-Quaker. But it must have made little difference to her; she at last had the opportunity to develop her true personality. She dressed as she had always wanted, in colorful, elegant clothes; she wore jewelry. She was learning to become an adept hostess, for she was fond of giving dinner parties. Within a short time, the Madison home received many guests.

In March of 1797, Madison retired from Congress; he and Dolley and her son John Payne Todd, now five years old, moved to "Montpelier," in Virginia, to live with his parents. They spent the next four years at "Montpelier," living quietly. It was a far different life from the excitement of Philadelphia, but if Dolley found it boring or disliked it in any way, she made no indication.

When Jefferson was elected third President, he appointed Madison Secretary of State. Dolley and James returned to the federal capital, now in the new city of Washington. Madison was then fifty, and Dolley thirty-three. It was also at this time that Madison's father died, and James became the new owner of "Montpelier."

Jefferson cared little for protocol or formal entertaining. Nevertheless, entertainment of some kind was required, and he called upon Dolley to act as his hostess when his older daughter, Patsy, was not available. The stiff, formal levees introduced by the Washingtons and the Adamses were discontinued. Jefferson's presidential dinners and receptions were intimate rather than lavish. The dazzling entertainment expected from a capital city was left to Dolley.

The city itself was still raw and unfinished; Pennsylvania Avenue was a swath of mud cut through the trees. But diplomats and statesmen from around the world were coming to the new capital. What they missed at the President's House they found at the Madison home. Dolley had become the undisputed hostess of Washington, and her parties more than made up for the Jeffersonian indifference to protocol.

Like Washington, Jefferson declined to run for a third term.

His personal choice as the man to succeed him was James Madison, who went on to an easy victory over his Federalist opponent, Charles C. Pinckney.

On March 4, 1809, Madison was inaugurated as fourth President of the United States. That evening, Washington, D.C.'s, first Inaugural Ball was held at Long's Hotel; it was undoubtedly the most brilliant celebration the young republic had ever seen.

All biographers agree that Dolley was a magnificent sight that evening. She lacked only attendants, for she "looked a queen," to quote one reporter on the scene. She wore a gown of pale, buff-colored velvet, with a train, topped by a string of pearls and by her ubiquitous turban and feathers—in this case, bird-of-paradise—(a turban with feathers had become her fashion trademark).

It was a triumph for Dolley. At dinner, she had the ministers of France and England, which were then at war with one another, seated on each side of her. Only she could have carried off such a feat. To quote another biographer: "Dolley's tact and physical amplitude, combined with the gentlemanly character of war in that day, kept the ministers at peace."

With Dolley now at the helm, the Executive Mansion became the focus of entertainment and fashion. For the first time, festivity was the keynote in presidential entertaining. Dolley restored the weekly "drawing rooms" of Martha Washington and Abigail Adams. But Dolley's receptions were far different. Where the others had been austere, Dolley's parties were festive and friendly. Her dinners and receptions, conducted on a grand scale, were the envy of hostesses everywhere. Dolley was the leader of fashion as well. She set the tone for the entire country. Whatever Dolley wore became the fad of the moment.

Aside from the threatening clouds of war, and occasional attacks of inflammatory rheumatism, there was only one other matter of real concern for Dolley. She and Madison never had children. She should have found comfort in her son, John Payne Todd. But she didn't, nor did Madison, who always tried to do his best for him.

As the President's stepson, Payne had every possible advantage, but squandered all of them. He was not the least interested in education, or in meaningful work. He preferred only to spend money. His mother, permissive, doting, indulgent, allowed him to do as he pleased, although she must have been privately concerned.

The second war with England began in June of 1812. Two years later, on August 24, 1814, a Wednesday, there occurred one of the most incredible events in the entire history of our country—the sacking of Washington by the British. Madison's role in this battle is not clear—some biographers insist that he ran off to escape the invaders; others insist, as strongly, that he rode everywhere amongst his troops, tirelessly attempting to salvage what he could from the debacle. He was sixty-three at the time; he had always been frail. It's possible he was able to spend hour upon grueling hour on horseback galloping back and forth to save the ghastly situation; or perhaps he was a more prudent hero simply trying to rejoin his wife.

Dolley stayed at the Executive Mansion throughout most of the day, although she could clearly hear the sound of cannon and could see soldiers running everywhere. Madison had given her instructions to leave at a moment's notice, and to take with her as many Cabinet papers as she could. She waited for his return, refusing to believe the British would actually enter the city. By late afternoon she knew Madison would not come back; she finally fled from the mansion, first making sure the portrait of George Washington was removed from the wall for safekeeping.

For the next two days, Madison pursued her from one village to another. They had previously arranged to meet at Wiley's Tavern a few miles to the northwest of Washington, on the south bank of the Potomac River. Dolley eventually made it to the tavern, but Madison did not. It wasn't until August 27 that they came together again, in Washington, after the British withdrew from the charred ruins of the city.

The War of 1812 had not been a glorious enterprise for the hapless Americans. The destruction of the capital did nothing for

Madison's waning popularity, nor did the Treaty of Ghent, concluded in Belgium on December 24, 1814, formally ending the
war. But Madison's popularity suddenly soared with the electrify-
ing news of a tremendous victory by General Andrew Jackson
over the British at New Orleans—two weeks after the war was
over.

Dolley reigned in Washington for two more years. She and
James never lived in the President's House again; only the shell
remained after the British had burned it. The mansion was rebuilt,
but was not ready to be occupied until the fall of 1817, after the
Madisons had officially departed from Washington.

Retirement did not find them forgotten, for guests were constantly dropping in upon them at "Montpelier." Twenty or so for
dinner were not unusual; as many as ninety at one time were entertained. Dolley, away from Washington, was still the hostess
without equal.

Toward the end of his life, James grew feeble. His financial
affairs had worsened. He had personally spent a great deal of
money on Dolley's son. John Payne Todd's way of life had become even more wasteful. He had taken to gambling, and to
drinking in any tavern he could find; he sometimes ended in jail.
He wrote to his mother only when he needed money. Unknown to
Dolley, Madison advanced him at least $40,000 through the years.
Though not in itself enough to bankrupt Madison, it was a drain,
particularly when coupled with poor tobacco crops, and the necessary support of his slaves.

On the twenty-eighth of June, 1836, James Madison died at
the age of eighty-five. As reported by one of his slaves, "He
ceased breathing as quietly as the snuff of a candle goes out."

For the next year, Dolley stayed on at "Montpelier," gathering
Madison's papers together. She was close to poverty and desperately needed the money that would come to her from publication
of her husband's documents. She turned to friends in Washington
for help; they succeeded in having Congress appropriate $30,000
for Madison's papers. It wasn't as much as she had expected, but

her circumstances gave her little choice. She paid her debts, including those of her son, and was left with $9,000.

Dolley, however, was never one to be dismayed by poverty or reverses. She moved to Washington and once again established a fashionable salon. She was sixty-nine, but in her approach to living, in her zest for making the most of each day, she was as youthful as ever. She was still tall and straight, with clear skin unmarked by age. Her ever-present turban and bird feathers had long gone out of style, but Dolley Madison could never be imagined without them.

The remaining years of her life were not easy, for she was constantly in need of funds. More of Madison's papers were sold, but once again John Payne Todd was making trouble. She wrote to him from Washington: "If you love me, my dear son, write to me —tell me when you will come to offer the papers to Congress. . . . We are without funds and those we owe are impatient."

Payne did nothing about her appeal. A few months later she sold "Montpelier," for much less than it should have brought. Her husband was buried on its grounds; the sale of the estate where he had spent so many years of a constructive life must have given her moments of anguish.

But Dolley was Dolley, as always. Her salon was constantly filled with friends and admirers. She was then, as she had been a generation before, the *grande dame* of Washington. She graced the functions of four more Presidents—Martin Van Buren, William Henry Harrison, John Tyler, and James Polk.

On July 12, 1849, at the age of eighty-one, the end came for the magnificent, the unbelievable Dolley Madison. Her funeral, attended by every notable in Washington, including the new President, Zachary Taylor, was as impressive for her in death as she had ever been in life.

She was buried in Washington, since she seemed to belong, for all ages, to the capital; but nine years later, her body was returned to "Montpelier" to rest beside the husband she had learned to cherish.

Elizabeth Monroe
1768–1830

The War of 1812 brought neither glory nor gain to the United States, yet it was not a complete fiasco. The New England states, before then dependent upon shipping for their economic survival, turned to manufacturing and the beginnings of a new and greater prosperity. A wave of nationalism and expansion swept the country, and with it, the "Era of Good Feelings."

One of the principal recipients of this renewed nationalism was James Monroe, who easily defeated his Federalist opponent in the election of 1816 to become the fifth President of the United States. In 1820, he won an almost unanimous reelection, with only one electoral vote cast against him.

By 1823, it was apparent some of the European powers coveted not only the riches of trade with newly formed Latin American countries, but perhaps the countries themselves. It was then that James Monroe enunciated his doctrine that was to become one of the principal elements in the basic foreign policy of the United States:

> We owe it therefore to candor and to the amicable relations existing between the United States and those powers, to declare that we should consider any attempt on their part to extend their system to any portion of this Hemisphere, as dangerous to our peace and safety.

The United States had come of age. It seems ironic it should have occurred during the administration of a President who was neither brilliant nor outstanding. Yet James Monroe happened at the right moment in history; on all fronts except one he had made the most of the Era of Good Feelings. Oddly, the exception was generated by his wife, Elizabeth Kortright Monroe. Her behavior as mistress of the White House endangered his popularity, at least on the governmental and diplomatic level.

Illness has been given as the excuse for Elizabeth Monroe's conduct as First Lady. But the nature of the illness has never been specified, or recorded. In his unfinished autobiography, James Monroe makes only a few brief mentions of his wife, none having to do with the state of her health.

The Van Kortryk family emigrated from Holland to the Dutch colony of Nieuw Amsterdam in April of 1633, and settled in Harlem; within a hundred years they were prosperous and prominent landowners and farmers. By then, Nieuw Amsterdam had become New York. The family name was Anglicized to Kortright, and part of the family settled in lower Manhattan, where Elizabeth Kortright was born on June 30, 1768. Elizabeth was the fourth of five children. Her mother was Hannah Aspinwall, and her father was Laurence Kortright, a wealthy merchant and privateer. During the French and Indians Wars, he was part owner of a number of ships authorized by the British Crown to wage legal piracy against French shipping. Privateering seems to have been the foundation of many colonial fortunes.

No records of Elizabeth's early years are available; in colonial days, only three events in a woman's life were normally recorded— her birth, her marriage, her death. But there can be no question that Elizabeth Kortright, as a child and then as a young lady, enjoyed all the benefits of her father's wealth and social position, for the Kortrights were one of the premier families of New York. She was fortunate as well in her appearance, for she was a most attractive young woman, tall and slender, with lovely arms and shoulders. Her hair was black, and her eyes were blue, with a touch of violet.

Elizabeth and Monroe met sometime in 1785, when she was seventeen and he was twenty-seven. Monroe was in New York as a representative of Virginia to the Congress of the Confederation. Elizabeth's Tory father did not approve of him as a prospective son-in-law, for he felt the young Virginian, from a family of modest means, was a poor choice for the beautiful Elizabeth; and Kortright may have preferred a suitor whose political views coincided more closely with his.

Elizabeth's friends apparently disapproved of Monroe as well, for they reportedly "twitted her with the amiable reflection that she was expected to have done better." But Elizabeth disregarded father and friends, and married James Monroe on February 16, 1786. As Monroe described it in a letter to Thomas Jefferson, written from New York City on May 11, 1786: "You will surpris'd to hear that I have form'd the most interesting connection in human life, with a young lady of this town . . . (a Miss Kortright, the daughter of a gent^n of respectable character and connection in this state)."

Ten months after their marriage, the Monroes had their first child, a daughter, whom they named Eliza. The date of her birth is given only as December of 1786. Unlike George Washington and Thomas Jefferson, both of whom carefully noted all important events in their diaries and account books, Monroe seems not to have recorded birth dates.

In August of 1789, the Monroes settled in Charlottesville, Virginia, not far from "Monticello." Monroe, together with James

ELIZABETH MONROE

Madison, had long been friendly with Thomas Jefferson, and it had been a persistent dream of his to be Jefferson's neighbor. He later bought a plantation much closer to "Monticello," where he planned to build a mansion with Jefferson's help.

Monroe was elected to the United States Senate as junior senator from Virginia in the winter of 1790. With that election, he gave up his practice as a lawyer. He decided to become a professional politician and devote his service to his country. The Monroes moved to Philadelphia, which was then the federal capital.

It was a far more social atmosphere for Elizabeth than she had found in Virginia. She was much sought after, and her popularity in the right circles did no harm to her husband, who was now considered one of the rising men of the country.

In 1794, President Washington appointed Monroe minister to France. In the latter part of June of that year, James, Elizabeth, and their daughter Eliza, then seven years old, sailed for France and arrived in Paris on the second of August.

Diplomatically and politically, their stay in Paris did not prove successful for Monroe. But Elizabeth scored a personal triumph. The French were much taken with *"la belle Americaine."*

Soon after their arrival, the Monroes heard that Madame Lafayette, wife of the Marquis de Lafayette, was in prison, presumably awaiting execution. They were horrified to learn that the wife of the American revolutionary hero was a prisoner in a filthy dungeon and might soon be beheaded, as her mother and grandmother both had been.

The Monroes were determined to do something for her but the problem facing them was a tricky one. They could not insult the French government by openly requesting her release, yet they could not permit her to be executed without at least attempting to help her. In Monroe's own words, they adopted "the following expedient":

> There were then no private carriages in Paris and the hacks were generally in the worst state. Mr. Monroe procured a carriage of his own as soon as he could, had it put

41

in the best order, and his servants dressed in like manner. In this carriage Mrs. Monroe drove directly to the prison in which Madame LaFayette was confined. As soon as it entered the street, the public attention was drawn to it, and at the prison gate the crowd gathered around it. Inquiry was made, whose carriage is it? The answer given was, that of the American Minister. Who is in it? His wife. What brought her here? To see Madame LaFayette.

The "expedient" did its work. The concierge immediately permitted Elizabeth to see Madame Lafayette. There is no record of what Elizabeth actually told Madame Lafayette, but presumably she assured her they were doing all in their power to secure her freedom. The story of Elizabeth's visit to the prison swept through all of Paris; the governing Committee on Public Safety, faced by popular support of this grand gesture of *la belle Americaine,* could do no less than release Madame Lafayette. The United States had repaid the Marquis de Lafayette some small measure of the tremendous debt it owed him.

By the summer of 1796, it was apparent the American leaders were not happy with their minister to France; they felt he did not adequately explain their position to the French and they requested that he come back. In the spring of 1797, the Monroes returned to the United States. Monroe, hurt and angry at his recall and at his failure as a diplomat, resolved to return to the practice of law. He and Elizabeth and their daughter Eliza went back to Charlottesville, Virginia. In May of 1799, their second child, a son, was born. So little is known of this second child he is often not mentioned in Monroe biographies. There is no knowledge of a name for him, or of his exact birth date, or the date of his death, which occurred in September of 1800.

Monroe, in the meantime, once again entered politics, and was elected governor of Virginia. In 1803, when President Thomas Jefferson asked him to travel to France on "an extraordinary mission," to help negotiate the purchase of New Orleans from Napoleon, Monroe was glad to accept. This new mission might help to vindicate the failure of the first.

Once again the Monroes sailed for France, where Elizabeth was greeted as an old friend. Their second daughter, Maria Hester, was born in Paris in 1803. Characteristically, Monroe made no record of the date.

As before, Paris was a personal triumph for Elizabeth. For Monroe, it represented a momentous decision. He had come to France expecting only to negotiate the purchase of New Orleans, but he and his fellow negotiator, Robert Livingston, were suddenly faced with Napoleon's offer for the entire Louisiana territory. Although they did not have instructions for such a huge purchase, they nevertheless concluded the deal with Napoleon; it turned out to be a master stroke.

Eliza, in the meantime, had returned to Madame Campan's Seminary, Montagne de Bon-Air (the Mountain of the Good Air) in St. Germain, a Paris suburb. She had been enrolled there during the Monroes' first stay in France, in 1794. A select academy for girls, it was here that Eliza became friendly with many young ladies of royal blood. A particular chum was Napoleon's stepdaughter, Hortense Beauharnais. The arrogant influence of the seminary and of its proud and haughty young women unfortunately manifested itself years later when the Monroes were in the White House.

After the successful conclusion of the negotiations resulting in the Louisiana Purchase, Monroe was sent to London as the new minister to the Court of St. James. This was in the summer of 1803. Eliza was left in Madame Campan's Seminary, and James and Elizabeth, together with their infant daughter, Maria Hester, crossed the Channel to England.

On the diplomatic level, Monroe was no more successful. The English looked upon Jefferson's Democratic-Republican administration as being pro-French; the Federalists, under George Washington and John Adams, had been pro-British. The English were polite, but Monroe was constantly frustrated in his attempts to discuss matters of importance affecting both countries.

By the time the Monroes returned to the United States in December of 1807, Elizabeth had experienced both friendship and disdain. She had learned the courtly ways of the European capitals. She had become cosmopolitan in every sense, in the worst and in the best way. She was to carry these traits with her into the White House in 1817, when she began eight years of uncertain dominion as mistress of the newly built Executive Mansion.

The Monroes spent seven years in Washington before moving into the White House as President and First Lady. Monroe served as both Secretary of State and Secretary of War in the cabinet of James Madison. At this time, Elizabeth's ailments may have begun to take their toll, for the Monroes did little entertaining during Madison's Presidency. Mrs. Margaret Bayard Smith, a prolific letter writer and observer of the Washington scene, wrote to her sister: "Altho' they have lived 7 years in W[ashington] both Mr. and Mrs. Monroe are perfect strangers not only to me but all the citizens."

The Executive Mansion, rebuilt after its destruction by the British in 1814, was ready for occupancy in December of 1817, although the East Room was not quite finished. It was a splendid new building, decorated with the Monroes' own elegant French furniture, which Congress bought from them. It is interesting to note that when the Monroe furniture arrived in Washington, there came along with it "thirty-nine cases containing twelve hundred bottles [of] Champagne and Burgundy wine."

The Monroes apparently intended to entertain on a grand scale, but it was not to be. Elizabeth discontinued Dolley Madison's custom of paying the first call on the ladies of Washington. Nor would she return calls if they were made upon her. Her health, it is said, was then not of the best, and she had no liking for the rigorous social rounds enjoyed by the indefatigable Dolley Madison. The women of Washington were outraged, but Elizabeth remained aloof. She preferred her solitude.

In the beginning of the Monroe administration, there was a storm of criticism leveled at Elizabeth. Most of the ladies boycotted her "drawing rooms" and levees. One such function was reported in this way: "The drawing room of the President was opened last night to a beggarly row of empty chairs. Only five females attended, three of whom were foreigners." But according to reports, Elizabeth was a gracious and stately hostess when she was well enough to hold her receptions.

Eliza was then living in the White House with her husband, George Hay, whom she had married in October of 1808. She was expected to carry on for Elizabeth as official hostess, but seems to have learned her lessons too well at Madame Campan's. Eliza must have thought of herself as Crown Princess, for she, too, refused to make the first call. She did make some return calls, but these were highly selective and only served to aggravate the diplomatic and social anger. Elizabeth, at least, retreated into solitude; Eliza made it all too plain that she cared not at all what others may have thought—the game was now to be played according to her rules.

The women of Washington were slow to forgive. Through almost the entire four years of Monroe's first term, they attended Elizabeth's formal, and often dull, receptions, only because they had to. Elizabeth intensified their displeasure when she refused to make an elaborate affair of her younger daughter's wedding, the first one of a presidential family ever to be held in the White House. When Maria Hester, who was seventeen, married Samuel Lawrence Gouverneur on March 9, 1820, Elizabeth insisted upon keeping it private, for relatives and close friends only, thereby excluding large segments of Washington society who had expected invitations.

In time, the "senseless war" ground to a grudging halt and the atmosphere improved considerably during Monroe's second term. Even though Elizabeth was often ill, and not happy with her role, the dry formalities of entertainment were continued; the White House receptions were now well attended. Perhaps more stately than fun, they were modeled on "the court etiquette of the Old World." One foreign diplomat made this observation: "A little to the left of the center of this room stood Mrs. Monroe. On arriving, all go up to her and bow, and she answers the greeting with a little nod of the head."

In February of 1825, the Monroes held their last "drawing room" as President and First Lady. A Mrs. Tuley of Virginia gives us this description of Elizabeth at her final reception: "Her dress was superb black velvet; neck and arms bare and beautifully formed; her hair in puffs and dressed high on the head and ornamented with white ostrich plumes; around her neck an elegant pearl necklace."

The Monroes retired to their new mansion in Loudoun County, Virginia—"Oak Hill"—and spent the next five years in unobtrusive, although troubled, retirement. They were quiet years for Elizabeth. For Monroe, they were years of financial struggle. He had borrowed heavily while he was President and his creditors were now pressing him.

On September 23, 1830, Elizabeth Kortright Monroe died at the age of sixty-two. As with her poor health, never explained (except for occasional references to rheumatism, a common complaint, along with migraine headaches), so there is no definite cause given for her death. She was buried at "Oak Hill," in a vault that Monroe designed for both of them. Monroe died the following year in New York City at the age of seventy-three. His death repeated a strange irony, for he died on July 4, 1831, exactly five years to the day after the deaths of John Adams and Thomas Jefferson.

Of all the First Ladies, Elizabeth Monroe is the most elusive. Yet, despite the lack of definitive information, we do have a fitting epilogue to her story in James Monroe's own words. Speaking of his marriage in 1786, he wrote this about Elizabeth in his unfinished autobiography:

> She moved with him to Virginia and has been the partner of all the toils and cares to which he has since been exposed in his public trusts abroad and at home. When the nature of these is considered, and the duties of a family devoted to

46

ELIZABETH MONROE

the honor and interest of their country . . . it will readily be conceived that her burdens and cares must have been great. . . . It was improbable for any female to have fulfilled all the duties of the partner in such cares, and of a wife and parent, with more attention, delicacy and propriety than she has done.

Louisa Adams
1775–1852

The 1820s found a spirit of liberalism sweeping across Europe. In the United States, growth was the governing element; the country was spreading, relentlessly. The common man demanded the vote. In some states, he won the right to choose his presidential electors; others states still clung to the outmoded system of choosing electors by the legislatures. But the shadow of the future had already fallen, and the old ways were doomed.

In the presidential election of 1824, in which five candidates participated, Andrew Jackson led the popular vote with 152,933; the second candidate, John Quincy Adams, received 115,696. The others trailed far behind. In the electoral vote, Andrew Jackson once again commandingly led the field. But he did not have a majority, and the election was thrown into the House of Representatives.

After much maneuvering, during which the Jackson forces an-

tunately, by the end of 1807, he had enraged the
f Massachusetts, who had originally placed him in the
n the Massachusetts legislature, in 1808, chose some-
resigned rather than suffer the ignominy of being

is career was once more revived when the new Pres-
Madison, appointed him as minister to Russia. Leav-
older children in the care of Grandmother Abigail,
and Louisa Catherine left Boston with their youngest
s Francis, on August 5, 1809, to sail to Russia. They
. Petersburg toward the end of October.

ial pomp of the Russian capital was far different from
ling and democratic ways of Washington. Louisa was
splendor and ceremony of the Czar's court, where she
ed shoulders with royalty and nobility of all ranks.
, on occasion, to overcome her shyness long enough
Alexander, emperor of all the Russias.

itself was not to her liking. The cold, harsh climate
with her; she was ill a great deal of the time. She
bly from migraine headaches, which sometimes in-
er for days. And there was the constant longing to
older sons. She had no way of knowing that seven
pass before they would be reunited.

1811, Louisa's fourth child was born. Her parents,
have a daughter at last, named her Louisa Cather-
nt lived for only a year. It was a bitter blow for
John Quincy, a stolid, unshakable New Englander,
s he wrote to his brother: "She was our only daugh-
as a seraph upon earth."

1814, John Quincy departed for Belgium, where he
egotiate a treaty of peace with England to end the
Louisa Catherine, in a land she did not like, was
only her six-year-old son to comfort her. Finally,
John Quincy sent word that she and Charles were
a and join him in Paris. The treaty with England

grily shouted "collusion," Henry Clay, one of the other candidates, gave his support to John Quincy Adams, and Adams was finally chosen as the sixth President of the United States. With characteristic lack of political acumen, Adams promptly appointed Henry Clay as his Secretary of State, and thereby set the stage for four years of bitter acrimony from the Andrew Jacksonites, who would never let John Quincy Adams forget that he was only a minority President, occupying the Executive chair by virtue of underhanded machinations. The Presidency, the Jacksonites insisted, belonged to their man, and they were determined he would have it by 1828.

They were right. John Quincy Adams, like his father before him, was rejected for a second term. Father and son, tactless, proud, obstinate, were alike in too many uncomfortable ways.

But not so their wives. John Quincy's wife, Louisa Catherine, was not at all like her incomparable mother-in-law. Louisa did not have Abigail's incisive intelligence; nor was she ever as sure of herself as Abigail had always been. For most of her married life, Louisa Catherine considered herself inadequate; with anyone else, she would have more than passed the test. But she had made the mistake of marrying an Adams. The Adamses demanded far too much.

Louisa Catherine was born in London on February 12, 1775, one of seven daughters. Her mother was Catherine Nuth, an Englishwoman, and her father was Joshua Johnson, an American who had been living in England for a number of years.

Joshua Johnson was London representative for an American tobacco firm. With the outbreak of revolutionary hostilities between his native country and England, Johnson moved his family to France, and Louisa Catherine spent much of her childhood in Nantes, a picturesque town on the Loire River. By the time they returned to London, where Johnson was to serve as American consul, Louisa Catherine had learned both English and French, which she spoke with equal facility.

John Quincy and Louisa met in England in 1795, where he had

been sent by the United States Government on diplomatic matters. John Quincy, twenty-eight, had spent much of his young life in public service, having been secretary to a diplomatic mission at the age of fourteen.

The twenty-year-old Louisa was a very pretty young woman, slight, with brown eyes and reddish-gold hair, which she usually wore in ringlets. John Quincy, almost totally inexperienced with women, was neither a dashing nor a romantic suitor. But he did have imposing credentials—his father was Vice President of the United States, he had graduated from Harvard at the age of twenty, and, at twenty-six, had been selected as minister to the Netherlands by President Washington.

There is evidence that John Quincy was at first far more interested in Louisa's older sister, Nancy. His ultimate choice of Louisa brought a temporary chill to relations between the sisters. Louisa Catherine later admitted in her memoirs that she was very much disturbed by her sister's silence. But distress over Nancy's unhappiness was not strong enough to prevent Louisa from marrying John Quincy. The marriage took place in London on July 26, 1797.

Two weeks later, Louisa's father was bankrupt. She imagined that her new husband was outraged by the true and alarming state of her father's finances, never properly revealed. Although John Quincy did not then, or later, indicate any such anger, Louisa was troubled for years by the thought that she may have deceived him.

On the political front, the marriage of John Quincy Adams and Louisa Catherine Johnson raised a loud hue and cry. John Adams had been President of the United States for about four months. Anti-Adams journalists bellowed that the President's son had married a foreigner, an Englishwoman, no less. It made no difference to them that Louisa was as much American as English, since she was, in actuality, half of each. To John Adams' opponents, she was all English.

The *Independent Chronicle* of Boston, although based in New England, was pro-Jefferson. With its usual lack of subtlety, the newspaper said: "Young John Adams' negotiations have termi-

had been concluded; the War of 1812 was ended. They could all go back to the United States.

His letter made it sound so simple; he beckoned, and she was to come. But it was the middle of winter; most of Russia was snowbound, and Paris was two thousand miles away.

On the afternoon of February 12, 1815, at a time when St. Petersburg was still in the grip of a bitter winter, Louisa and Charles Francis started off for Paris in a coach which had for its insignia the Russian Imperial Eagle. Three servants accompanied them.

The journey took six weeks—in biting cold, across deep snow drifts, over ice-clogged rivers. In Louisa's own words, they were "jolted over hills, through swamps and holes, and into valleys into which no carriage had surely ever passed before, and my whole heart was filled with unspeakable terrors for the safety of the child." But the worst terror was to occur almost at the end of their long journey.

Napoleon had escaped from Elba. He was on his triumphant way back to Paris, and men were rallying to join him. The closer Louisa came to Paris, the more her Russian coach drew anger and violent threats. The shouting soldiers who were now clogging the roads were often drunk and openly belligerent. The Russian Imperial Eagle on Louisa's coach inflamed them, for it was the symbol of their hated enemy. Only her fluent French and her constant shouts of "Vive Napoleon!" saved them.

On the night of March 23, almost at the stroke of midnight, Louisa's carriage rolled into the courtyard of the hotel where her husband was waiting for them. John Quincy, ever the stern and upright Puritan of New England, greeted them with annoyance for being late. He had been to the theater that night and had come back to his hotel expecting them to be there. He had not seen them for almost a year; they had endured unbelievable hardships; and this was how he welcomed them. Still, he listened to Louisa's lengthy and impassioned description of her travels and admitted that he was "perfectly astonished at her adventures."

But they were not yet to return home. John Quincy was appointed minister to England. Their two oldest boys came from Boston to join them in London; for the first time in seven years the entire family was together again. George Washington and John had been small boys when their parents had last seen them—now they were young men, on their way to maturity.

In April of 1817, President Monroe asked John Quincy to be his Secretary of State. The family arrived back in the United States on August 6, 1817, exactly eight years and one day after they had left.

John Quincy's record as Secretary of State was, in the beginning, far more impressive than Louisa's activities as an official hostess in the Monroe administration. She was in the direct line of critical fire aimed at the President's wife. But Louisa, in time, overcame the feminine hostility. She established a custom of entertaining once a week, sometimes lavishly; her "Tuesday evenings" were famous in the capital.

On January 8, 1824, on the anniversary of the Battle of New Orleans, Louisa and John Quincy hosted a party for its hero, General Andrew Jackson. It was a hugely successful affair, with one thousand people attending. Washington talked about it for months. It was even immortalized in a poem written by a gentleman named Agg. Two lines were quoted by everyone:

> Belles and matrons, maids and madames.
> All are gone to Mrs. Adams'. . . .

When John Quincy became the sixth President of the United States in 1825, the social requirements were more demanding. It was expected there would be presidential receptions, and Louisa held levees every other week. They were well attended, but unexciting. In a book published in 1829, the author wrote: "At the President's levees there is commonly no other amusement but conversation."

Other accounts of the John Quincy Adams administration give

the impression that life in the White House from 1825 to 1829 was well ordered, that Louisa was, always, a gracious and charming hostesss, that her receptions were models of entertainment. Much the opposite is true. Louisa was constantly ill, and her migraine headaches had grown worse. There was tension among the sons. The President was vilified at every turn by the Jacksonite press. They were not happy years for Louisa.

Despite Louisa's health, which had grown worse in 1828, and despite John Quincy's failure to achieve his one abiding goal, reelection as President, they were determined that at least one reception should be memorable. In December of 1828 they hosted a glittering affair that elicited these comments from the ubiquitous chronicler of early Washington society, Margaret Bayard Smith:

> Mr. and Mrs. Adams have gone a little too far in this *assumed* gaiety. At the last drawing room they laid aside the manners which until now they have always worn and came out in a brilliant masquerade dress of social, gay, frank, cordial manners. What a change from the silent, repulsive, haughty reserve by which they have hitherto been distinguished.

The loss of the Presidency, though profoundly painful to the proud and obdurate John Quincy, could not compare to the loss Louisa and her husband suffered without warning in May of 1829. George Washington Adams, their oldest son, either jumped or fell from a steamship traveling through Long Island Sound, and was never seen again. Twenty-eight and unmarried, he had not lived up to the expectations of his father. Whether his death was accident or suicide was not definitely established, but his brother Charles Francis reported he found a note in George's effects requesting that "his debts should be paid and the balance given to a little girl he had seduced."

At the age of sixty-two, the former President now expected he would be politely forgotten by his fellow countrymen. Permanent retirement, however, was to elude him. In 1831, at the age of sixty-four, he was elected by the voters of the Plymouth district to serve in the United States House of Representatives. Against his wife's wishes and the protestations of friends and family that it was unbecoming for a former President to become a simple congressman, John Quincy gladly accepted his seat in the House, for he considered it a challenge and an obligation to his country.

Louisa and John Quincy went back to Washington, where he served as a congressman for seventeen years. A fighter despite his age, he was known as "Old Man Eloquent." Now that it was no longer necessary for Louisa to endure the rigorous rounds of presidential entertaining, she became a gentle, elderly woman, often in a lonely world of her own choosing, waiting for the fiercely dedicated and forgetful John Quincy to return from his desk at the House, where he might stay until midnight.

Washington, however, was not always lonely for Louisa. Her many grandchildren frequently came to visit. Summers, she and John Quincy returned to Massachusetts, and here, too, Louisa was surrounded by her family.

On February 21, 1848, John Quincy Adams, representative to Congress, former President of the United States, collapsed at his desk in the House. Louisa hurried to his side, but he did not know her. He died two days later, not quite eighty-one years old. Louisa was grieved at his death and his failure to recognize her, as she wrote to her sister, Harriet: "Oh, can anything compensate for the agony of this last sad parting on earth, after fifty years of union, without even the privilege of indulging the feelings which all hold sacred at such moments."

Louisa lived four more years. She died on May 14, 1852, at the home in Washington, D.C., she and John Quincy had shared for the years he had been in Congress. She was seventy-seven at her death. Her son Charles Francis had her body removed from Washington, D.C., and reburied in the Adams burial plot in Quincy, Massachusetts, next to her husband.

In her memoirs, Louisa Catherine Adams made frequent references to her inadequacies and failings as a wife and mother. But she was not being fair to herself, for her family had far different memories of her. One of her grandsons, in a famous autobiography written in 1905, *The Education of Henry Adams,* spoke of her with the greatest reverence:

> The Madam was a little more remote than the President, but more decorative. She . . . seemed a fragile creature to a boy who sometimes brought her a note or a message, and took distinct pleasure in looking at her delicate face. . . . He liked her refined figure; her gentle voice and manner; her vague effect of not belonging there, but to Washington or to Europe, like her furniture. . . . Try as she might, the Madam could never be Bostonian, and it was her cross in life, but to the boy it was her charm. . . . She seemed singularly peaceful, a vision of silver gray, an exotic, like her Sèvres china; an object of deference to every one . . . but hardly more Bostonian than she had been fifty years before, on her wedding-day, in the shadow of the Tower of London.

Rachel Jackson
1767–1828

When Andrew Jackson became the seventh President of the United States in 1829, he brought a new age of politics to Washington. With his election, the dynasty of the Founding Fathers came to an end.

Tall, spare, rugged and tough as the tree that gave him his nickname, "Old Hickory" had been a hero to the common man ever since his stunning victory over the British at New Orleans in January, 1815. The people, not the wealthy aristocrats, put Jackson into the White House, and he was there to protect their interests.

Jackson, a self-educated, self-made product of the frontier, was a man of violent moods—volatile, hot-tempered, and quick to take offense. Furiously upright and honorable, he had fought many duels in his younger days. He still bore the scars as proof and two bullets that had never been removed. Many of the duels were fought to defend the honor and reputation of his wife; she had been maligned, slandered, and abused for most of their married life; she deserved none of it.

Rachel Donelson Jackson died only a few weeks after Jackson was elected President. Her death brought intense grief to her husband and sorrow to thousands of others, but it may have spared her years of agony. She had been terrified of living in the White House, for she had been tragically unsuited for the role of First Lady, and she must have known it. Shortly before she died, she reportedly said: "I had rather be a door-keeper in the house of God than to live in that palace."

In early 1780, a large party of women and children, escorted by Colonel John Donelson, arrived at a frontier settlement in western Tennessee, on the Cumberland River. They had come to join their men who had fought their way past hostile Indians to hack a new village out of the wilderness. The Donelson party had traveled two thousand miles by inland waterways from Virginia to Tennessee, on a journey that lasted four months.

One of the children was the colonel's daughter, Rachel. Rachel, whose mother was Rachel Stockley, had been born twelve years before in Halifax County, Virginia, on June 15, 1767. Although her father had been fairly prosperous and prominent (he served in the Virginia House of Burgesses), Rachel had had almost no schooling beyond the usual colonial functions of sewing, cooking, and music. At the backwoods settlement in Tennessee, there was little time for education but she did learn to read and write.

When Rachel was seventeen, Colonel Donelson decided his fortune was to be made in Kentucky rather than Tennessee, so he moved his family once more. By then, Rachel had become a vivacious and attractive young lady. She was not a beauty in the classic sense, but her black hair and deep brown eyes, coupled with a happy and lively spirit, brought her more than her share of attention.

Shortly after the Donelsons arrived in Kentucky, Rachel met Lewis Robards. Like so many others of the day, Robards had a military title (he called himself "Captain") although he did little soldiering. He was well educated, literate, and handsome. He was also, as it turned out, almost insanely jealous. Rachel married him in Mercer County, Kentucky, in 1784. Her parents returned to Tennessee, leaving the seventeen-year-old bride to cope with her new husband.

Domestic trouble was not long in coming. From the beginning, Captain Robards imagined his wife to be guilty of all sorts of wrongdoing. He constantly accused her of infidelity; actually, quite the opposite was true. It was Robards himself who strayed. As if to conceal his own transgressions, he created dreadful scenes. He refused to believe Rachel was innocent of his frenzied accusations. More and more, she found it impossible to stay with him; in 1788, she went back to Tennessee. Her father had died in 1785, killed either by Indians or renegade whites. Her mother operated a boarding house in the Nashville settlement, and it was there that Rachel met Andrew Jackson.

Jackson had come to Nashville to practice law, and had, within a short time, established himself as the leading lawyer of the rough frontier area. He was tall and wiry—he was over six feet and weighed no more than 140 pounds—with fierce red hair and a manner that was both carefree and intense.

From the first, Jackson appears to have been drawn to the young woman, now separated from her wildly jealous husband. Whatever the relationship between Jackson and Rachel may actually have been, Robards believed the worst. He had followed Rachel to plead with her to return with him to Kentucky. When he heard of the attentions the fiery young lawyer had been paying to his lovely black-haired wife, Robards flew into one of his uncontrollable rages, and he and Jackson challenged each other—Robards offered to fight with his fists, Jackson preferred a duel. Nothing happened, and Rachel did go back to Kentucky with her husband.

By July, 1790, conditions in the Robards household had again become unbearable for Rachel. Jackson, bowing to the impassioned entreaties of Rachel's family to rescue her, went to Kentucky and spirited her away before Robards was aware of it. When

Robards learned that Rachel had gone back to Nashville with Jackson, he stormed after them. This time Jackson threatened to cut off Robards' ears. and Robards stomped off, muttering empty threats. To avoid any further confrontation with Robards, Jackson took Rachel to Natchez, Mississippi, to stay with friends.

In 1791, Jackson learned that Robards had been granted a divorce, and he quickly married Rachel in August of that year, in Natchez. The marriage can hardly be called precipitate, for Jackson had waited three years, ever since he had met her in 1788; it turned out to be a hasty and ill-conceived decision, one that would haunt both him and Rachel for the rest of their lives.

Jackson was always an astute man; he was one of the best lawyers in the West, with a keen and analytical mind. It is incredible that he did not take the time or trouble to investigate the validity of Robards' divorce. Robards had, in fact, not been granted a divorce at all, but only the right to sue for one. In effect, the marriage ceremony between Jackson and Rachel was not valid, and Jackson was now living with another man's wife.

Robards did eventually get his divorce, on September 23, 1793. His grounds were simple. He was able to prove with no difficulty whatsoever that his wife, Rachel Robards, "doth still live in adultery with another man." This astounding news spread quickly throughout the territory; Rachel was now living a life of bitter shame. Jackson's loyalty to her and to her good name never wavered, either then or through the painful years that followed. On January 17, 1794, in Nashville, Tennessee, Rachel and Jackson were married once more, this time in a ceremony that was legal but certainly could not have been more binding than the first. Rachel and Jackson were then almost twenty-seven, with Rachel the younger by four months.

The charge of adultery was never forgotten by Jackson's enemies and political opponents. He fought many duels as a result; most of them ended with comparatively simple wounds or none at all. One, however, had the most serious possible consequences; another had all the ludicrous elements of tragic farce.

There are several versions of this latter duel, which took place in 1803, between Jackson and John Sevier, governor of Tennessee. After a bitter dispute that had been smoldering for years, Sevier encountered Jackson in Knoxville. The governor sneeringly referred to Jackson's running off to Natchez with another man's wife. "Great God!" Jackson bellowed, "do you dare mention *her* sacred name?" The inevitable result was a challenge, and the two men arranged to meet just over the border of the state, in Indian territory.

Jackson arrived at the appointed time, but the governor was delayed. Jackson waited for two days, his frustration and anger growing with each hour that passed. Finally, he could wait no longer and he mounted his horse to search for his enemy. He suddenly saw the governor and his party riding toward him. Jackson, overcome with the righteousness of his fury, raised his cane, and, leveling it like a lance, galloped full tilt at Governor Sevier. The fierce and skinny knight was determined to defend the honor of his fair lady with the last ounce of his chivalry.

Governor Sevier, gaping at this wild Don Quixote bearing down upon him, tried to dismount, but he became tangled in the scabbard of his sword; he tumbled off his horse and disappeared from sight. Jackson rode around furiously and aimlessly, searching for someone to attack. In the confusion that followed, tempers cooled, the combatants were mollified, and the duel canceled.

Three years later, another slur against Rachel, uttered this time by one of the best marksmen in the territory, Charles Dickinson, brought Jackson and Dickinson to the banks of the Red River, in Logan County, Kentucky. The two combatants stood facing each other exactly twenty-four feet apart. At the shout of "Fire!" Dickinson got off the first shot. Jackson should have been instantly killed, for Dickinson never missed. Jackson flinched as the bullet struck him near his heart, but he did not fall. With his left hand covering a gaping wound in his chest, he took careful aim, his right hand never wavering, and shot Dickinson just below the ribs. The leaded ball passed entirely through Dickinson's body, from one hip to the other. He died that night. Although Jackson was severely wounded, he rode off without assistance. Mysteriously,

Dickinson's unerring aim had faltered a fraction of an inch; by that much, Andrew Jackson lived to become the seventh President of the United States.

Rachel Jackson would have preferred a simple, unassuming life, but it was not possible. Her husband was marked for greatness, and Rachel could not escape the responsibilities that now fell upon her. As the wife of a man who was successively, in the course of six years, a congressman, a United States senator, and a judge of the Supreme Court of Tennessee, Rachel found public attention upon her. She was still only a woman from the backwoods, despite the prestige of her husband's name. Unlettered, untutored in the niceties of cosmopolitan society, Rachel Jackson was happiest when working on the Jackson plantation, "Hunter's Hill."

In a comparatively short time, Jackson had managed to accumulate a great deal of land and a number of slaves. Like most of the wealthy southerners, Jackson's attitude toward his slaves was proprietary and often demanding; Rachel was far more tolerant. In time, the supervision of the slaves was left entirely to her, as was the administration of the plantation itself. With the help of Eli Whitney's newly invented cotton gin, production at "Hunter's Hill" expanded enormously, and the Jacksons were more than comfortable. As their prosperity grew, so did their social activities, and their house was often filled with noisy visitors and casual passersby.

In 1804, business reverses forced Jackson to give up his "Hunter's Hill" plantation, and he moved with Rachel to an undeveloped tract a few miles north of Nashville. He built a log cabin that he named "The Hermitage," and it was here, over the years, that he was able to rebuild his fortune and to replace the original log cabin with the beautiful mansion that later became widely known throughout the entire country.

The Jacksons never had children; in 1809 they adopted one of a pair of twins born to Rachel's brother, Savern Donelson. The boy was named Andrew Jackson, Jr.; he was always treated by both Rachel and Jackson as if he had been their natural-born son. Some years later, another nephew, Andrew Jackson Donelson, came to live with them, and he, too, was treated like a son, though never formally adopted.

Rachel, at the time they adopted Andrew, Jr., was forty-two, and no longer the slim and lovely girl Jackson had first met more than twenty years before. But she was as warm-hearted and generous as ever; people meeting her for the first time quickly forgot her obvious lack of education and breeding, and came away remembering only her friendliness and warmth.

James Parton, an Englishman who became Jackson's first major biographer in 1860, quotes a letter written by a young lady whose father had been an officer under General Jackson. The young lady said in part:

> Picture to yourself a military-looking man, above the ordinary height, dressed plainly, but with great neatness; dignified and grave. . . . Side by side with him stands a coarse-looking, stout, little old woman. . . . Her eyes are bright, and express great kindness of heart . . . her face is so good-natured and motherly, that you immediately feel at ease with her, however shy you may be of the stately person at her side. . . . Their affection for each other was of the tenderest kind. The General always treated her as if she were his pride and glory, and words can faintly describe her devotion to him.

The young lady was right; Rachel was, in fact, Jackson's pride and glory, despite the figure that had grown too stout, the skin too coarse. His affection was complete and genuine; it mattered not what others thought of her, or how she appeared in their eyes. To Jackson, she was the beautiful Rachel, as he had first known her and as he would always remember her. Oddly, he never addressed her by her first name; he called her "Mrs. Jackson," or "Wife," and she addressed him as "General," or "Mr. Jackson."

A member of the Tennessee state militia, Jackson was spending more and more time at his military duties. The separations were often unbearable for Rachel, who was happy only when he was with her. Very little of her correspondence survives, but there are letters she wrote to Jackson in 1813 that demonstrate how deeply she loved "the General." With all her imperfections of syntax, Rachel's own words illustrate more tellingly than can the most accomplished spinner of prose the depth of her feelings for her husband:

> . . . Shall I see you in twenty Days o God send Showers on Scorching withering grass will not be more reviving Gladly will I meete you when ever you bid me. . . . I could write you all Day Long but such a Pen I feare you never Can read it . . . and may The Lord bless you health safely restore you to my armes in mutuel Love is the prayers of your affectionate wife Rawchel Jackson.

After the Battle of New Orleans, in January of 1815, Jackson was placed in command of the city. Rachel came from Nashville to join him; as the wife of the country's newest hero, she was eagerly awaited by the Creole ladies of New Orleans. They were not prepared to find a short, dumpy, and unassuming woman, but they fluttered over her to make certain she dressed properly, said the right things, and appeared in public as the majestic lady of the conquering general.

When the Jacksons returned to "The Hermitage," Rachel suddenly found religion in the person of the Reverend Gideon Blackburn, who brought her whole-heartedly into the church. Jackson refused to be converted, but he had no objections to her religious devotions. In 1821, when Jackson was made governor of Florida, recently sold to the United States, Rachel attempted to inject her own brand of Presbyterianism upon the Spaniards of Pensacola. Fiddling and dancing were prohibited upon the Sabbath. Rachel did not endear herself to the Floridians, who were as Spanish as ever, despite their new status as Americans.

The presidential election of 1824, which Jackson lost to John Quincy Adams, began four years of vilification and abuse from the Adams people and the supporters of Jackson. As the election of 1828 approached, the lies and accusations from each side mounted in unbelievable viciousness and lack of taste. The pro-Adams newspapers exhumed the disgraceful story of the first false marriage between Rachel and Jackson. "Ought a convicted adulteress and her paramour husband to be placed in the highest offices of this free and christian land?"

Andrew Jackson raged at the slanderous attack, but he was helpless, for he couldn't personally punish all of his opponents. Efforts were made to keep the sordid campaign from Rachel, but she did learn of it. She was horrified and deeply ashamed at the story now spread over the entire country. Her shame was compounded by the intensity of her religion, for adultery was the cardinal sin. Sick with mortification, she retired to her room and refused to face the constant stream of visitors now coming to "The Hermitage." She wrote to a friend: "The enemys of the Genls have dipt their arrows in wormwood and gall and sped them at me. . . . They have Disquieted one that thaey had no rite to do."

When the results of the election made it clear that Jackson was to be the next President, Rachel withdrew even more. She lost interest in everything around her, and barely spoke. One of the few visitors permitted to see her reported that "Mrs. Jackson was once a form of rotund and rubiscund beauty, but now [is] very plethoric and obese . . . with a short and wheezing breath."

In December Rachel reluctantly permitted well-meaning friends to escort her to Nashville for fittings for the wardrobe she was to take to Washington. She overheard some women remarking that she would be impossible as the First Lady of the Land. Her friends later found her crouching in a corner, weeping hysterically. That was the beginning of the end. On December 17, 1828, she suffered a severe heart attack. Despite the constant attentions of her husband and the best efforts of her doctors, including several bleedings, she died on December 22, at the age of sixty-one.

Her funeral on December 24 brought thousands of mourners to "The Hermitage." Never before had Nashville seen such a genuine exhibition of grief. The path from the house to the grave, where she was to be buried in the garden, was covered with cotton. The ladies of Nashville dressed her in the white satin gown and kid gloves and slippers she had planned to wear to her husband's Inaugural Ball in March. Rachel Robards Jackson, the unlettered little woman of the backwoods, was buried with tenderness, love, and honor.

Jackson survived her by more than sixteen years. He wore a miniature of her every day of those remaining years, and at night he carefully placed it on his bedside table next to his Bible and his spectacles. He died on June 8, 1845, at the age of seventy-eight. He was buried beside her, in the rose garden where she had spent so many quiet and untroubled hours.

Andrew Jackson never forgave those who had maligned her. An eyewitness at Rachel's funeral described the scene in this way:

> As the friends of the dead gathered about to look for the last time upon her face, General Jackson lifted his cane as if appealing to Heaven, and by a look commanding silence, said slowly and painfully and with a voice full of bitter tears: "In the presence of this dead saint I can and do forgive all my enemies. But those vile wretches who have slandered her must look to God for mercy."

Hannah Van Buren
1783–1819

In the election of 1836, Martin Van Buren, a man who had been born in an obscure Dutch village on the Hudson River, defeated a coalition of four other candidates to become the eighth President of the United States. Van Buren had been personally chosen by Andrew Jackson to be his successor, and Jackson's party, now known as the Democrats, dutifully gave their support to his choice. Anti-Jacksonites formed a new party; calling themselves the Whigs, they ran four sectional candidates against Van Buren in an effort to split the vote and to keep him from winning an electoral majority. But the four candidates, including an old warhorse and Indian fighter, William Henry Harrison, could not muster enough votes among them to defeat Van Buren. The dandyish, five-foot-six little Dutchman from Kinderhook, New York, thus realized a lifetime dream. He had risen from obscurity to the highest office in the land, despite a lisp and a Dutch accent he was never able to lose.

Martin Van Buren was a political artist. He planned and devised his course to the White House with the exactitude of a master tactician. His enemies called him "The Little Magician," "The American Talleyrand," "The Red Fox of Kinderhook." To his friends, he was "Little Mat" or "Matty."

Like Thomas Jefferson and Andrew Jackson, Van Buren came to the White House a widower. Hannah Hoes Van Buren had died eighteen years before; they had been married for only twelve years. Not one letter of hers remains, nor one scrap of paper to tell us what she thought, but one can only wonder how she felt about her husband's political opportunism. Hannah was a gentle, charitable woman. She could not have approved of Van Buren's pragmatic, cynical tactics.

Kinderhook in the 1780s was a completely Dutch village. Its church was Dutch Reformed, its language was Dutch; many of its inhabitants were descendants of Dutch immigrants who had been brought from Holland 150 years before as indentured servants to the local patroon, Kiliaen Van Rensselaer. The town had received its name in 1609 from the Dutch crew of Henry Hudson's *Half Moon*. Sailing inland up the wide river, the ship had dropped anchor. Suddenly there were scores of Indian children on shore gaping at this strange and wonderful craft. The crew later referred to the spot as Kinder-hoeck, the "children's corner."

Two of the families who settled in this lovely and peaceful little village on the Hudson River were the Quackenbosses and the Hoes. On February 4, 1776, Johannes Hoes married Maria Quackenboss. Of their five children, three sons and two daughters, their fourth child was Hannah, born in Kinderhook on March 8, 1783. Hannah thus became the first presidential wife to be born an American citizen. The other First Ladies before her were British subjects.

It was an odd twist of fate that Hannah Hoes should have become the first wife of a United States President to be born a citizen of her country, for Hannah was far more Dutch than American. Born and raised in an insular community that never lost its Old Netherland quality, Hannah rarely spoke English; when she did, a Dutch accent more marked than Martin's immediately betrayed her heritage.

Hannah and Martin, who was only four months older than she, grew up together; both attended a tiny school in Kinderhook where they were taught by a lone teacher who later served as the model for Washington Irving's Ichabod Crane in "The Legend of Sleepy Hollow." Their schooling was sporadic at best, for the village could not afford to maintain the teacher on a full-time schedule; it was necessary for him to supplement his income with any odd job he could find, and this often took him away from the classroom. For Hannah, this casual education was not serious; most Dutch girls of the time were taught on a limited scale. Emphasis was placed on needlework, housework, cooking, and the Bible, which they learned to read in Dutch. The Calvinistic households of Kinderhook saw little importance in learning English, either to read or write.

The relationship between Martin and Jannetje (as her family and friends knew her) was a close one from the start. Hannah was related to his mother, for Mrs. Van Buren had been a Hoes as well. Martin had left school when he was fourteen, and had gone to work for a local lawyer, Francis Sylvester. By the time he and Hannah were eighteen, they apparently had an understanding, if not a formal engagement. Hannah was as shy and frail then as she had been as a child. She had blue eyes and soft, golden-brownish hair; her face was perhaps more round than oval, with a quality of sweet and pleasant repose. Martin, too, had blue eyes, with reddish hair that sometimes showed a touch of yellow.

Van Buren decided to study law, and he was off to New York City to work with William Van Ness, a Kinderhook neighbor who had become a successful and prominent lawyer in the big city to the south. Though there is no mention in Van Buren's memoirs of Hannah's presence at the tavern where he awaited the stage coach that was to take him to New York, the shy and soft-spoken girl must have been there with his family. He was to be away for some time, and surely she would have come to say good-bye.

Van Buren left Kinderhook in 1802; exactly one year later he was admitted to the bar. His tutelage under Van Ness was highly successful, for not only did he become a full-fledged lawyer in that single year, but he also made the acquaintance of many people who were prominent in New York political circles and would later prove most useful to him.

The separation between Martin and Jannetje proved not to be as long as she had feared, for he returned to Kinderhook in 1803 to set up his own practice in partnership with his half-brother James Van Alen. (Martin's mother had been a widow with three children when she married Martin's father, Abraham Van Buren, in 1776. Her first husband had been Johannes Van Alen.) James Van Alen was more of a farmer than a lawyer, but his young half-brother had plans for him. Under Martin's careful planning and campaigning, James was elected to the New York State Assembly, and soon after was appointed a surrogate judge. The financial rewards for the law firm of Van Alen and Van Buren were immediate. Little Mat was on his way.

Hannah was then twenty; she had every right to expect a proposal from her childhood sweetheart. But Van Buren made no move to marry her, despite the growth of his law practice. Decades later, an elderly resident of Kinderhook, who claimed to have known Van Buren, asserted that Martin had loved another girl; and after her death, had gone, in secret, to visit her grave in Valatie, a village a mile or two from Kinderhook. There has never been confirmation of this tale, but the fact does remain that Van Buren waited for four years after his return from New York to propose marriage to Hannah.

In 1807, Martin Van Buren made a decision marked with the shrewdness that was to characterize the next thirty years of his political life. He backed Daniel D. Tompkins for governor of New York, instead of the incumbent, Morgan Lewis, who had confidently expected Little Mat to carry the Kinderhook area for him. When Tompkins defeated Lewis to become the new governor, he remembered Van Buren's help by appointing him surrogate judge to replace his half-brother James Van Alen, who had resigned not long before. Martin Van Buren had won his gamble, in more ways than one.

On February 21, 1807, Martin and Hannah had suddenly gone off through the deep snows and across the ice-bound Hudson River to the town of Catskill, where they were married in the home of Hannah's sister. To Hannah, who had waited so long a time, it may have seemed an impulsive gesture; she would have preferred a traditional Dutch wedding, which would have meant a long and boisterous celebration. But Martin Van Buren never made a move without considering every possible implication. A quiet and private wedding permitted him to leave his new bride after the briefest of honeymoons so that he might begin, as quickly as possible, the arduous campaign that was to follow.

During the first year of their marriage, Hannah was frequently alone, while Martin traveled over the countryside lining up support for Tompkins. But Hannah had the happiest of consolations; on November 27, 1807, her first child, Abraham Van Buren, was born. A few months later, in 1808, after Martin's appointment as surrogate judge, the Van Burens moved to Hudson, the new county seat, a few miles downriver from Kinderhook.

It was a difficult move for the shy Hannah, for she had spent her life in a small, inbred community. Hudson, a busy shipbuilding town and center of commerce, was a far different matter. She did eventually manage to adjust to the ways of the Hudson inhabitants, although she missed the Dutch Reformed Church. There was none in Hudson, and since religion was important to her, she joined the First Presbyterian Church, where the services were conducted entirely in English. Martin himself did not join, though he often accompanied her.

On February 18, 1810, a second son was born to Martin and Hannah. They named him John. In 1812, two more events of importance occurred for Hannah; her third son, Martin, Jr., was born on December 20, and her husband was elected to the New

York Senate. Out of a total of forty thousand votes, the thirty-year-old Martin defeated his better-known and far more experienced opponent, E. P. Livingston, by a scant two hundred votes. The margin, small as it was, sent Van Buren to Albany. For Hannah, it would mean more years of separation and loneliness; for Van Buren, it would lead to full and complete control of the New York political machine.

From 1812 to 1816, Hannah and the three boys stayed on in Hudson, while Martin carefully began the construction of the Albany Regency, a collection of politicians, legislators, and king-makers that was destined to be the most effective political organism of its time. One of its members was William Marcy, who gave an immortal slogan to the country and helped to perpetuate a patronage system that still plagues us today: "To the victors belong the spoils." It was partisanship carried to an extreme—the winning party simply threw out of office all the appointees of the losers, and replaced them with their own. For the man in a position to dispense this political largesse, it meant unlimited power and influence. For Martin Van Buren, who became undisputed leader of the Albany Regency, it meant eventual control of 6,600 state jobs, 8,000 military commissions, and state contracts by the score. The Little Dutchman of Kinderhook had laid and executed his plans with meticulous care.

Van Buren added to his duties by having himself appointed attorney general of New York State in 1815. This meant more absences from Hudson and from Hannah and the children. But Hannah kept herself busy; she had the house to take care of, and the three boys. She must have had help at home, for there is mention in Van Buren's papers of a slave named Tom. Hannah had other activities to occupy her: she had always been concerned about the poor and the needy, and she gave as much time to charitable work as her health would permit. She was not as strong as she could have wished, and she found herself tiring too easily.

In 1816, Van Buren moved Hannah and the children to Albany; Tom came with them. But Tom apparently did not get along with other black slaves in the state capital, and he ran away.

Van Buren made no effort to find him; he replaced Tom with a hired man, a former slave.

A fourth son, whom they named Smith Thompson, was born to Hannah and Martin on January 16, 1817. It is not certain whether it was the birth of this fourth child that weakened her, or the harsh winter; whatever the reason, Hannah began to develop alarming symptoms. She had a persistent cough, and she often had to stay in bed. In February of 1818, Van Buren suddenly received word that his mother was dying, and he hurried back to Kinderhook. Hannah had pleaded to be taken along, but Martin refused to allow her to venture out in the severe February weather. His mother died shortly after he arrived in Kinderhook. When he returned to Albany, Hannah was no better.

The months that followed were difficult for Van Buren. He knew that Hannah was dying; she had tuberculosis (which they knew then as consumption) and there was no chance of her recovery. Toward the end she began to cough up blood; she herself must have known that she had only a short time left to her. She asked Martin to conduct her funeral "with the utmost simplicity, and the money that would otherwise have been devoted to mourning emblems be given to the needy."

On February 5, 1819, just sixteen days short of their twelfth anniversary, Hannah died of the disease that had wasted her frail body. She was buried in Albany, and this legend was inscribed on her stone: "Beneath this tomb rest the remains of the first person interred in this cemetery."

Many years later, Van Buren had her reburied in Kinderhook. This time her tombstone had a different inscription: "Sacred to the memory of Mrs. Hannah Van Buren, wife of Martin Van Buren, who departed this life on the 5th day of Feb. A.D. 1818, in the 36th year of her age. She was a sincere christian, dutiful child, tender mother, and most affectionate wife; precious shall be the memory of her virtues."

In the entire length of Van Buren's autobiography there is not a single mention of Hannah. He spoke freely of himself and of

74

his career, but spoke not at all of her. After her death, he left their four sons in the care of relatives and friends, and closed up the home he had shared with Hannah. Three years later he proposed to Ellen Randolph, Thomas Jefferson's granddaughter; the story is she rejected him because she didn't want to be a stepmother.

The climax of Martin Van Buren's career came with his election in 1836 as the eighth President, but his triumph did not bring him the place in history he had so ardently sought. Although he was far from being a bad President, he had the misfortune to inherit the business panic of 1837, sown with the seeds of Andrew Jackson's policies. If Martin Van Buren is remembered for anything, it is for the crushing depression that took place during the four unfortunate years of his administration.

In 1840, Martin Van Buren failed to win reelection; he tried twice more after that to regain the prize that had been his for much too short a time, and twice more the people of his country rejected him; and consigned him, in the end, to oblivion. He retired to Kinderhook, where he realized at least one of his final ambitions—he bought the grand and beautiful home of the Van Ness family. He named it "Lindenwald." It was exactly such a magnificent mansion he had worked so hard to achieve, where he might quietly live out the remainder of his days, basking in the glory and the honors due to a former President. But he spent the final years of his life alone and almost forgotten; he must have realized then how different it all would have been if Hannah had lived to share these last desolate and lonely moments with him.

On July 24, 1862, Martin Van Buren passed away at the age of seventy-nine. He was buried in the Kinderhook Cemetery, next to Hannah. He had died of old age, complicated by asthma, loneliness, and the short memories of the people he had both used and served for over thirty years.

Anna Harrison
1775–1864

On November 7, 1811, William Henry Harrison, superintendent of the Northwest Indians and governor of the Indiana Territory, led an attack against the Shawnee twin brothers, Tecumseh and Tenskwatawa, better remembered as the Prophet. With eleven hundred soldiers, Harrison marched against Tecumseh's village on the Tippecanoe River in Indiana, and decisively destroyed forever Tecumseh's hope of regaining his lands and leading his people back to their former glory. But the glory that was lost to Tecumseh was to be Harrison's. Years later, this dim but never-forgotten feat burst into flame, and overwhelmed Martin Van Buren, one of the most able and well-trained men ever to hold public office.

When the promotional drums began their insistent frenzy for Harrison in the presidential campaign of 1840, a religious and almost hysterical fervor gripped the electorate. "Tippecanoe and Tyler too!" swept through every state and territory. Voters flocked to the polls for their rediscovered hero. By a popular vote of 1,275,-612 for the Whig candidate, William Henry Harrison, against 1,130,033 for Martin Van Buren, the incumbent Democratic-Republican seeking reelection, and by a far more convincing electoral margin of 234 to 60 in Harrison's favor, a man totally unfit for the office was elected ninth President of the United States. Martin Van Buren was swept into oblivion by a phrase destined to become an historic political slogan: "Tippecanoe and Tyler too!" On such a slender thread was hung the fabric of government and the destiny of a powerful nation.

For the second time, the voters selected a man of the frontier to lead them. The new First Lady, like the President-elect, was a product of the expanding West. Anna Symmes Harrison had come to Ohio in 1795, when it was still a rough, uncultivated land. She had chosen to leave behind her a life of comparative comfort and social graces to be with her soldier husband in the sparsely settled outposts of Ohio and Indiana.

Anna Harrison was the only First Lady whose lifetime spanned four major wars in the eighteenth and nineteenth centuries—the American Revolution, the War of 1812, the Mexican War, and the Civil War. She was the wife of one President, and was to be the grandmother of another, yet she never saw or lived in the White House, and, in fact, never set foot in the city of Washington.

Anna's parents, John Cleves Symmes and Anna Tuthill, were married in Southold, Long Island, in 1760. Two years later, a daughter, Maria, was born. In 1770, the family moved to Sussex County, New Jersey, and settled on a farm bordering the Flatbrook River in Walpack Township, not far from Morristown. On July 25, 1775, in the farmhouse which John Symmes had named "Solitude," Anna was born. Exactly one year after her birth, her mother died.

During the third year of the American Revolution, in 1778, the Americans, under the command of George Washington, and the British, led by Sir Henry Clinton, pursued each other up and down the state of New Jersey, and came far too close to Morristown for comfort. John Symmes, serving as a colonel in the Continental Army, decided that Anna, four years old, would be safer with her maternal grandparents, who were still living in Southold, Long Island.

He managed to acquire from somewhere, possibly from a dead or captured redcoat, a British officer's uniform. Tucking Anna securely onto the front of his saddle, Colonel Symmes, disguised as a British officer, rode with her across New Jersey through the British lines; several days later, he and Anna arrived in Southold. He deposited her with her grandparents, and returned to Morristown. She was not to see him again until 1783.

Anna attended the Clinton Academy of Long Island for a number of years. When her father remarried, he brought her to New York and enrolled her in Mrs. Isabella Graham's School for Young Ladies. With the training she received at these two schools, Anna became the first wife of a President to have a formal education.

After the death of his second wife, Symmes journeyed to the territory near the Ohio River and purchased, with others, a vast area of land totaling a half-million acres. In addition, he was appointed a judge in this new northwest territory. He returned to New York in 1794, to marry for the third time. His third wife was Susanna Livingston.

John and Susanna Symmes moved to Ohio in 1795, taking Anna with them. Judge Symmes built a substantial log cabin home in a small settlement named North Bend, sixteen miles west of Cincinnati, which was then, seven years after its founding, "a miserable village of log cabins." The pioneer population of the area numbered about fifteen thousand, widely scattered over the vastness of the Northwest Territory.

When the Symmes family arrived, Lieutenant William Henry Harrison was stationed at Fort Washington (where Cincinnati was established). The fort was under the command of General (Mad Anthony) Wayne. General Wayne, one of the popular military leaders of the Revolution, had been sent to the Northwest by President Washington to keep the Indians in check.

Harrison had briefly studied medicine under the noted physician, Dr. Benjamin Rush, but had forsaken the art of healing for the art of warfare. Armed with a copy of *Cicero* and an officer's commission wangled out of President Washington (Harrison's father had been one of the signers of the Declaration of Independence), William Henry Harrison was on his way to the Northwest "an Ensign in the 1st U.S. Reg of Infantry." He was a gallant and daring soldier. In one encounter with the Indians, he rallied his men with a spirited cry: "Onward, my brave fellows! the enemy are flying—one fire more, and the day is ours." His reward for courage was a promotion to lieutenant.

He met Anna Symmes in the spring of 1795, in Lexington, Kentucky, while on business for General Wayne. Anna had come to Lexington to visit her sister Maria, who was married to Major Peyton Short. Harrison fell instantly in love with Anna, described by some as "a remarkably beautiful girl." She was slender and dark, not too tall, with dark eyes. To the erudite Harrison, himself only of medium height, the quiet, pious, and educated young lady of nineteen must have seemed like a refreshing breath of spring after years of exposure to the hearty roughness of the frontier women.

Judge Symmes did not immediately approve of Harrison as a suitor for his daughter. Harrison, who had inherited very little money from his prominent though land-poor father, had no future but the Army. In 1795, this seemed a meager prospect to the wealthy and influential judge, and he suggested that the young lieutenant pay court elsewhere.

Despite the disapproval of her father, Anna Symmes and William Henry Harrison were married on November 25, 1795, in North Bend, Ohio, at the home of Dr. Stephen Wood. Their host, a justice of the peace, performed the ceremony. (The father of the bride was away on business.) The bridal couple rode off to Fort Washington, where Lieutenant Harrison had to report back for duty.

Two weeks later, Judge Symmes was a guest at a farewell dinner for General Wayne, who was to return to Philadelphia. When Symmes encountered his new son-in-law at the dinner, he angrily asked how the young lieutenant expected to support his daughter. The actual words of Harrison's reply have been reported in differing versions; the most widely quoted has him saying, with a manly flourish: "By my sword and my own right arm, sir!"

His boastful words were not entirely correct. Although he was promoted to captain and given command of Fort Washington, he resigned from the Army in 1798 to become Secretary of the Northwest Territory at an annual salary of $1,200. In 1801, he was appointed territorial governor of Indiana and superintendent of Indian Affairs.

The Harrisons were parents of ten children. Their first, Elizabeth Bassett, was born on September 29, 1796, at Fort Washington. Their second, a son whom they named for Anna's father, was also born at Fort Washington, on October 28, 1798. The others, three girls and five boys, were born in Richmond, Vincennes, Cincinnati, and North Bend.

In the forty-five years of their marriage, Anna and William Henry Harrison had two permanent homes. The first, a simple log cabin, was built at North Bend, Ohio. The second, a far more substantial building, was completed in Vincennes, Indiana, in 1804. They occupied this house, which they called "Grouseland," for only a few years, but it has been considered a national shrine and is now a museum.

Before their family grew to its sizable proportions, Anna joined William Henry on an occasional journey. She went with him to Philadelphia in 1799; while he was serving as a territorial delegate in the House of Representatives, she went on to Richmond, Virginia, to visit with his family. It was there, in September of 1800, that her third child, a daughter, Lucy Singleton, was born. By the time their Vincennes home was ready to be occupied, their family had grown to five, and Anna no longer had the time or the energy to make further travels with her husband. Their fourth and fifth children, both boys, were born in Vincennes, capital of the Indiana Territory.

Harrison, as territorial governor, made "Grouseland" his head-quarters. Anna often had dozens of visitors to accommodate, including Indian chiefs who came to Vincennes to negotiate with Harrison for the ceding of their lands to the Americans. Governor Harrison, under the "unofficial and private" instructions of President Jefferson, had become adept at persuading the Indians to part with huge parcels of their land.

Anna had no objections to entertaining the many people who came to her house, but would permit no official business to be conducted on Sunday. From her grandparents she had acquired a devout Presbyterianism, and she remained true to her piety and religion for the rest of her life.

She liked to read, and was far more literate than most women of her day, and better informed on political issues, although she did not interfere with her husband's policies, or attempt to shape them in any way. Her place was in the home, and it was there she stayed.

Physically, Anna was a slight woman. Though not robust, she found enough endurance to maintain their large house, to rear her ever-growing family, and to supervise the many properties her husband had acquired through the years. Harrison, with all his land and influence, was constantly in debt, and Anna often made do with less, despite an outward appearance of prosperity.

Anna's father, John Cleves Symmes, had never forgiven Harrison for eloping with his daughter against his wishes. Through the years, he refused to reconcile completely with Harrison, though he always remained close to Anna and his grandchildren. Anna and her father both had the strongest of family ties, with fond memories and a distinct longing for their homes in New Jersey and Long Island. Despite this dual nostalgia for the comfortable past, they willingly chose to remain in the rough and unsettled frontier, for each felt that the future of the country lay in the expanding West.

In February, 1811, Anna wrote to her father pleading with him to visit his grandchildren in Vincennes:

> Make up your mind arrainge all your affair's and be quite
> ready to accompany Mr. Wallace in his Boat as far as the
> Falls or the Red Banks which ever place he gits out at and
> we will have a horse there ready for you Mr. Harrison men-
> tioned it to him before he left this and he said he would be
> extreemly happy in your company he will stop at Cincin-
> natta if you perfer.

Anna's pleas and instructions apparently were successful, for
Symmes did forgive Harrison, as Anna had so strongly hoped.
Symme's wife, Susanna Livingston, had returned to New York,
for unlike Anna, she could not adjust to frontier life, and Symmes
now turned to the Harrisons for solace and love.

After the Battle of Tippecanoe, in November of 1811, Harrison
sent Anna and their eight children, the oldest aged fifteen, back
to North Bend. Harrison himself left Vincennes some months later
when he resigned as territorial governor of Indiana to become a
major-general in the Kentucky militia during the War of 1812.

For much of the next three years, Harrison was away fighting in
the war, and the problems of raising their large family, grown to
ten with the births of Anna Tuthill in 1813 and James Findlay in
1814, were left entirely to Anna. The original log cabin had been
greatly expanded, so there was room enough for all the children,
and for the children of neighbors. Anna had set up a school in
their North Bend home and hired a tutor for the education of her
family. Any other children who wished to join them were welcome.

Anna Harrison was to know much grief in the many years that
still faced her. Her sister Maria Short died after only thirteen
years of marriage; on February 26, 1814, Anna's father, John
Cleves Symmes, died of cancer. Once the owner of immense
tracts of land on the Ohio frontier, Symmes was penniless and
embittered at the end. He had been ruined by bad luck and poor
management of his affairs.

In 1817, the last-born of Anna's children, James Findlay, was the
first to die, at the age of three. Anna was then forty-two, and her
husband forty-five. By 1840, when Harrison was elected the ninth

President, they were to see a daughter die and four more of their sons, two of them in disgrace. Their first-born son, namesake of Anna's father, had been unjustly accused of embezzling funds while holding a government position. Whether justified or not, he died owing the government over $12,000, a debt his father was forced to assume. William Henry, Jr., died in 1838, possibly the result of excessive drinking, a lifelong problem he could never control. Harrison assumed his debts as well; the widows and families of these two sons moved into the North Bend home, and Anna and William Henry Harrison again had a houseful of young people to support.

The nation danced with delirium when "Old Tippecanoe" was elected in 1840. Once more, as they had with Washington and Jackson, they turned to a military hero for leadership. But Anna, the hero's wife, was a reluctant heroine. Harrison was sixty-seven and she was sixty-five. They had lived most of their lives on the frontier. She wasn't sure she could adjust to the ways of the capital, teeming with officials and representatives of every civilized country in the world. She faced her coming role as hostess of the Executive Mansion with trepidation, doubting she would measure up to its immense responsibilities. And she wasn't well. The deaths of three of her sons in consecutive years had left her shaken with grief.

In February of 1841, when her husband journeyed from North Bend to Washington for his Inauguration in March, Anna was too ill to accompany him. She stayed behind, making plans to join him later in the spring. The day of his Inauguration was bitterly cold; against all advice he refused to wear either hat or coat. He stood outside in the bone-chilling March day delivering the longest Inaugural speech on record. One month later, he died of pneumonia, the first President to die in office. He was sixty-eight. He was buried temporarily in the congressional burial vault in Washington, D.C., and was then reburied in North Bend, Ohio.

Anna continued to stay on at their North Bend home. Always deeply religious, she turned more and more to her Bible and to her church. In 1855, the North Bend house burned down and Anna moved in with her sole surviving child, John Scott. All the others had died within six years of her husband's death.

On February 25, 1864, almost eighty-nine years old, Anna Symmes Harrison died, and was buried in North Bend, near her husband and her father. Her funeral services were conducted by her long-time pastor and friend, the Reverend Horace Bushnell, a blind preacher from Cincinnati. The text of his sermon had been personally selected by Anna: "Be still and know that I am God." Perhaps a more fitting testimonial might be these words, written about her in 1883:

> Every public and private charity was near her heart, and received liberally from her hand. But those who enjoyed her bounty knew not of its source. To a poor minister she would write: "Accept this trifle from a friend." To the Bethel Sabbath school, "This is but a widow's mite." To the suffering poor of the city, "Please distribute this from one who wishes it was a thousand times more."

Letitia Tyler
1790–1842

In the early morning hours of April 5, 1841, two special emissaries from Washington, D.C., arrived at the Williamsburg, Virginia, home of John Tyler with an urgent message, dated Washington, April 4, 1841:

> To John Tyler, Vice President of the United States.
> *Sir:*—It has become our most painful duty to inform you that WILLIAM HENRY HARRISON, late President of the United States, has departed this life.
> This distressing event took place this day, at the President's mansion in this city, at thirty minutes before one in the morning.
> We lose no time in dispatching the chief clerk in the State Department, as a special messenger, to bring you these melancholy tidings.

We have the honor to be, with the highest regard, your obedient servants."

The letter was signed by the six members of Harrison's Cabinet, including Daniel Webster, Secretary of State.

In the most unexpected of fashions, a southern, slaveowning aristocrat, stubborn defender of states' rights, had suddenly been thrust into the center of the governmental stage. For the first time in American history, a President had died in office. The Whig leaders, who had selected the Virginia-born John Tyler as Harrison's running mate simply to balance the ticket and to placate the influential slaveowners of the South, now confidently expected the puppet Tyler to dance to their tune; he would be "Vice President Acting as President." But Tyler refused to let them pull the strings. He insisted that he would *serve* as President, not *act* as President. He won his point, and established the most important of all presidential precedents: Upon the death of the President, the Vice President automatically becomes the President in fact.

Neither radical nor rebel, John Tyler maintained a spirit of independence in his public and private lives. He was married twice, to Letitia Christian and to Julia Gardiner. Both wives were beautiful and wealthy, but there the similarity ended. Letitia, born and bred in the Virginia plantation country, was a self-effacing woman, content to occupy the background. Julia, born in New York and thirty years younger than Tyler, was far more ambitious and outspoken than the reserved Letitia. John Tyler had a full life with each of them, though each brought him happiness in her own distinctive way.

Colonel Robert Christian, married to Mary Brown, owned a large plantation in New Kent County, Virginia. Like so many other Tidewater estates, "Cedar Grove" was built on a grand and magnificent scale. The Christians were a family of substance, and lived accordingly. President Washington was a close friend.

Letitia was born at "Cedar Grove" on November 12, 1790, the

third of six daughters. There were two sons as well. The house and the wealth of Letitia's father were more than enough to care for all of them in the best possible manner. Their every wish and need was attended to by personal servants and slaves. There was no lack of company, for the Christian family, in the Tidewater tradition, welcomed visitors and did a great deal of entertaining, both formal and informal.

There is no mention made of Letitia's education; it is known that she spent most of her life, before her marriage to Tyler, on the plantation, so there is little likelihood she was sent anywhere for schooling. She and her sisters were probably tutored at home. Their formal training concentrated on preparing them for the same role their mother occupied—to be mistress of an extensive plantation; it was assumed the lovely young ladies would each make a match suitable to her background.

In Letitia's case, the preparation was successful, for it is reported she had no lack of suitors, despite the obvious fact that she was "modest," "refined," and "genteel." She may have been too modest; many years later, one of her daughters wrote that Tyler did not even dare to kiss Letitia's hand until three weeks before the wedding, and this after an engagement that lasted almost five years.

Tyler and Letitia met in the spring of 1808, when he was eighteen and she was seventeen (he was eight months older than she). Tyler was a young man of prodigious intellect. He had graduated from William and Mary College at the age of seventeen; he was more than a fair violinist; he composed; he wrote sonnets. Slender, intense, his political philosophy of the supremacy of states' rights was already firmly ingrained.

Letitia was slight, with a quiet, patrician quality to her face. She had black hair, dark eyes, and an olive complexion. Tyler was immediately attracted to her, and she to him. Objections of her parents to their early marriage may have had to do with their extreme youth, or Tyler's lack of personal wealth. Although he became a lawyer at the age of twenty, and was elected to the Virginia House of Delegates one year later, in 1811, it wasn't until his father's death in 1812, when he inherited part of his father's plantation and some of his slaves, that marriage plans were finally made. John and Letitia were married on his twenty-third birthday, March 29, 1813; they moved into a home on the "Greenway" plantation, his father's property.

Tyler's career in politics was already defined. Between 1811 and 1816, he served in the Virginia House of Delegates; in 1817, he was elected to the United States Congress, as a representative from Virginia; from 1823 to 1825, he again was a member of the Virginia House of Delegates; from 1825 to 1827 he was governor of Virginia; and finally, in a period that established him as a national figure, he served in the United States Senate from 1827 to 1836.

Letitia's training, which had so well prepared her for her position as mistress of Tyler's house, was put to immediate use. Tyler's private practice as a lawyer in Charles City County and his membership in the House of Delegates left him no time for his five-hundred–acre plantation. Actual supervision of the fields, the many houses, the field hands and the other slaves fell upon Letitia. There was much to be looked after, including a kitchen-garden, fruit-orchards, a dairy, a laundry, poultry yards, spinning, weaving, knitting, sewing, the ordinary household affairs, and the purely decorative task of overseeing the lawns and gardens. It was a full-time job, and Letitia performed it admirably, as well, say a number of Tyler biographers, as did Abigail Adams, who supervised her husband's properties. Letitia's success as a plantation supervisor, coupled with the money and property she had inherited upon the death of her parents, freed Tyler from financial burdens, and permitted him to concentrate upon politics.

The first of the Tyler children arrived on April 15, 1815. She was named Mary. During the next fifteen years, seven more children were born, all in Virginia. All lived to maturity, except for the sixth child, Anne Contesse, who lived only for three months. Of the seven surviving, four were daughters—Mary, Letitia, Elizabeth, and Alice; and three were sons—Robert, John, Jr., and

Tazewell. Tazewell, the last of the eight, was born on December 6, 1830, when Letitia was forty, and Tyler not yet forty-one.

Letitia refused to leave Virginia, and only once did she agree to visit Washington, in the winter of 1828–29, while her husband was serving as senator. The capital was not to her liking. During heavy rains, it was one huge mudhole; with the wind from the right direction, it smelled abominably, of livestock and other assorted odors. By 1841, when the Tylers moved into the White House, conditions had improved and Letitia did not have the same objections. But, sadly, she then had no need to decry the state of the capital. She had been invalided by a paralytic stroke in 1839, and from that moment was confined to a wheelchair; she never left the seclusion of her own room, either at her home in Williamsburg, Virginia, or later at the White House, except for one occasion.

Five of Letitia's children were married while she was still alive. Of the five marriages, only three proved happy; the two failures involved John, Jr., who married Martha Rochelle in October of 1838, and daughter Letitia, who married James A. Semple in February of 1839. John, Jr.'s, marriage floundered because of his distressing record of failure, compounded by addiction to alcohol (a disease shared by other presidential families). The precise reasons for the ultimate estrangement between daughter Letitia and her husband, James Semple, are vague, but it appears that her father lent a helping hand to Letty in 1844, while he was President. He appointed Semple a purser in the United States Navy; for much of the time thereafter, Semple was off at sea, and Letty was spared the agony of continuing marital strife.

On September 12, 1839, the Tylers' oldest son, Robert, married Priscilla Cooper, daughter of Thomas Abthorpe Cooper, one of the great dramatic actors of the day. Robert had seen Priscilla, herself an actress, performing Desdemona to her father's Othello in Richmond, Virginia, and fell instantly in love with her. The romance, which began in 1837, blossomed into marriage only after six proposals and many love letters laden with poetry. Robert brought his new bride, whom he had married in Pennsylvania, to meet his family in Virginia. Priscilla wrote a lengthy letter to her sisters giving her impressions of her in-laws. She had this to say about Letitia:

> She must have been very beautiful in her youth, for she is still beautiful now in her declining years and wretched health. Her skin is as smooth and soft as a baby's; she has sweet, loving black eyes, and her features are delicately moulded. . . . The room in the main dwelling furthest removed and most retired is "the chamber," as the bedroom of the mistress of the house is always called in Virginia . . . here mother with a smile of welcome on her sweet, calm face, is always found seated on her large arm-chair with a small stand by her side, which holds her Bible and her prayer-book—the only books she ever reads now. . . .

John Tyler's term as President, shortened by the one month Harrison had served, was marked by constant friction between Tyler and the congressional leaders. His insistence that he alone was President had stunned not only his opponents, but his own followers. Within a short time, Tyler vetoed a number of major bills, all of them proposed by his party. The angry Whig leaders were further frustrated when they could not muster enough congressional votes to override his vetoes, whereupon, for the first time in the history of the country, a presidential impeachment resolution was presented to Congress. The resolution was eventually withdrawn; the Whig leaders, bent upon some form of retaliation, read Tyler out of their ranks, and John Tyler became a President without a party.

During all of this governmental turmoil and political in-fighting, Letitia remained calm and removed. She never attempted to influence her husband's views, and kept herself withdrawn, both spiritually and physically. She lived in her own apartment at the White House, where family and intimate friends came to visit. Her daughter-in-law, Priscilla Cooper Tyler, acted as hostess of the Executive Mansion in her stead.

Letitia's only public appearance as First Lady took place on

January 31, 1842, when Elizabeth was married to Walter Waller. Elizabeth was the second presidential daughter to be married at the White House (the first was Maria Hester Monroe). Letitia's daughter-in-law Priscilla, in another letter written to her family in February of 1842, described Letitia at the wedding:

> She gained by comparison with all the fine ladies around her. I felt proud of her, in her perfectly faultless, yet unostentatious dress . . . receiving in her sweet, gentle, self-possessed manner, all the important people who were led up and presented to her. She was far more attractive to me in her appearance and bearing than any other lady in the room. [Dolley Madison, who was then almost seventy-two, was one of the guests.]

Letitia returned to her private apartment, and never again came downstairs. On Friday, September 9 of that same year, 1842, she suffered another stroke; she died the following day, Saturday, September 10, two months short of her fifty-second birthday. She was buried at "Cedar Grove" in Virginia, where she had been born.

The twenty-nine years of marriage between John and Letitia Tyler had been peaceful and restrained, compassionate rather than impassioned, but they had been years of contentment. With Letitia suddenly gone, Tyler was plunged into gloom. He ordered the White House to be hung with black crepe, and a long period of mourning was begun. Letitia's daughter-in-law Priscilla described the atmosphere of the Executive Mansion: "Nothing can exceed the loneliness of this large and gloomy mansion, hung with black, its walls echoing with sighs."

Twenty-one months later, John Tyler's period of mourning came to an end when he married the twenty-four-year-old Julia Gardiner, a vivacious, outgoing favorite of the New York social set and prospective heiress to a number of valuable real estate properties in lower Manhattan.

Julia Tyler
1820–1889

Lying off the eastern tip of Long Island, in a body of water now called Gardiners Bay, is a 3300-acre mass of land once known to the Montauk Indians as Manchonake. In 1639, the Montauks sold this island "ffor ten coates of trading cloth" to an English soldier and adventurer by the name of Lion Gardiner. The following year, in March of 1640, Gardiner's title to Manchonake was made irrevocable by a grant from King Charles I of England, transferring all rights to Lion Gardiner and his descendants. The name of the island was changed from Manchonake to Gardiners Island, and remains today the only seventeenth-century British royal grant to be held in this country by the descendants of the original owner.

On May 4, 1820, or July 23, 1820 (she herself never knew the exact date), Julia Gardiner was born on Gardiners Island. She was the third of four children. Her father, David Gardiner, was serving as overseer of the island, though he was not in the direct line of succession. Through his wife, Juliana McLachlan, who inherited considerable property in lower Manhattan from her father in 1819, David Gardiner became a man of wealth. In 1822, he moved his family to East Hampton, Long Island, a few miles from the ancestral home. He entered politics, and served as a New York state senator from 1824 to 1828 (Gardiner never again held public office, yet he always referred to himself as "Senator").

When Julia was not quite fifteen, in April, 1835, she was enrolled in Madame N. D. Chagaray's Institute, a select school for well-born young ladies on Houston Street in New York City. Madame Chagaray's curriculum was planned to instill an adequate understanding of the classic requirements—music, French, literature, among other subjects—but the girls were carefully shielded from the harsh realities of the outside world. Yet, somehow, Julia learned exactly how to conduct herself in the real world Madame Chagaray seemed to have forgotten.

Toward the end of 1839, when Julia was nineteen, she posed for an advertisement for Bogert and Mecamly, a department store in New York City. Julia, described in the ad as "the Rose of Long Island," was depicted carrying a placard that read: "I'll Purchase at Bogert & Mecamly's *No. 86* 9th Avenue. Their Goods are Beautiful & Astonishingly Cheap." The advertisement brought instant notoriety to Julia and much embarrassment to her parents, heightened a few months later by the appearance of a poem on the front page of the Brooklyn *Daily News*. The poem, written by "Romeo Ringdove," was clearly an impassioned statement of love for "Julia—the Rose of Long Island." Her parents had seen enough. They promptly whisked Julia and her sister off to Europe.

The trip to Europe was later followed by an extended visit to Washington, in the winter of 1841–42. Everywhere, the flirtatious, extroverted Julia left broken hearts behind her, and men of various ages sighing in defeat.

Julia and John Tyler met briefly in January of 1842, at a White House reception, but it wasn't until the following year, 1843, five months after the death of his wife, that Tyler began to take serious notice of Julia. Like Letitia, Julia had glossy black hair and dark eyes. Her skin was light, and her face round. She was five foot three in height, and her figure attracted glances of frank admiration and open envy.

Tyler proposed for the first time at a White House Washington's Birthday ball, on February 22, 1843. Julia, only twenty-two, was taken aback by this sudden proposal from the President, whom she had seen but a few times and never in private; her immediate reaction was a stunned, "No, no, no." Tyler persisted, although much of the courtship was conducted by mail, for the Gardiners left Washington at the end of March.

Rumors of Tyler's romance with a popular girl so many years younger alarmed his family and friends. Nor did his political opponents approve. John Quincy Adams, who was then seventy-seven, referred to the romance as "the old fable of January and May." Adams had never been a Tyler admirer.

The Gardiners returned to Washington on February 24, 1844. Four days later, on February 28, there occurred an event that shocked the nation, and probably provided the final impetus for Julia. The new steam frigate *Princeton* was making a gala excursion trip down the Potomac River, with President Tyler aboard, and about 350 specially invited guests, including Julia and her father, David Gardiner.

The *Princeton* carried the world's largest naval gun, a weapon called the "Peacemaker." It was fired three times during the leisurely trip. The first two firings brought lusty cheers from the onlookers gathered on the deck. On the third firing (during which President Tyler and Julia were, most fortunately, at a "sumptuous collation" in the salon) something went wrong.

The breech of the Peacemaker exploded, and sprayed a violent path of death and injury into the crowd pressed around it. Eight people were killed, and more than a dozen injured. Among the dead were Tyler's Secretary of State, his Secretary of the Navy, and the former senator from New York, David Gardiner.

The death of her father had a dramatic impact upon Julia. She now had an entirely different view of Tyler; he replaced, in her mind, the father she had lost with such tragic suddenness. Tyler seemed to her "to be more agreeable in every way than any younger man ever was or could be."

Four months after the accident, on June 26, 1844, the fifty-four-year-old President of the United States married the twenty-four-year-old Julia Gardiner at New York's Church of the Ascension, on Fifth Avenue at Tenth Street. The wedding was conducted under conditions of the utmost secrecy, so that not even Tyler's daughters were aware of it. News of the wedding created a sensation all over the country, and evoked remarks both flattering and uncomplimentary. Those men who had seen the quite remarkable figure of the beautiful bride now referred to Tyler as "Lucky Honest John." Another comment, from the diary of New York's caustic chronicler of the social scene, George Templeton Strong, called Tyler a "poor, unfortunate, deluded old jackass."

When Tyler's three older daughters received word of the wedding, they were outraged, not because of the marriage, which they had accepted as inevitable, but because of the secrecy, and because it seemed to come too soon after their mother's death. Oddly, the oldest daughter, Mary, who was five years older than her new stepmother, was the first to relent; Elizabeth, the third daughter, did eventually come around; Alice, the fourth daughter, who was seventeen, didn't seem to mind too much; it was only Letitia Semple who refused to accept Julia. With Tyler's three sons, the marriage never was a problem.

Julia was gloriously happy in her new role as First Lady of the land. She made no secret of her delight; she reveled both in her role and in her much older husband. She was determined that her reign as mistress of the Executive Mansion would indeed be royal and auspicious. To develop a proper image, she asked for, and received from Tyler, an Italian greyhound; she surrounded herself with a "court." Her pretensions, benevolently accepted by her devoted and fascinated husband, were often ridiculed in the press:

> We understand . . . that the lovely lady Presidentress is attended on reception-days by twelve maids of honor, six on either side, dressed all alike; and that her serene loveliness

"receives" upon a raised platform with a headdress formed of bugles and resembling a crown.

The Lady Presidentress, however, was not shaken by her critics. She hired a New York newspaperman to extol her virtues, and thereby became the first First Lady to have her own press agent. He dutifully planted in the friendly press such beguiling items as a description of Julia's court—"an irresistible bodyguard of modesty and beauty." The First Lady, he wrote, was "beautiful, winning, as rosy as a summer's morning on the mountains of Mexico. . . ."

But there were a few clouds on Julia's horizon. One of them was the deplorable condition of the White House. Congress, because of its long-standing feud with Tyler, refused to appropriate funds to repair and refurbish the Executive Mansion; hordes of visitors constantly streaming in and out had left the President's dwelling looking like a seedy, rundown, third-rate hotel, with tobacco stains on the pillars, threadbare carpeting, and furniture literally falling apart and coming out at the seams. Julia's mother generously provided Gardiner money to set the White House gleaming once again, as befitted the home of her daughter.

Julia concurred wholeheartedly with Tyler's political views. There was too little time left to influence his presidential decisions, but unquestionably she supported him in everything he did. Tyler's last major official act as President was the signing of a joint resolution, passed in March of 1845 by both houses of Congress, inviting the Republic of Texas to join the Union as the twenty-eighth state. Texas was not admitted officially until December 29, 1845, eight months after the close of Tyler's term, but Tyler and Julia always thought of Texas as an accomplishment of his administration.

As her own last major effort in the White House, Julia planned a ball that would be unforgettable. The date was February 18, 1845, a Wednesday. She invited two thousand people; reportedly, almost three thousand attended. The magnificent chandeliers in the East Room glittered with more than six hundred candles; music for dancing was provided by a Marine band in vivid scarlet uniforms. There were a hundred bottles of champagne, wine by the barrel. The numerous tables, set up buffet style, continually groaned under the weight of food, but the crushing crowds emptied them as fast as they could be restocked. It was, in truth, a memorable affair; the cost to Tyler was estimated at over $2,000. For Julia, it was the highlight of her brief and glowing reign in the White House, where she regally served for eight months.

With the Inauguration of James Knox Polk as the eleventh President, Tyler and his young bride retired to his new plantation, "Sherwood Forest," a property about two miles from "Greenway," where Tyler had been born and where he had spent much of his life. At the time he bought "Sherwood Forest," Tyler had not planned on using it to house youngsters, but its purchase was a master stroke. A year after his retirement from the Executive chair, there began what can only be described as a presidential phenomenon—Tyler's second family.

With Letitia, his first wife, Tyler had had eight children. With Julia, he had seven more, five sons and two daughters. The first, a son, arrived on July 12, 1846, when Tyler was fifty-six, and the last, a daughter, on June 20, 1860, when he was seventy. Some of the children from his first set had, in the meantime, passed away— Mary in 1848; Elizabeth in 1850, at the age of thirty-seven; and Alice in 1854, only twenty-seven. Letitia's three sons and one daughter were still alive.

Despite Julia's northern birth, she was as prosouthern as her husband, and as fierce in her support of states' rights. The use of slaves at "Sherwood Forest" did not disturb her at all. Slavery had been an accepted tradition on Gardiners Island for well over a century, and she therefore endorsed it completely without giving a second thought to the moral or ethical question.

Tyler's views, like Julia's, always conservative and politically fundamentalist, moved closer, with each year, to the position of the southern plantation owners. Outwardly opposed to secession, Tyler and Julia nevertheless wished for it, and did nothing to resist it. In February, 1861, Tyler presided over a Peace Conference convened in Washington, D.C., in a vain attempt to stop the on-rush of the War Between the States. From the beginning, the Peace Conference was doomed to failure; the moment it ended, both Tyler and Julia openly worked for secession of the South.

The Tyler course was now evident. Tyler helped to create the government of the Confederate States, and he was elected a member from the State of Virginia to the Confederate House of Representatives. His sons and grandsons, those who were old enough to participate actively, flocked to the southern colors, and either joined the Confederate Army, or served with the Confederate Government. A Tyler grandson, William G. Waller, son of Elizabeth, married Jefferson Davis' sister-in-law. The Tylers were committed, without limit, to the cause of the southern states.

In January, 1862, before Tyler had time to take his seat in the Confederate Congress, he became ill. Julia, at home in "Sherwood Forest," dreamed he was dying, and she hurried to Richmond to be with him. When she arrived, she found him perfectly well, but he died a few days later, on January 18, 1862, of "bilious fever," a catch-all phrase designed to cover the ignorance of the attending physicians. Tyler was not quite seventy-two.

For the first time in its history, the federal government ignored the death of a former President; no announcement that Tyler had passed away came from Washington nor was a formal proclamation of mourning issued, as had been the custom in the past. It was as if, in the eyes of the federal government, John Tyler, tenth President of the United States, had never existed. To the Confederacy, John Tyler was a fallen hero, and he was given a state funeral.

The Civil War years, immediately following her husband's death, were desperately trying for Julia. She moved with her children to a northern sanctuary, the Staten Island home of her mother. "Sherwood Forest" was occupied by Union troops in 1864 and virtually destroyed. In October of that same year, Julia's mother died, and with her death came three years of bitter litigation and family discord between Julia and her brother, David

Gardiner, over the equitable disposition of their mother's property. The dissension was heightened by David Gardiner's refusal to switch his allegiance to the South, as most of the other Gardiners had. He was as resolute in his support of the North, as Julia was of the South. Brother and sister broke completely; never again were they cordial or friendly.

Julia's troubles with David were complicated by many suits against her husband's estate, so that she was plagued for a number of years by legal difficulties; and the country-wide panic of 1873 once again almost wiped her out, as had the Civil War and the Reconstruction. But somehow, with her usual style and elegance, Julia survived adversity. She flitted back and forth between Washington and Virginia, participating in the social events of the capital. And no matter how hard pressed she may have been for money, she always managed to dress impeccably, in the height of fashion.

The panic of 1873 passed; her mother's estate, in which she now shared, again gave Julia an income. With the help of her oldest son, David Gardiner Tyler, "Sherwood Forest" slowly came back to life. And finally, in 1882, she was awarded by an act of Congress, a lifetime pension of $5,000 a year as the widow of a President. Three other presidential widows were given similar pensions.

On the personal side, her daughter Julia was the first to marry, when she was twenty. She married William H. Spencer, on June 26, 1869, the twenty-fifth anniversary of her parents' wedding, in the same church. Two years later, in May of 1871, she died in childbirth. Julia grieved as much for her as she had ever grieved for her own husband, but she found some solace by conversion to the Roman Catholic faith. John Alexander was the next to be married, to his third cousin, Sarah Griswold Gardiner, in August of 1875. He was also the next to die, in New Mexico in 1883. On a surveying trip for the Government, he died of alkaline poisoning after running out of fresh water.

Only two of Julia's stepchildren were living by this time—John, Jr., and Letitia Semple, who still refused to reconcile with her. Robert died in 1877 at the age of sixty-one; Tazewell, forty-three, died in

1874. Tazewell, who had been a doctor, never forgave Julia for leaving "Sherwood Forest" during the Civil War.

Of her own surviving children, her fifth-born, Lyon Gardiner, had the most auspicious career. He became a successful author, with the publication in 1885 of a comprehensive, two-volume collective biography, *The Letters and Times of the Tylers.* Lyon's books were a source of great pride to Julia.

In July of 1889, in the same Richmond hotel where John Tyler had died, Julia Gardiner Tyler suffered a stroke. She had been ill for a number of years. At 11 A.M. of July 10, 1889, doctors were hurriedly summoned to her room, and diagnosed her attack as "congestive chill." There was nothing they could do to help her; she was unconscious and on the point of death. Her five surviving children were quickly notified, but not one of them arrived in time; she died at 5:15 P.M. at the age of sixty-nine. She was buried in Hollywood Cemetery in Richmond, next to her husband.

Mrs. Ex-President Tyler, as she often referred to herself in her correspondence, would have preferred an ending more suited to her flamboyant and romantic manner. For Julia Gardiner Tyler was truly an original; she lived in a grand style; it would have been fitting if she had died in the same way.

Sarah Polk
1803–1891

After seven ballots, the Democratic convention, meeting in Baltimore in the spring of 1844, could not agree between former President Martin Van Buren and General Lewis Cass as their presidential candidate to face Henry Clay, the Whig nominee. Suddenly, prior to the eighth ballot, the name of James Knox Polk was placed in nomination.

The delegates were electrified; it was apparent that a feeble old man, totally blind in one eye, almost blind in the other, and closer to death than he was to life, had thrust upon the convention his personal choice. Andrew Jackson, who had selected Van Buren to succeed him in 1837, now wanted his party to nominate Polk, his fellow Tennessean. The message was clear: Van Buren, opposed to the annexation of Texas, was to be dumped, despite his eminence as a former President, in favor of the lesser-known Polk. Like his long-time friend and mentor, Andrew Jackson, Polk strongly favored the annexation of Texas as the twenty-eighth state.

On the eighth ballot, Polk received forty-four votes; on the ninth, he was chosen by acclamation, and became the first dark horse in the history of American politics. "Old Hickory," sick and weary, still spoke with immense authority.

Henry Clay and the Whigs were jubilant. They were certain the Democrats had made a gigantic blunder; Polk would go down to certain defeat and drag the Democratic party with him. But Clay overlooked the old soldier. Jackson, too ill to leave his bed, countered the joyous Whig cry of "Who is James K. Polk?" with a barrage of letters dictated to his niece. He wrote to Democratic leaders, wardheelers, petty officials, anyone who could help. Almost single-handedly, Jackson made good on a pledge to Polk's wife, Sarah Childress Polk: "Daughter, I will put you in the White House if it costs me my life." Final election results gave Polk 1,339,368 votes to 1,300,687 for Clay.

The Whigs' electioneering question, "Who is James K. Polk?" was now joined by another: "Who is Sarah Childress Polk?" The country soon had the answer, for Sarah Polk was entirely different from her ebullient predecessor, Julia Tyler. The White House was to experience four years of "Puritan austerity."

Prominent amongst the early settlers in Tennessee were Andrew Jackson, the Childress family, the Whitsitts, and the Polks. Like many others, Captain Joel Childress became a wealthy planter. Married to Elizabeth Whitsitt, he settled in Rutherford County, not far from Murfreesborough, the county seat. On September 4, 1803, a second daughter, Sarah, was born to Joel and Elizabeth Childress; there were two sons as well.

For a short time, Sarah and her sister went to the common school nearby, and later attended a private school in Nashville (about thirty miles away) when Sarah was thirteen. The two girls boarded with the family of Colonel Butler, a member of General Andrew Jackson's staff. Sarah frequently saw the tall, lanky general and his short, stocky wife, Rachel. In later years, Sarah particularly remembered a ball she attended at the Jackson home.

When Sarah was fifteen, she and her sister were sent to Salem, North Carolina, to attend the Moravian Female Academy. Salem (now part of Winston-Salem) was perhaps four hundred miles from Murfreesborough; it was a long trip, tedious, and especially taxing for two young ladies who had to make the entire journey on horseback. But the girls had adequate escort in their older brother Anderson and a slave from their father's plantation. To speed them on their way, Captain Childress gave each of his daughters a louis d'or, a French gold coin. Sarah kept hers for the rest of her life; it remains a prized relic amongst the Polk mementoes.

The Moravian Academy was the best school of its kind in the entire South. With emphasis on religion, and valuable training in needlework and music, it did not overlook reading, writing, arithmetic, and history. It proved to have a profound influence upon Sarah, for it helped to shape her personality and her attitudes.

In 1819, Captain Childress died, and Sarah and her sister returned to Rutherford County. Once they left the academy, their formal education ended. Sarah brought back with her at least one tangible product of her stay at Salem—a piece of needlework depicting a white tomb gleaming in a stand of weeping willows.

It is not known precisely when James Polk met Sarah, but the most likely time was 1815, when Polk was nineteen and she was twelve. Polk, who had started school much later than most young men of his time, was sent to the academy in Murfreesborough. His family were well-to-do planters near Columbia, in Maury County, about fifty miles away. As a boy, he had been sickly, and was kept out of school because it was thought he wasn't strong enough for the rigors of education. In time, his father did permit him to enter a Presbyterian academy at the age of eighteen. He was sent, the following year, to Murfreesborough, where he met Sarah; he later enrolled in the state university at Chapel Hill, North Carolina.

Polk was a prim, humorless young man, medium in height, of slender physique, and hair brushed long behind his ears. Sarah, at the age of twelve, must have been a striking child. As an adult, she has been variously described as a "raven-haired beauty" and "not beautiful." Beautiful or not, the girl with the dark, almost Spanish complexion had in time a lasting effect upon James Polk.

In 1819, when Sarah was sixteen, Polk once again came to Murfreesborough, this time as clerk of the Tennessee Senate. Bustling and dusty Murfreesborough had been selected as the state capital, and though the legislature met only for a month at a time, it was enough for Polk to begin a courtship of Sarah Childress that was to cover four years.

After his graduation from the University of North Carolina, James Polk studied law under Felix Grundy, Nashville's most celebrated lawyer. Polk later returned to Maury County, where his father had a plantation, and went into the practice of law in partnership with another young attorney. In addition, his fortunes improved considerably from speculation in land, which he acquired through his father's generosity and wise counsel.

There is a story, neither verified nor refuted, that it was Sarah who urged Polk to pursue a career in politics. Whoever offered the impetus, he became a candidate in 1823 and won election to the Tennessee state legislature.

On January 1, 1824, James Polk and Sarah Childress were married at the Childress plantation, with Parson Henderson performing the ceremony and many guests from both families in attendance. The celebrations continued for a number of days, and spilled over into Columbia, fifty miles away, when Polk brought his bride home to meet the rest of his "kin" and neighbors.

In 1825, Polk ran for Congress, at the specific request of the Jackson people, who had singled him out with good reason. He was ardently pro-Jackson; a better-than-average speaker; he had the ambition and zeal of youth; his political philosophy paralleled Jackson's; and he was pliable. Much to Sarah's gratification, Polk won his election, and began a congressional career that lasted fourteen years.

Polk made his first trip to Washington in the fall of 1825. Sarah did not join him. She did come with him to the next session, and accompanied him to Washington every year thereafter except for one. They always traveled by carriage, accompanied by at least two servants. The trips were leisurely and relaxing, for the Polks had no financial problems; James had inherited a large share of his deceased father's estate, including land and slaves, and he later bought his own plantation in Mississippi.

Sarah enjoyed life in Washington. She took a thorough interest in politics, and was better informed than many of her husband's colleagues and acquaintances. Deeply religious, with a moralistic inflexibility and standards of righteousness that some people found distasteful, she was nevertheless a good conversationalist, often witty. Men found pleasure in her company, although they learned not to visit the Polks on Sunday morning. Anyone in the Polk parlor at that time was carefully herded to church by the self-proclaimed shepherdess, Sarah Polk.

The Polks never had children. Through the years they surrounded themselves with various nephews and nieces; in 1844, they adopted one of Polk's nephews, son of his brother Marshall.

Polk rose steadily in the Democratic party hierarchy; in 1835, he was chosen Speaker of the House of Representatives and held that position until 1839, when he returned to Tennessee to serve a term as governor.

In a try for reelection, he suffered two crushing defeats, in 1841 and 1843, losing both times to James C. Jones. Polk thought he had reached the end of the road. But in 1844, at the age of forty-nine, he was plucked from the ignominy of political oblivion by the canny Jackson.

Polk's defeat of the seasoned campaigner, Henry Clay, to become the eleventh President of the United States, must be considered one of the great upsets in American history, and a personal victory for Sarah Polk and Andrew Jackson, who never doubted that Polk would win.

In January, 1845, on their way to Washington for the Inauguration, the Polks stopped off at "The Hermitage" in Nashville to pay their respects to the elderly gentleman himself, General Andrew Jackson. This is the scene, as later recorded by a Polk biographer:

> The leave-taking was affectionate and impressive, for each felt conscious, that, in all probability, it was a farewell forever. It was the son, in his pride of manhood, going forth to fulfill his high destiny, from the threshold of his political godfather, whose trembling lips, palsied with the touch of age, could scarce invoke the benediction which his heart would prompt.

Sarah and James Polk never saw Jackson again. He died four months later, on June 8, 1845.

The Inauguration of James Polk took place on a rainy, blustery day, March 4, 1845. Polk shouted his Inaugural Address into the teeth of a wet and driving wind "to a large assemblage of umbrellas," as John Quincy Adams drily noted. Throughout the drenching rain, Sarah Polk stood calmly, unprotected, clutching a useless ivory fan presented to her as a remembrance of the solemn occasion.

That evening, at a gala Inaugural Ball, the keynote for Sarah's term as First Lady was sounded. The moment the Polks entered the large and crowded hall all dancing stopped and did not resume until two hours later, when the new President and his lady left. It was to be the same at all public receptions in the White House. Heeding the strictures of her rigid Presbyterian code, Sarah abolished dancing, drinking, and playing of cards. Nor was food to be served; the assembled guests were to have nothing but conversation. As always, the doors of the White House were open, and anyone was welcome. Sarah's gatherings were often crowded to the point of suffocation, although one was described by a Washington newspaper in this way: "Crowd thin,—conversation stiff, frigid, hard, affected, and altogether so-soish."

Despite the stiffness and austerity of her receptions, Sarah herself was popular; she read a great deal, and knew how to comment on what she had read, whether it was a current novel or an event of political importance. And somehow, despite her dictum that the President must live within his $25,000 annual salary, she managed to dress in elegant silks and satins and velvets (the colors, though muted, were always tasteful, and reflected the latest fashion trends).

Socially, Sarah's four years as First Lady were not successful; she must receive credit, however, for establishing the annual custom of a Thanksgiving dinner at the White House. And her receptions will always be memorable for the presence of the aging but still remarkable Dolley Madison, who was then in her late seventies. As President Polk noted in his diary: "Towards the close of the evening I passed through the crowded rooms with the venerable Mrs. Madison on my arm."

Sarah and James Polk were the hardest-working couple ever to occupy the White House. They were never separated; Sarah became Polk's personal secretary, working at his side for twelve and fourteen hours a day. As custom demanded, they held twice-weekly public receptions and more formal official dinners. But they resented time lost from work, and would often make up for it by returning to their papers long after their guests had gone. The Polks never took a vacation, and spent a total of only three days away from the White House.

Publicly, Polk's opinions and policies were his; privately, there can be no doubt that Sarah exerted much influence upon his thinking. She scanned the newspapers for him, marking articles she thought he should read; he discussed his work with her, and unquestionably permitted her to voice her opinions freely. It was inevitable that the First Lady's philosophy was reflected in the President's deeds. A Polk opponent once commented that James K. Polk was one of the "most henpecked" men he had ever known.

Polk may have been influenced by another source. In July of 1845, John L. O'Sullivan, writing in the *Democratic Review,* stated his belief that it was "our manifest destiny to overspread the continent . . . for the free development of our yearly multiplying millions." There were many who were gripped by the sentiment;

"manifest destiny" had the fervent ring of a holy pronouncement. Expansion became more than a byword; it was a mandate for the President, and Polk set about fulfilling it.

By the time his single term came to an end, his administration was responsible for the acquisition of 800,000 square miles of land, including the vast Oregon Territory, whose boundary was set at the present parallel of 49 degrees, and the California Territory. The latter acquisition covered all of the far Southwest from the Rio Grande to the Pacific Ocean, ceded to the United States as a result of the Mexican War, which may well be one of the most unjustified conflicts in American history.

It was thought that Polk's grueling schedule and devotion to his office shortened his life; when he and Sarah left the White House in 1849, he was thin to the point of emaciation, his hair white, his hands trembling and supported by a cane. He died three months later, on June 15, 1849, at "Polk Place," his new home in Nashville. He was buried in a marble tomb Sarah had copied from the needlework she had made at the Moravian Female Academy thirty years before. Polk was fifty-three.

Sarah never remarried, although she was only forty-five when her husband died, and she survived him by more than forty-two years. Polk had requested, in his will, that his slaves be freed, but Sarah refused to free them. She had use for them on the Polk plantation in Mississippi. As absentee owner, she conducted the affairs of her large property with a firm and orderly hand. In 1860, sensing perhaps that the era of the gentle, magnolia-scented South was coming to an end, she sold her plantation and thereby rid herself of possible guilt; her slaves were now someone else's responsibility.

During the Civil War, her house in Nashville was left untouched by invading northern armies. Union generals treated her with the same courtesy and respect as did her southern neighbors. She was, as always, staunchly pro-South, yet she was, above all else, the widow of the eleventh President of the United States. As she told a Polk biographer; "I have always belonged, and do now belong, to the whole country."

In the entire forty-two years after her husband's death, she never left "Polk Place" except to go to church. She welcomed all visitors, and proudly conducted them through her husband's study, which had been left exactly as it had been when he died. She permitted no one else to clean or dust it. In his memory, she wore, until the day she died, an article of black. And she undoubtedly remembered Polk's last words, spoken just before he closed his eyes: "I love you, Sarah, for all eternity, I love you."

Sarah Childress Polk passed away on August 14, 1891, almost eighty-eight years old. She was buried next to her husband, in the tomb she herself had designed.

There is a postscript to the story of James and Sarah Polk. In his will, Polk had directed that "Polk Place" be maintained as a perpetual shrine:

> My beloved wife Sarah Polk and myself have mutually agreed with each other, that at our respective deaths, it is desired that our bodies may be interred on the said premises . . . the said house, lot and premises shall never pass into the hands of strangers . . . nor shall any buildings or improvements be placed over the spot where [our] tomb may be.

Despite a public demand that the terms of Polk's will must be honored, Tennessee refused to do so. The will was broken, the house was sold, and on September 18, 1893, James and Sarah Polk were reburied by the sovereign state of Tennessee, "with appropriate ceremonies" on Nashville's Capitol Hill.

Margaret Taylor *

1788–1852

On May 11, 1846, President Polk sent an historic message to Congress requesting a declaration of war against Mexico. "The cup of forbearance has been exhausted. . . . After reiterated menaces, Mexico has passed the boundary of the United States, has invaded our territory and shed American blood upon American soil." Congress did as he asked; war against their Latin neighbor was declared the following day. A bizarre and extraordinary chain of events was thereby set in motion, and culminated, two and half years later, in the election of a well-meaning, good-natured, and politically inept professional solder as the twelfth President of the United States.

The Mexican War brought instant fame to General Zachary Taylor. He had never exercised his right to vote, and, in fact, did not know where his party allegiance lay, but he suddenly found himself promoted for the Presidency, under the sure hand of Thurlow Weed, undisputed boss of the Whigs. Weed had decided, in 1846, that the inexperienced Taylor would be the next President; his party, which had lost to Polk in 1844, would make its triumphant comeback in 1848 with a military hero, "Old Rough and Ready."

Thurlow Weed's assessment was shrewdly correct. Once again, a skillful campaign of promotion and bombast created a giant for American history; a man of mediocre talent stepped onto the illustrious pages of governmental folklore. Zachary Taylor was ready to take his place alongside George Washington and Andrew Jackson, two other generals who had towered above their peers. He had fought bravely and dutifully in the war with Mexico; the American people could do no less than reward him with the Presidency.

No portrait of Margaret Taylor is extant.

110

Betty Taylor Bliss

(Daughter of Margaret and Zachary Taylor)

There was one who did not agree. Margaret Smith Taylor, the new First Lady, had no desire to go to Washington, and never wanted her husband to be President. She prayed for his defeat, and considered his victory a plot to deprive her of his company and shorten his life. She was right in at least one respect; she did not belong in the White House. Of all the First Ladies who had come before her, Margaret Taylor was the least prepared for her position, and the most unwilling to serve.

General James John Mackall, Margaret's grandfather, was one of the wealthier landowners in Calvert County, Maryland. He numbered among his assets a large plantation, many slaves, and eight beautiful daughters. One daughter, Ann, married Walter Smith of St. Leonard's Creek Hundred, located in a neighboring area, near the Patuxent River. Smith had come into proprietorship of his own plantation by way of inheritance.

Little is known of the family life of Walter and Ann Smith, nor is it certain exactly how many children they had. There is mention of at least two sons and two daughters. One daughter, Margaret, was born on September 21, 1788, in Calvert County.

111

Of Margaret's childhood and schooling, nothing has been recorded. Many Calvert County records were lost, and the Smiths, who had no reason to expect that one of their own would be a First Lady of the land, did not save correspondence and other papers. Margaret's early years are therefore shadowy. Many years later, when she actually lived in the White House and could have told her story to others, either no one asked or she would not say. She wrote no letters; if she had, they were not found. Posterity was never to know of Margaret Taylor's childhood and some of her later years.

In 1809, when Margaret was twenty-one, she was visiting her sister, Mrs. Samuel Chew, in Jefferson County, Kentucky. Her father had died a few years before. In Kentucky she met a young lieutenant, stocky, with rather short legs and a broad face. She herself was slender, and probably had brown hair and light eyes. A portrait of her does exist, but her descendants deny its authenticity; they claim she "never wished to sit for her portrait, and . . . no likeness of her was extant."

The twenty-four-year-old lieutenant was Zachary Taylor, a professional soldier. He was home on leave, visiting with his family at their plantation near Beargrass Creek, not far from Louisville. The home of Mr. and Mrs. Samuel Chew, where Margaret was staying, was a few miles away. Lieutenant Taylor and Margaret were introduced by a mutual friend. The introduction was successful, for Taylor and Margaret were married the following year on June 21, 1810, at her sister's log cabin. Although Margaret brought no dowry with her (her brothers had inherited the Smith property in Maryland) there was no financial concern, despite the low pay of a first lieutenant. Zachary's father presented them with 324 acres of his own plantation.

Taylor apparently had no specific military assignment for the next year. He and Margaret were living in Jefferson County, where the birth of their first daughter, Ann Mackall Taylor, occurred on April 9, 1811. In November of the same year, Taylor was promoted to captain and assigned to Fort Knox at Vincennes, Indiana Territory (William Henry Harrison was then governor of the territory). On

March 6, 1814, a second daughter was born to Margaret and Zachary. They named her Sarah Knox, in honor of the fort where she was born; for the rest of her life, she was known more simply as Knox.

Margaret's trip from Kentucky to join her husband at Fort Knox was the first of many she was to take over the next twenty-seven years. In all that time, she was never to have a permanent home; she would spend more time separated from her children than with them. Her husband's welfare was her overriding concern.

Four more children were born to the Taylors, all in Jefferson County. There were three daughters: Octavia Pannel, on August 16, 1816; Margaret Smith, July 27, 1819; and Mary Elizabeth (later known as "Betty"), on April 20, 1824. The Taylors' only son, Richard, was born on January 27, 1826.

The War of 1812 found Taylor a brevet major (brevet was a promotion to a higher rank, generally temporary, without an increase in pay). By 1819, he had become a lieutenant colonel, and was transferred, in August of that year, to Louisiana. He settled Margaret and their four daughters with Margaret's sister, living at Bayou Sara in the Louisiana delta. Taylor then went on to his assignment.

Less than one year later, in July of 1820, there began a crushing series of blows. The bayou country, damp and misty, was a breeding ground for malaria. The disease could strike without warning, as it suddenly did against Margaret and the children. Octavia, not quite four, died quickly; by September, Margaret was dangerously ill. The two older children, not affected as much as the others, gradually recovered, as finally did Margaret. But in October, the youngest died at the age of fifteen months. Within the space of less than four months, Margaret and Zachary had lost two of their four children to "a violent bilious fever" (as Taylor wrote of it) and Margaret herself had almost gone.

Margaret was now determined that her surviving children, Ann and Knox, must be spared further exposures, and she sent them off to relatives for schooling. She did the same with her next two children, Betty and Richard, as they grew old enough for education. She and Zachary were together in a variety of forts; she was often lonely to a point of depression, for not only were her children away, but Zachary many times had to leave her because of military matters.

At Fort Crawford, in the Michigan Territory, their eldest daughter, Ann, at the age of eighteen, married an Army surgeon, Dr. Robert Wood. Three years later, at the same fort, a fateful meeting took place that was to lead to one of the major tragedies in Margaret's life.

Knox, now a lovely and graceful eighteen, returned from school to rejoin her parents. In the late summer of 1832, she met a young lieutenant stationed at Fort Crawford, Jefferson Davis (the same Jefferson Davis who later became President of the Confederate States). The young people fell instantly in love, but Colonel Taylor objected to a marriage between them. He had seen first-hand, through Margaret, what Army life could mean to the wife of a soldier. One daughter, Ann, had already married a military man, and he would "be damned if another daughter of his shall marry into the Army." But despite his unconcealed resistance, Davis and Knox did finally marry, on June 17, 1835. Davis resigned from the Army, and took Knox to Louisiana, where he intended to start a plantation.

Margaret remembered all too vividly what Louisiana had done to two of her other daughters, and she could not help but worry about Knox. Knox, however, did not share her mother's fears. On June 17, her wedding day, Knox wrote to her mother, and included these words: "The part of the country to which I am going is quite healthy." On August 11, there was another letter, with further assurance: "Do not make yourself uneasy about me; the country is quite healthy." Knox died of malaria a month later, on September 15, at the age of twenty-one. Jefferson Davis became a recluse, and did not remarry for several years. Of Margaret's grief there is no eyewitness testimony, but the only letters she ever kept were those two from Knox, which became worn from constant rereading.

From 1813 to 1840, Margaret and Zachary shared the loneliness and desolation of frontier posts from Indiana to Florida. At times, separation from their children was more than they could bear. In March of 1837, Taylor asked for an extended leave of absence "for the purpose of visiting [our] children who are at school . . . and who have been absent from us for . . . several years." The leave was granted, but could not be used, for once again military necessity took precedence over personal needs; this time it was a war against the Seminole Indians.

In 1841, Taylor, a brigadier-general, was placed in command of a large area of the Southwest, with headquarters at Baton Rouge, Louisiana. And here, for the first time in her life, at the age of fifty-three, Margaret Taylor made a permanent home for herself and her husband.

Although she had her choice of several imposing brick buildings reserved for officers, she chose, instead, "a cottage in sad disrepair on the river bank." It was a small, rundown house of four rooms, built forty years before for the Spanish commandant. The cottage, empty and neglected, was away from the center of the bustling headquarters; perhaps this was the reason it appealed to Margaret. It was isolated and peaceful, overlooking the river.

With the help of her younger daughter, Betty, two slaves, and assorted "invalid soldiers unfit for military duties," Margaret soon had the little house gleaming and clean, and furnished in a simple, comfortable way. For Margaret, it was a "dream cottage," where she would be happy to spend the rest of her life, for she assumed that she and Zachary would never again be separated. But history has a way of sweeping before it the trifles we consider significant; a four-room cottage doesn't stand a chance against "manifest destiny." With the Inauguration of President Polk in 1845, and the joint resolution of Congress to annex the Republic of Texas as the twenty-eighth state, trouble with Mexico was inevitable. In July of 1845, General Taylor and his Army embarked for Corpus Christi, Texas, to await the start of hostilities. And Margaret Taylor, fifty-seven, gray and tired and ill, was alone, except for her daughter Betty.

Ironically, the first two battles of the Mexican War, which

spread the name of General Zachary Taylor across the entire United States, were fought *before* the actual declaration of war on May 12, 1846. The Battle of Palo Alto (Mexico) took place on May 8; the next day, the American Army, under General Taylor's command, advanced a few miles further into Mexico and engaged the enemy at Resaca de la Palma. The numerically superior Mexicans, under the uncertain leadership of General Mariano Arista (who supposedly was still in his tent, in his underwear), were completely routed. And the fame of General Zachary Taylor, "Old Rough and Ready," was assured.

By the time the Whig convention assembled in Philadelphia in June of 1848, Thurlow Weed and his cohorts had executed their plans with precision. Zachary Taylor, never behind in the voting, was nominated on the fourth ballot, with Millard Fillmore of New York as his running mate. When Margaret heard the news of Zachary's nomination, she reportedly cried out "that it was a plot to deprive her of his society, and shorten his life by unnecessary care and responsibility." Perhaps she did say something very much like that, for by then she had deliberately withdrawn from the mainstream of social activity. During the war, she had been in "a dreadful state of mind"; Zachary, despite his rank, was as vulnerable as any of his fellows, for officers too were killed, and she did not know a moment without worry.

She was even less pleased with his election; she did not accompany him to Washington in March of 1849. She was said to have been a semi-invalid by then, though nothing definite of her illness has ever been stated. There are reports of her in perfectly good health at the White House after she arrived, yet there is conflicting and reliable testimony that she was indeed not well.

Whispers about this strange woman from the frontier had circulated before her arrival: she smoked a corncob pipe (not true—she hated the smell of tobacco); she was "a poor-white of the wilds" (again not true, for she was a descendant of distinguished Maryland families on both sides). It *was* true that she had spent too many years at isolated military posts; she may have felt ill at ease in the teeming turmoil of Washington diplomacy.

She did not assume the role of First Lady at the White House; she was not only a semi-invalid, she was a semi-recluse. She was content to leave the chores of entertaining in the hands of her daughter Betty, now married to Colonel William Bliss. Betty acted in her place as official hostess, while Margaret remained in the apartment she had chosen on the second floor of the Executive Mansion. One of those privileged to see her was Varina Howell Davis, Jefferson Davis' second wife, whom he had married in February of 1845. Jefferson Davis was now a senator from Mississippi, and he was on close terms with the Taylors, who still thought of him as part of the family.

Varina Davis wrote many letters; in a number of them she spoke of Margaret: "I always found the most pleasant part of my visit to the White House to be passed in Mrs. Taylor's bright pretty room where the invalid, full of interest in the passing show in which she had not the strength to take her part, talked most agreeably and kindly to the many friends admitted to her presence." Later, in May of 1850, the picture becomes more poignant: "I went upstairs to see Mrs. Taylor. I found the old lady sitting with her feet in the fender shivering, and she seemed so charmed to see me, said she felt so wretchedly lonesome, and chilly."

The White House, despite the absence of its First Lady from its public functions, was a far gayer and more pleasant establishment than it had been under Sarah Polk. President Taylor was a gregarious man, and liked having many people about him, including noisy grandchildren and nephews and nieces. As a President, he left little for historians to praise, but his administration at least was an enjoyable one.

On July 4, 1850, President Taylor spent a grueling afternoon enduring, under a relentless and baking sun, a long-winded tribute to our first President at the new Washington Monument. When the interminable speeches were at last over, he hurried to the White House, where he greedily consumed huge quantities of iced milk and cherries. His alarmed physician pleaded with him to stop, but he would not. That night he was seized with violent cramps and died five days later, on July 9, at the age of sixty-five. The cause of his death was listed, variously, as "bilious fever, typhoid fever, or cholera morbus." A more accurate diagnosis would have been acute gastroenteritis.

The effect of his death upon Margaret was ghastly. Varina Davis, who was in his room when he died, describes the scene: "The tearing Mrs. Taylor away from the body nearly killed me— she would listen to his heart, and feel his pulse, and insist he did not die without speaking to her." Nor was it easier for Margaret during Taylor's funeral, once more described by Mrs. Davis: "I saw her endure all the torture of a state funeral. [She] was worn to a shadow, and lay without uttering a sound, but trembled silently from head to foot as one band after another blared the funeral music . . . and the heavy guns boomed . . . to announce the final parting."

Zachary Taylor was buried, with honors, in Washington, D.C., and later reburied in the Taylor family plot near Louisville, Kentucky. He had served only sixteen months of his four-year term.

Margaret Taylor, not quite sixty-two, had lost the one important prop in her life. She went to live with her son in Pascagoula, Mississippi. She died two years later, on August 14, 1852, one month short of sixty-four, of causes not mentioned, but if a broken heart is medically possible, she died of that; she was buried next to Zachary, in the Taylor family plot.

She never thought of herself as a public figure, and would have been astonished at the many mentions of her passing in the American press. The *Daily Picayune* of New Orleans sadly noted that her death "will carry a sentiment of profound regret among a numerous circle of connexions and friends," while the *New York Daily Times* of August 17, 1852, put it more succinctly: "Mrs. General TAYLOR, relict of the late President, died at East Pascagoula on Saturday night." (Relict is an archaic word for widow.)

Abigail Fillmore
1798–1853

Disaster struck a double blow at the once mighty Whigs; twice they emerged triumphant in presidential elections, and both times their successful candidates died in office. Zachary Taylor's death in July of 1850 signaled the beginning of the end for them; within a few years they would disappear entirely from the American scene.

Millard Fillmore, Taylor's Vice President, was a bland, handsome man who was neither equipped nor prepared to handle the affairs of state. When he took the oath of office on July 10, 1850, to become the thirteenth President of the United States, he faced a task that pleaded for wisdom to rival Solomon's and for statesmanship of the highest order. The tense and tenuous peace that had been maintained between slave-owning South and industrial North since the Missouri Compromise of 1820 was ripping apart. South-

119

ern militants were screaming for secession. Disunion was clearly in the air.

Once again, mutual concession seemed the only way out, and a set of resolutions, engineered by Henry Clay and designed to placate both intensely sectional factions, was introduced into Congress. Their two salient points included the Fugitive Slave Act and the admission of California into the Union as a free state. The first would appease the South; the second would soothe the North.

Fillmore now faced a most difficult decision. If he signed the repressive Fugitive Slave Act, it might well be "the death blow of his personal popularity in the North," according to one of his biographers. "Great portions of his political friends would be alienated forever." But Fillmore was convinced that a middle course was the only way to preserve the country against the "ravings of Southern Disunionists and the curses of extreme Abolitionists at the North," and he signed the act into law on September 18, 1850.

Whether the new First Lady, Abigail Powers Fillmore, approved of the Fugitive Slave Act cannot properly be determined. It is known that she had warned her husband of the damage to his political life if he signed the act, although there is no indication that she exerted any pressure upon him for or against it. She did much to influence him throughout their marriage, but she preferred the background, and publicly, the decision was his. Years later a close friend wrote that Fillmore had been "heard to say that he never took any important step without her counsel and advice." If her advice extended to the Fugitive Slave Act, it was a calculated risk they both lost.

In that same fateful year of 1850, a man named Enoch Sherman Leland compiled *The Leland Magazine, or a Genealogical Record of Henry Leland and His Descendants, Containing an Account of Nine Thousand Six Hundred and Twenty-Four Persons, in Ten Generations.* One of this multitude of Leland relatives and decendants was Abigail Powers.

ABIGAIL FILLMORE

Abigail, whose mother was Abigail Newland, was born in Stillwater, New York, in Saratoga County, on March 13, 1798. Abigail's father, the Reverend Lemuel Powers, died in 1800, when she was two. Mrs. Powers was left with the young Abigail, an older son, a library extensive for its day, and no funds. Believing that she could do better in the still uncultivated western part of New York, Mrs. Powers moved her children and her books to Moravia in the Finger Lakes area of Cayuga County.

There could not have been much opportunity for schooling in the frontier hamlet, yet Abigail and her brother, who became a lawyer and a judge, were taught by someone. Or they may have taught themselves, by using the many books their father had bequeathed them as his only legacy. By the time she was sixteen, Abigail was educated to the point where she could teach others.

A few miles to the east, on a farm near Sempronius, there lived another family, the Fillmores. Nathaniel Fillmore was neither sagacious nor lucky; a series of misfortunes led him to Cayuga County, where he did his best to extract a living from the clayey soil. He could not afford tutors or schooling for his children. At least one of them, Millard, was determined to learn, and over the years he did manage a bit of education. At the age of ten he was "drilled most thoroughly in Webster's spelling-book." As he himself later spoke of that meager training: "I think I went through that book without missing in the spelling of a word; but I did not learn the definition of a single one."

Though they lived only a few miles apart, Abigail and Millard did not meet until the fall of 1819, when she was twenty-one and he was nineteen. Abigail was then teaching school in New Hope, a village a few miles to the north of Sempronius and northeast of Moravia, her own home. Millard's search for education had brought him to New Hope, and the academy where Abigail was teaching.

When Millard first entered Abigail's class, she was struck not only by his age (at nineteen he was the oldest of her students, and only two years younger than she) but by his bearing as well. He was a solid, well-built young man, with fair hair, blue eyes, and smooth skin. He had been raised on a farm, yet he had the confident air of a successful townsman, despite the constant poverty of early years.

Abigail, too, carried herself well. At five feet six inches she was taller than most women of her time. As a child, her hair was reddish; it turned darker as she grew older. Her eyes were light. She wore her hair parted in the middle, and twisted into tight curls hanging over each side of her head. No one has ever claimed that she was a great beauty, but certainly she was attractive.

The relationship between Abigail and Millard had both immediate and long-range rewards. For the first time in his life (as he wrote in his autobiography) he heard a sentence parsed, and had the opportunity to study geography with a map. He went on to say: "I pursued much of my study with, and perhaps was unconsciously stimulated by the companionship of, a young lady whom I afterward married."

The romance, however, was years in developing. After only a few months in New Hope, he left to study law with Judge Walter Wood in Montville, a village just outside of Moravia. From there he went to Aurora, some 150 miles to the west, not far from Buffalo, in Erie County. This was in September of 1821. He had been seeing Abigail while he lived in Montville, for that was only seven or eight miles from New Hope. For an ardent young suitor, it was merely a brisk walk (he did not own a horse). From Erie County, it would have meant at least a week or more of steady hiking.

Unfortunately, his letters to Abigail have not been preserved, so we have no way of knowing why he waited so long to come back. He spent a number of years in Aurora and Buffalo, studying and working. Eventually, he did return to Cayuga County, and, to quote a recent biographer, "This time Fillmore abandoned foot-travel and like a successful man arrived in Abigail's home town by stagecoach." Soon after, Abigail and Millard were married, on February 5, 1826, at the Moravia home of her brother, now a judge. Abigail was almost twenty-eight, and Millard had just turned twenty-six. More than seven years had elapsed since their first meeting.

The Fillmores moved to Aurora, where he had been practicing law and building a house. It was expected that Abigail, like every woman of her time and place, would become a housewife. But that was not for her. She had flaunted convention by working before her marriage; as Mrs. Fillmore, she continued working, for she was a teacher, and there was a need of her skills and knowledge.

In 1819, when she had first met Millard, she had helped to mold his education, and no doubt had mapped a course of study for him and the proper books to read when he left New Hope the following year. She herself was literate and well read, as evidenced by a letter she wrote from her new home in Aurora on August 27, 1826.

This letter, written to a relative with whom she had been living in Moravia prior to her marriage, is one of the only examples of her correspondence still in existence. All of her letters were ordered burned, together with other family correspondence and papers, by direction of her son's will. His instructions were followed soon after his death in 1889, and almost nothing written by Abigail remains, except for this letter and perhaps one or two others. Writing to Miss Maria Fuller, Abigail said, in part:

> My mind often reverts to the pleasant hours I have passed at your house. . . . Oh, that I may again have the pleasure of spending a happy evening in your family with the little children sitting near me, asking a thousand interesting questions.

Life in Aurora meant an adjustment for Abigail. It was a larger town than she had known. Her husband was considered one of the leading citizens of the area. Apprenticed to a wool-carder and cloth-dresser at the age of fifteen, Fillmore had become a gentleman of substance.

In 1828, Abigail was faced with another, and greater, adjustment. On April 25, a son was born to her; he was named Millard Powers Fillmore. She was thirty at the time. Her only other child, Mary Abigail, was born four years later, in Buffalo, on March 27, 1832.

With an infant son and a home in Aurora to keep her busy, Abigail no longer had time for teaching. Fillmore, in the meantime, had risen rapidly in political circles. In 1829 he was elected to the New York State Assembly, and served until 1831.

Fillmore's growing practice in Aurora and his service in the State Assembly brought him an offer of a law partnership from one of the leading attorneys of Buffalo. In 1830, Fillmore, Abigail, and their two-year-old son moved to Buffalo, a town of eight thousand. This time Fillmore did not have to build a house for his family; he bought a six-room frame structure two blocks from the main street.

Settled soon after the close of the American Revolution, Buffalo for many years was no more than a village, until the completion of the Erie Canal in 1825. From then on, its growth in size and importance was spectacular. Its upper social stratum was polished and worldly, despite the distances of the town from the main centers of culture and sophistication. For the first time, Abigail indulged her love of music (she played both the harp and the piano); there were chamber recitals and dances, as well as concerts, plays, lectures, and formal dinners. The Buffalonians, friendly and sociable, accepted Abigail and Millard Fillmore as their own.

Life in Buffalo was not all play or work. Both Abigail and Millard were believers in religion, though not to the point of extremism. They joined the Unitarian Church, which would seem to have been their last choice. Though Fillmore had been a member of no particular sect, his family were Methodist; Abigail's father had been a minister in the Baptist church; and they had been married by an Episcopalian. They never explained why they became Unitarians, but they were faithful to their choice. Sunday worship was a lifelong habit; they tolerated no business of any kind on the Sabbath.

Abigail now indulged another of her passions—her love of books. Fillmore bought books for her by the carton, until their library reached four thousand volumes. But there was little in the way of literature. Abigail's choices were dull and prosaic, as were Millard's.

A close friend, Mrs. S. G. Haven, wife of Fillmore's law partner, described the Fillmores in a paper delivered before the Buffalo Historical Society: "[Their] private life [was] so domestic and so quiet and uneventful as to present but few salient points for the narrator, and none whatever for the sensationalist."

In 1848, Abigail and Millard moved once again, this time to Albany, New York. He had been elected comptroller of the state. By then he was one of the most prominent men in the entire State of New York. He had served a number of terms in Congress, as representative from Erie County; in 1844, a year when the Democrats were overwhelming the Whigs in most parts of the country, he ran for governor of New York on the Whig ticket, and lost to the Democratic candidate, Silas Wright. Four years later he convincingly won election as comptroller and proved that the voters had not forgotten him.

The Fillmores rented their house in Buffalo and moved into an apartment in Albany, the state capital. Mary Abigail, now sixteen, was sent to a finishing school, and Millard Powers, twenty-one, was sent to Harvard.

Abigail, at the age of fifty, expected no more honors for her husband, and she would have preferred none, for the infirmities of middle and older years had begun to take their toll. But she made no objection when the Whig convention, meeting in Philadelphia in June of 1848, nominated her husband for the office of Vice President. Nor did his election to the second highest office in the land disturb her; like millions of others, she never dreamed the President would die, almost without warning. During most of the sixteen months Fillmore served as Vice President, she lived in Buffalo, with short visits to Washington. She and Mary spent the spring of 1850 in the capital city, living at the Willard Hotel. They went back to Buffalo in June, and so were not present when Taylor died and Fillmore suddenly found himself the focus of attention the world over.

Abigail, not feeling well, did not return to Washington for her husband's Inauguration, nor was she there when the storm broke over his signing of the Fugitive Slave Act in September. Sensitive as she was to political nuances, she must have been deeply disturbed by the vituperation being heaped upon him. But she must have found solace in the knowledge that her husband's actions had saved the Union—at least for the time being. Southern militants no longer threatened to secede, and northern anger over the Fugitive Slave Act gradually subsided, so that a sense of normalcy was restored to Washington.

By October, Abigail was well enough to travel and she came at last to the White House to take her place as First Lady. Mary Abigail, at eighteen a poised young lady and accomplished musician (she, too, played the harp and piano), served as official hostess until her Mother's arrival.

Abigail's stay at the White House was unspectacular, although she was responsible for a number of innovations. When she moved in, she found the Executive Mansion totally devoid of books (it did not even have a Bible), and she thereupon persuaded her husband to request an appropriation from Congress for a library, which she established in a lovely oval room on the second floor; she had a bathtub installed (Washington gossip was titillated by the stories that President Fillmore *bathed regularly* with Corinthian Oil of Cream and concentrated extract of eglantine); and an iron cookstove was brought in to replace the huge fireplace where all the cooking had previously been done.

Abigail continued the custom of Tuesday afternoon receptions, without food or drink, and Friday night levees, with music only. There were many times she could not attend, because of a painful ankle injury she had suffered some time before. Mary, as she often did, would stand in for her as hostess.

Culturally, the Executive Mansion reflected Abigail's tastes, for she often invited writers to the White House, including William Makepeace Thackeray and Washington Irving. The Fillmores enjoyed concerts; of the many they attended one was a Jenny Lind recital.

One of the more sensational events during the Fillmore administration was the publication of Harriet Beecher Stowe's *Uncle Tom's Cabin*. For the first time, many northerners read of conditions in the South, and were horrified, although Mrs. Stowe's book was not entirely accurate.

The Presidency of Millard Fillmore ended on a quiet note; he had contributed little of value to history. Most of his party had turned against him, for many of them could not forget that he had signed the Fugitive Slave Act; they refused to nominate him for a second term. Millard Fillmore had but a brief moment of glory. His term as President lasted exactly two years and 236 days.

As First Lady, Abigail's record was as unimpressive as her husband's. The performance of her last official act, however, had a tragic and unlooked-for consequence. The Inauguration of the new President, Franklin Pierce, took place on March 4, 1853, a day that was raw and blustery, with masses of wet snow. No one would have blamed Abigail for not attending, but she believed in conventions and proper appearances. It was her place to be there; she suffered through the slush and chill and the wet, icy snow. By next morning, it was evident she was ill; that evening she ran a high fever, and soon developed pneumonia. Less than one month later, on March 30, 1853, Abigail Fillmore died in her suite at the Willard Hotel at the age of fifty-five.

Her daughter, Mary Abigail, twenty-two, died the following year of cholera in Aurora, New York, Fillmore himself lived for twenty-one years after Abigail's death. In 1858, he remarried; his second wife was a widow named Caroline Carmichael McIntosh. She was forty-four and Fillmore was fifty-eight. He died on March 8, 1874, at the age of seventy-four. He and Abigail are both buried in Forest Lawn Cemetery, Buffalo, New York.

The Buffalo Historical Society, which has done much to preserve the surviving Fillmore papers, has an eloquent (though stilted) description of Abigail's death: "She had long been a sufferer of ill-health and was looking forward eagerly to a return to her old home, when she was taken away to those temples not made with hands."

Jane Pierce
1806–1863

The presidential campaign of 1852 found both major political parties in a state of confusion and disarray. The Whigs, on the point of extinction, desperately attempted to repeat what they had done twice before—they hoped to win with an elderly military hero. On the fifty-third ballot, they turned to General Winfield Scott.

On the Democratic side, the problem was no less acute. After forty-six ballots, which saw an excess of backstage maneuvering, no decision could be reached among the four leading contenders. On the next two ballots, a new name received a few tentative votes. On the forty-ninth ballot, there was a sudden bandwagon rush to the new man, and, for the second time in the history of American politics, a dark horse triumphed. Forty-seven-year-old Franklin Pierce of New Hampshire was the Democratic nominee by a vote of 282 to 7.

The nomination of Pierce might well have been a fatal miscalculation, for he was vulnerable to criticism. He was a known alcoholic. The Whigs, in a gross display of bad taste, chortled that Pierce was the "hero of many a well-fought bottle."

Despite his vulnerability and the virulence of the Whig attack, Pierce scored a smashing victory. He defeated General Scott, "Old Fuss and Feathers," by a popular vote of 1,601,274 to 1,386,580 and an electoral margin of 254 to 42, twenty-seven states against four. It was a spectacular feat for Franklin Pierce, but the confidence shown him by the electorate was unwarranted. He was the worst of a series of bad Presidents; his wife, Jane Appleton Pierce, was as unsuccessful a First Lady as those immediately preceding her. Yet in fairness to both, Jane and Franklin Pierce came into the White House suffering intolerable grief and sorrow. In time, Pierce found some solace in his work; but for Jane, there was no forgetting a terrible moment that had taken place only two short months before her husband's Inauguration. It clouded the four years she lived in the White House, and haunted her for the rest of her life.

In 1807, the tiny college of Bowdoin, situated in a remote section of the District of Maine, selected as its second president the Reverend Jesse Appleton, a Congregational minister. Appleton, married to Elizabeth Means of Amherst, New Hampshire, was not a wealthy man, but his wife's father was one of the richest merchants in the area. Jesse and Elizabeth Appleton had six children, three sons and three daughters. Their youngest daughter, Jane, who was born on March 12, 1806, in Hampton, New Hampshire, was one year old when her father received his appointment.

Bowdoin, near the village of Brunswick, was devoted exclusively to the education of well-born young men. There was little opportunity for the Appleton children to attend school, and yet they received excellent training, undoubtedly from their father and students of the college impressed into service as tutors. Just before his death in 1819 at the age of forty-seven, the Reverend Appleton remarked to a minister friend: "I have endeavored faithfully to instruct my children, and they have conducted so as greatly to endear themselves to me." Whether he was referring to spiritual or lay instruction is not clear (in later life, Jane was a deeply religious woman).

In 1820, Jesse Appleton's widow, Elizabeth Appleton, moved with her children to her father's home in Amherst, New Hampshire. He gave them an empty farmhouse, which Elizabeth, with the help of a servant girl, soon made habitable for her family. By this time, Jane was beginning to reveal signs of frail health, which was to plague her for the better part of her life. On June 17, 1820, Elizabeth Appleton wrote to her sister (Jane was then fourteen): "Jane, William, and Robert go to school and attend I should hope pretty well to their studies. . . . Jane's health is improved."

Shortly after the Appletons left Bowdoin in 1820, Franklin Pierce enrolled in the college at the age of sixteen, and graduated four years later. The exact circumstances of his meeting with Jane Appleton are vague. Some misinformed biographers place the meeting at Bowdoin, but that wasn't possible, for the Appletons had left Bowdoin before he arrived.

Pierce, born and raised in Hillsborough, New Hampshire, returned there in 1824 after his graduation. Amherst, New Hampshire, where Jane was living, was perhaps twenty miles away. It is probable that he traveled from Hillsborough to pay a courtesy call on the widow of President Appleton. He therefore could have met Jane any time after 1824; Jane would have been eighteen, and Pierce twenty.

If their first meeting did occur in 1824, there is a curious feature to their romance that has never been adequately explained. They did not marry until many years later. Nor is the marriage itself fully understood. Pierce was a convivial young man rising rapidly, with a minimum of ability, in a political milieu characterized by hearty good-fellowship. Jane was a moralistic young woman thoroughly indoctrinated with the sober and proper ideals of her Congregationalist father and matriarchal grandmother.

Pierce was already a victim of his weakness; his mother had been an alcoholic and he was convinced he had inherited her uncontrollable tendencies, though his major fault may have been not addiction to alcohol but rather his inability to hold liquor in quantity. The politicians of his day were hard drinkers as well as hard manipulators; Pierce, who thought it was expected of him to keep up, did his best, but often to a point of illness.

Another mark against him, in the eyes of Jane's relatives, was his lack of family tradition; his father had been a fighting soldier in the American Revolution, had risen to the rank of general in the New Hampshire militia and had served as governor of his state. But the rough old general was a farmer; his background was rustic and ordinary. Jane Appleton, on her maternal side, came from a family of aristocrats. They were rich, haughty, and unapproachable except by their own. It may well be that they objected to the gregarious and bibulous Franklin Pierce because he lacked suitable background. (They conveniently forgot that Jane's maternal grandfather, Robert Means, had started his climb to wealth and prestige as a New Hampshire peddler.)

Jane was lovely in a quiet, unobtrusive manner. Small, with delicate features, she had dark hair and dark eyes. She could not have lacked for suitors, yet she did wait for Pierce. Or perhaps, by the time she reached twenty-eight and had not yet found the ideal man, she settled for less. Or, and this is a real possibility, Jane may have truly loved this procrastinating young man who took so long to make up his mind about her.

Pierce and his "dearest Jeanie" were married in the parlor of the Means's Amherst mansion on November 19, 1834. Jane was not quite twenty-nine and Pierce was a few days short of thirty. Pierce, a successful lawyer (he had been admitted to the bar in 1827), had served for four years as a legislator in the New Hampshire House of Representatives, and was, at the time of their marriage, representative from New Hampshire to the United States Congress.

Jane and Pierce set out for Washington soon after their wedding, and arrived there on November 28, 1834. Jane's concern for her husband's weakness was even then apparent, as she wrote to her father-in-law, General Benjamin Pierce:

"Frank does very well thus far, sir, and is as you say a *pretty good boy*—it is to be sure rather *soon* to judge but I hope I shall have no reason to alter my opinion—in *such a case,* I shall appeal to you, who I am sure will lend me your *countenance.*"

At the close of the session, Jane and Pierce went to Hillsborough, New Hampshire. He had purchased a house from General McNeil, and they now set about the task of becoming settled married people. Pierce returned to the practice of law, and took in, as his clerk, Albert Baker, whose sister, Mary Baker Eddy, was to establish the First Church of Christ, Scientist.

For the next session of Congress, Pierce set out alone. Jane was pregnant and could not make the tedious trip to the capital. He was in Washington when their first son, Franklin Pierce, Jr., was born on February 2, 1836. His joy was short-lived; the infant boy died three days later. Pierce was thrown into a state of melancholy, eased not at all by drink. For Jane, it was a most difficult period, for she was ill, and it took her some time to regain her strength.

In the early summer of 1836, after Pierce had returned from Washington, they moved to Concord, where they lived in a boarding house. Pierce learned in the fall that he had been elected to the United States Senate; Jane accompanied him for his first session as a senator. As before, she did not like Washington, and made little effort to join its varied activities. By the following summer, in 1838, Jane was more than happy to return to the cool hills of New Hampshire, for she had been both ill and depressed. There had recently been a number of deaths in her family; coupled with her continuing state of bad health, she was in no condition for the humid and swampy capital.

On August 27, 1839, a second son, Frank Robert, was born in Concord. Not quite two years later, a third son, named for his paternal grandfather Benjamin, was born on April 13, 1841, also in Concord. Both boys, fortunately, were healthy. Now, with a family to think of, Jane's continual pleas to Pierce that he give up politics brought a positive response. Although he was the youngest member of the Senate, he was no more than a competent follower who knew how to obey orders. His law practice had suffered while he was in Washington; with little future as a politician, he at last did as Jane asked and retired from the Senate in 1842.

The Pierces bought a house in Concord, on Montgomery Street; it was their first real home since they had left Hillsborough six years before. Jane had lived in a series of boarding houses, both in Washington and Concord, and she now looked forward to a life of contentment with her husband and her young family. But it was not to be. Frank Robert, at the age of four, developed typhus fever and died on November 14, 1843. Jane and Pierce inscribed on his tombstone: "A loved and precious treasure lost to us here but safe in the Redeemer's care."

Jane was now left only with Benny, two years old. She herself was thirty-seven. Pierce, in the meantime, had reformed, and was active in a temperance society. In August, 1846, President Polk invited Pierce to join his Cabinet as Attorney-General. It was a tempting offer, but Pierce was forced to decline, as he wrote to the President: "Mrs. Pierce's health, while at Washington, was very delicate. It is, I fear, even more so now: and the responsibilities which the proposed change would necessarily impose upon her, ought, probably, in themselves to constitute an insurmountable objection to leaving our quiet home for a public station at Washington."

Yet he had no objection to leaving her when a military career beckoned. With the outbreak of the Mexican war, Pierce offered his services; in February of 1847 he was commissioned a colonel in the Regular Army and one month later he was a brigadier-general. By April he was recruiting an Army and making preparations to leave for Mexico. Jane, in a constant state of depression, could do nothing to persuade him to stay with her and Benny.

His service in Mexico lasted a total of eight months; he saw violent action, during which he badly wrenched his left knee. He returned to Jane at the end of the year, and from then until 1852, life was peaceful for them. Jane began to feel better, though both Pierce and Benny learned that it was not always easy to be with her. She was often short-tempered; there were times when she was happy, but her years of melancholy made it impossible for her to show affection. She particularly wanted Benny to know how dearly she loved him; he was the focus of her attention, yet her aloofness and her many attacks of nervous tension would not permit natural demonstrations of love for the child.

When news came in June of 1852 that the Democratic convention had selected Pierce as their presidential candidate, Jane was horrified. She had no desire for her husband to return to political office, even to so exalted a position as Chief Executive of their country. Little Benny, too, was distressed, as he said in a letter to his mother: "I hope he won't be elected for I should not like to be at Washington and I know you would not either."

Pierce's overwhelming victory in the November election was submerged two months later by one of the most tragic events in presidential history. It occurred on January 6, 1853, while Pierce, Jane, and Benny were returning by train to Concord; they had been in Boston to attend the funeral of Jane's uncle. Just outside of Andover, some twenty miles to the north of Boston, the coupling on their car suddenly snapped, and the car was whirled violently around, tumbling off the tracks to a crashing and splintering halt at the bottom of the embankment. The car was destroyed, and yet there was only one fatality—eleven-year-old Benny Pierce.

Of the many reports of this appalling accident, there is a graphic and vivid account in a letter by one of Jane's cousins on January 7, 1853:

> Mr. Pierce's last voluntary act before [the car] rolled over was to seize Jane in one arm and reach the other towards Benny. But he did not grasp him and when it was over Mr. Pierce found Benny lying by his side & saw that something, a seat perhaps, that had grazed his head and left many splinters in his hair had taken off the back of Benny's head & killed him instantly. Jane he kept in his arm, I believe she saw that dreadful sight for one moment, but Mr. Pierce threw a shawl over the precious little form and drew her away. . . . Jane has shed few tears, she lies on the bed her eyes closed,

now and then uttering a short ejaculation sometimes a prayer, sometimes a question "why was my boy killed? Oh tell them not to go on railroads!"

Jane and Pierce were both gripped by an uncontrollable grief. The same cousin wrote a few days later, on January 10: "It was enough to break one's heart when Mr. Pierce would come into her room nearly bent double by his bruises & muscular strains and throw himself on the bed by her side and mingle his woe with hers. . . . Jane says in her anguish, 'Oh, was it to humble us, oh, we were not proud—' "

But the Inauguration in March was still to be faced. Pierce, who had looked forward to sharing his triumph with his wife and son, came to Washington alone. Jane had learned somehow that he had actively worked for the Democratic nomination while swearing to her he did not want it. She no longer had any faith in him; it was a disconsolate and crushed Franklin Pierce who was sworn in on Friday, March 4, 1853, as the fourteenth President.

Jane came to the White House two weeks later, but she was in no condition to officiate as First Lady. Her aunt by marriage, Abby Kent Means, acted as hostess for her. Sometimes Varina Davis, wife of Jefferson Davis, who was Pierce's Secretary of War, would stand in for Jane as official hostess. The Davises and the Pierces became close friends. Varina would often visit with Jane in her private quarters at the White House, and did her best to comfort the still grieving mother. She would sometimes find Jane writing pathetic pencil notes to the dead Benny, assuring him of her love, pleading with him to forgive her for not having been more demonstrative in her affection.

For almost two years the White House was a gloomy mansion; there were official levees, receptions, and dinners, at which Abby Kent Means or Varina Davis would act as hostess, yet there was no gaiety of any kind. Finally, on January 1, 1855, at the traditional New Year's Day reception, Jane Pierce made her first public appearance as First Lady. There is this description of her as she stood at her husband's side for the first time in twenty-two months: "Her woe-begone face, with its sunken dark eyes, and skin like yellowed ivory, banished all animation in others." But at least it was a beginning, and from then until the end of Pierce's term in March, 1857, she occasionally attended public White House functions. During this time, she went to church as often as she was well enough to leave her quarters, and she insisted that the White House staff attend.

Pierce had come to the White House shaken by his son's death and his wife's loss of faith in his integrity. He had completely lost any capacity for leadership he may have had; his administration accomplished nothing except to add a few more coals to the smoldering fires of enmity between North and South. In 1854, he signed the controversial Kansas–Nebraska bill, which declared the Missouri Compromise of 1820 to be "inoperative and void." Slavery in the new territories was permissible at the will of the people; no longer would it be prohibited by law. The slave-owners had won another significant victory. Pierce's signature on this bill, together with his efforts to push it through Congress, revealed his extreme prosouthern bias; there was no chance whatever of his renomination in 1856, and he retired from politics.

Pierce had planned to build a new house in Concord, but in the summer of 1857, Jane was ill again. Her aunt and dear friend Abby Means had died; Jane was despondent. Pierce took her on an extended trip to Europe and to the island of Madeira, off the coast of Portugal. There were other trips, and Jane would occasionally brighten and seem to recover. But her melancholia had become chronic, and the disease that killed her father was slowly devouring her. On December 2, 1863, at the age of fifty-seven, Jane Appleton Pierce died of tuberculosis in Andover, Massachusetts.

Pierce's faithful friend, Nathaniel Hawthorne, came as soon as he heard the news. When he looked at the shrunken figure in the coffin, it seemed to him "like a carven image laid in its richly embossed enclosure [with] a remote expression about it as if it had nothing to do with things present."

Jane Pierce was buried in Concord, New Hampshire. Not quite six years later, Franklin Pierce himself died at the age of sixty-four. The years after Jane's death had been aimless and full of pain, and he had taken to excessive drinking again. During the Civil War, he had been accused of disloyalty to the Union. When he died on October 8, 1869, he was a man who had spent much of his life in torment; he had seen few of his dreams realized. The house he had planned to build for himself and his "dearest Jeanie" had never been started. But in death his country honored him with a period of national mourning. He was buried in Old North Cemetery in Concord, next to his wife and children.

Mary Lincoln
1818–1882

From the very birth of the republic, the issue of slavery was a festering sore that never healed. Various compromises pieced together through the years offered no permanent remedy or cure; the wound was always there, lying beneath the surface, ready to erupt. By the time James Buchanan, the only bachelor ever to serve as Chief Executive, entered the White House on March 4, 1857, it may have been too late. The Civil War, in effect, had already begun, for the proslavery and antislavery forces in the country had polarized beyond further concession.

Against this grim background, Abraham Lincoln was elected in 1860 as the sixteenth President of the United States. His election brought bitter denunciation from the South and virulent criticism of his antislavery position. The break between North and South was completed with the formation of the Confederate States of America on February 8, 1861, with Jefferson Davis as its president.

Lincoln was inaugurated on Monday, March 4, 1861; six weeks later, on April 12, southern forces fired upon the regular troops in Fort Sumter, South Carolina. A flotilla of federal ships had steamed into the harbor to relieve the besieged garrison, but Confederate guns kept them away. Total, destructive, and bloody warfare had begun.

In the White House, two principal characters in another tragedy, smaller, more personal, but no less poignant, were settling into their roles. Abraham Lincoln was faced with the massive problems of fighting an all-out war; his wife, Mary Todd Lincoln, faced a battle within herself. Her entrance into the White House had been a moment of supreme triumph; there would be few such moments left to her. She was to know more anguish than joy, more of despair than happiness. Her life was to be a maze of uncontrollable complexities, with pain and misery her constant companions. Mary Todd Lincoln was an intricate, fascinating, and troubled human being.

Slavery was a common practice in Lexington, Kentucky, as it was throughout the South; in Lexington, as elsewhere, there were benevolent slave-owners who abhorred the slavepens, the auction block, and the whipping posts, yet did nothing more than turn their backs on the thrashings and the cruelty. Horrified at what they heard and would not see, they had no desire to destroy the foundation and life-blood of southern wealth.

One of the more enterprising and successful men in Lexington was Robert Smith Todd, married to Elizabeth Parker, herself a member of a wealthy and illustrious Kentucky family. Robert and Eliza Todd had seven children, four daughters and three sons; their fourth oldest, Mary Ann Todd, was born on December 13, 1818. Eliza Todd passed away in 1825.

A year later, when Mary was eight, her father sent her to the academy of Dr. John Ward, an Episcopal minister who believed in coeducation (most people did not). On November 1, 1826, Mary's widower father remarried, to the dismay of Mary's maternal grandmother, who later did her best to destroy the marriage.

The new stepmother apparently presented no obstacle to Mary and the other children. This phase of Mary's life was placid and easy-going, with a number of household slaves to take care of the family's smallest wants. For her entire life, Mary's attitude toward slaves was friendly and kind. While she lived in Kentucky she accepted the facts of slavery without question.

In 1832, Mary entered a select boarding school, where the principal subjects were French, music, and "a truly useful & 'Solid' English Education in all its branches," including the arts of conversation and letter writing.

That same year of 1832, her older sister Elizabeth married a student attending Lexington's Transylvania Seminary, Ninian W. Edwards, son of the governor of Illinois. Edwards and Elizabeth moved to Illinois, where they settled in Springfield. Three of the sisters were to follow.

When Mary completed her schooling, she was a bright, friendly, impulsive young lady, short, on the plump side though certainly with an appealing figure. Her favorite dresses were low cut, to reveal her smooth neck and shoulders. She had brown hair, blue eyes, a short, straight nose, and a round face. Fluent in French, she could be caustic in English, for she had a cutting tongue, although her charm and gracefulness more than atoned for the bite of her words. She enjoyed being a southern belle in a totally southern environment, but she felt there was no one in Lexington who would make a suitable husband, so she went off to Springfield in 1837, when she was nineteen, to survey the northern fields.

She did not meet Lincoln that summer, although she must have heard of the tall, gangling man with the somber face and quiet, ready wit, for he had already served a term in the Illinois General Assembly. Mary stayed in Springfield only for a few months and returned to Lexington. But this time, relations between Mary and her stepmother had become strained, for the second Mrs. Todd had a houseful of her own children, and the constant friction between Mrs. Todd and Mary's maternal grandmother did not help.

Finally, in the fall of 1839, Mary left her father's house for good and went back to Springfield to live with her sister, Mrs. Ninian Edwards.

Mary found the growing town of Springfield much to her liking; she soon became part of "the coterie," a lively group of bright, politically minded young people who regularly gathered in the parlor of Ninian Edwards' house. (The brilliant "Little Giant," Stephen A. Douglas, Illinois secretary of state, occasionally joined them.)

One of her nieces wrote that Mary and Lincoln met at a cotillion, where he said to her, "Miss Todd, I want to dance with you in the worst way." According to Mary's comment, "he certainly did."

Although Lincoln had a ready tongue in a courtroom, he was often silent in Mary's presence. He would "gaze on her as if drawn by some superior power, irresistibly so; he listened—never scarcely said a word." He did finally find some way to speak up, for by the end of 1840, he and Mary had come to an understanding. There is a story, now a well-worked legend, that Mary Todd, who did not really love Lincoln, recognized greatness in him, and her ambition to enter the White House one day as its First Lady overshadowed any romantic notions she may have had about other men. Perhaps, in her quickly changing moods, flashes of prescience did happen for her, and she may have seen more in "the plainest looking man in Springfield" than anyone else, for she and Lincoln were married on November 4, 1842, in the Edwards home. Despite his previous hesitations, Lincoln had inscribed in her ring, "Love is Eternal."

The newlyweds moved into a room in the Globe Tavern, where they paid $4 a week, including board. Her family and friends were horrified at this comedown for the patrician "Molly," as Lincoln affectionately called her before the children came. But Mary gave no sign of dissatisfaction, though her early years with Lincoln must have been trying. He was a melancholy man, often given to periods of silent depression; Mary herself had a volatile temperament. She would suddenly erupt in a flash of anger; her particular targets were tradesmen, servants, anyone she felt was beneath her. Moments later the anger would pass, and she would be calm again, the exhibition of temper forgotten. More and more, Lincoln learned to be tolerant of her outbursts, although his own attacks of melancholia continued.

To make matters worse, Mary suffered from migraine headaches, which would develop without warning. The combination of near poverty, a morose husband, and recurrent pain could not have been easy for her. But there were compensations. Lincoln was a witty and humorous man with a marvelous knack of storytelling in the Mark Twain tradition. Life with him had satisfaction and happiness as well as struggle and despair.

On August 1, 1843, their first son, Robert Todd Lincoln, was born, in the Globe Tavern. A year and a half later, with Lincoln's law career slowly improving, they bought a house and moved in early in 1844. On March 10, 1846, their second son was born; they named him Edward Baker Lincoln.

Lincoln, who had never given up thoughts of politics, was elected to Congress the same year his second son was born. He served in the House of Representatives for one term, from March, 1847, to March, 1849. He was not impressive as a congressman, although he did voice his opposition to the Mexican War.

Lincoln's election to Congress was the first moment of real triumph for Mary. But she did not care for Washington, and she went to Lexington in 1848 with her sons.

Some of the letters Lincoln and Mary wrote to each other during the time he was in Washington without her reveal small signs of the coming storms that were to batter Mary. In May of 1848, Mary wrote from Lexington: "MY DEAR HUSBAND—You will think indeed, that *old age* has set *its seal,* upon my humble self, that in few or none of my letters, I can remember the day of the month, I must confess it as one of my peculiarities. . . ." Then she adds, after much chitchat: "How much, I wish instead of writing, we were together this evening, I feel very sad away from you." Lincoln's answer, written the following month, has this comment:

"The leading matter in your letter is your wish to return to this side of the Mountains [Washington, D.C.]. Will you be a *good girl* in all things, if I consent?"

In July, Lincoln wrote again and mentioned two unpaid bills Mary left behind her in Washington, one for $5.38 to P. H. Hood & Co. and the second for $8.50, owed to Walter Harper & Co., "for goods which they say you bought. I hesitated to pay them, because my recollection is that you told me when you went away, there was nothing left unpaid." It has never been learned whether Mary forgot to tell him, or deliberately did not. In later years, he was to remain ignorant of debts totaling far greater amounts.

The only death that had affected Mary personally had been that of her mother in 1825. Now, in a space of seven months, she lost three people very dear to her. On July 16, 1849, her father died of cholera; six months later, in January, 1850, her maternal grandmother, Mrs. Elizabeth Parker "died at an advanced age"; and within a week, on February 1, 1850, the Lincolns' second-born son, Edward Baker, died of diphtheria at the age of four.

The pain of Eddie's loss was alleviated by the birth of a third son. On December 21, 1850, William Wallace Lincoln was born in Springfield. Two and a half years later, on April 4, 1853, Thomas (later to be affectionately known as "Tad") was born, and the Lincoln family was complete. Mary was no longer "Molly" to her husband; she was "Mother," and Lincoln was "Father" or "Mr. Lincoln."

For the next few years, Lincoln's prosperity grew with his law practice. He was now well known in political circles, and in 1856, when the newly formed Republican party was searching for a vice-presidential candidate, his name was mentioned. Lincoln, on hearing the news, was said to have remarked: "I reckon that ain't me; there's another great man in Massachusetts named Lincoln, and I reckon it's him."

He did not receive the nomination for the Vice-Presidency but his fame was spreading. One of his memorable speeches, to the Republican convention of Illinois in June of 1858, contained these lines: " 'A house divided against itself cannot stand.' I believe this government cannot endure, permanently half *slave* and half *free*." He had publicly stated his opposition to slavery, although in a letter written by Mary in 1856, she assured her half-sister, Emilie Todd Helm, that Lincoln was not an "Abolitionist. In principle he is far from it, all he desires is that slavery shall not be extended, let it remain where it is."

In the presidential election of 1860, Lincoln easily defeated three other candidates. The Democratic party, badly divided on the slavery question, had split in two parts; the northern Democrats, with Stephen Douglas as their nominee, received 1,375,157 votes, while the southern Democrats, with John Cabell Breckenridge of Kentucky as their choice, received 847,953 votes. Tennessee's John Bell, candidate of the fourth party in the race, the Constitutional Union, received 590,631 votes. The four-year-old Republican party now became a power in American politics with a total of 1,866,352 votes for its candidate, Abraham Lincoln, and its first major victory.

For Mary Lincoln, a plump and motherly forty-two, her husband's election was the supreme moment. As the wife of the President-elect, she was the best-known woman in the country. And she had to be the best dressed. In January of 1861, she traveled to New York for a shopping spree that knew no bounds. She bought what she pleased, without regard for price or eventual payment. For the first time she exhibited traces of the failing that would one day bring abuse and public accusations—she had a compulsive need to spend money in huge amounts and to dress in the costliest and most elaborate of costumes.

Mary's first year in the White House did not go as she would have liked. Though Washington was the federal capital, it was largely a southern city, and Mary was resented as a former southerner who had defected to the North; many of the more prominent Washingtonians openly snubbed her. Others considered her to be far less worldly than she herself thought she was, for Springfield, Illinois, to them was a frontier town without polish or elegance.

Mary was handicapped on the entertainment level as well. Because of the war, receptions were curtailed; further, it was expected that Mrs. Lincoln would do as other women were doing and would give up buying fancy clothes and traveling to New York to do her shopping. But the wife of the President did not agree; she traveled and shopped as she chose, despite the censure of those who voluntarily deprived themselves.

Her family in Kentucky also proved to be a source of pain and embarrassment for her. One brother and three half-brothers were fighting with the Confederate Army, and Mary's loyalty to the Union was questioned. As reported by her mulatto dressmaker, Mrs. Elizabeth Keckley, Mary said of her relatives who had joined the Confederates: "Why should I sympathize with the rebels, are they not against me? They would hang my husband tomorrow if it was in their power, and perhaps gibbet me with him." But the attacks against her continued, until Lincoln himself was forced to appear before a Senate committee to swear before that body that his wife was not a traitor.

On February 20, 1862, eleven-year-old Willie Lincoln died in the White House of typhoid fever. And from the moment of his death, Mary was never the same again. Her children and their friends had been given the run of the White House; its corridors had resounded with their shouts, but it would no longer be a happy mansion of love and childish enjoyment. For her, it was a building of gloom and grief almost too great to bear. There was a kind of disordered madness now in everything Mary did; at first she withdrew completely, and then when she took her place next to her husband again she often shrilled her jealousy of other women who came near him. Her buying sprees went on, and her debts piled up. By the summer of 1864, she owed $27,000, principally to merchants in New York City. Lincoln knew nothing of this huge sum, and Mary was terrified that he would not be reelected, for then her creditors would demand payment and Lincoln would learn how much she had been spending. The buying and the jealousy, together with excruciating headaches, were symptoms of a disease that was consuming her sanity, though it was not to be known for some years.

When Lincoln was reelected in the fall of 1864 (the southern states of course did not participate in the voting), Mary found momentary relief from the desperation of her debts. Now that she was "Mrs. President" again, her creditors no longer threatened her. But she couldn't stop herself from buying; for her husband's second Inauguration, she spent $2,000 on a gown of white silk and lace, and she bought three hundred pairs of gloves in four months.

On April 14, 1865, Good Friday, Mary accompanied her husband to Ford's Theater to witness a performance of *Our American Cousin*. They had a private box, well guarded, but somehow a southern sympathizer, an actor named John Wilkes Booth, eluded the elaborate security and, from a space of five feet, standing at the rear of the loge, shot Lincoln in the back of the head. The following morning, at twenty-two minutes and ten seconds past the hour of 7 A.M., Lincoln died at the age of fifty-six.

For Mary, the next five weeks were weeks of darkness; she remembered nothing of them. During that time, with no one to supervise the Executive Mansion, the public looted the White House of many valuable articles. An eyewitness reported: "The rabble ranged through it all at will. . . . It was plundered not only of ornaments but of heavy articles of furniture. . . . Exquisite lace curtains were torn into rags and carried off in pieces."

When Mary at last emerged, shaken, gray, she left the White House with her two surviving sons, Robert and Tad, and moved to Chicago, where she hoped to find peace and solitude. But poverty became a terrifying delusion; she imagined she was totally without funds, although Lincoln had left an estate of $83,000, which grew to $110,000 before it was liquidated. A good part of the money went to pay the debts that had piled up remorselessly during her four years in the White House, yet she had a great deal of money left, and there was no need for her to cry out that she was a pauper.

In her growing anxiety, she hit upon a scheme to raise funds—
she permitted the New York *World* to print a letter advising that
her second-hand clothes were for sale. No one bought them, and
the country was outraged at her ill-considered exhibition, as was
her son Robert. With the help of friends, she escaped to Europe
and took Tad with her. The boy, who had a cleft palate and had
learned to read at a late age, was now her only joy. He was a bright
and friendly child, despite his speech handicap. Four years later
they returned to America and went back to Chicago, where, Tad,
at the age of eighteen, died of pneumonia on July 15, 1871. Mary,
who had been forty-seven at her husband's death, was fifty-three
when her third son died, leaving only Robert of all her family.

Mary Lincoln lived for eleven more years. During that time she
knew much loneliness and pain; there were periods of hallucina-
tions, although she was more often rational. Robert had married.
Because of his mother's erratic behavior, Robert's wife refused to
have her visit at their home, and Mary understood.

Without a house of her own, and unwelcome in Robert's, Mary
lived in a succession of hotel rooms, many of them unfashionable
and rundown. She went off to Florida to find surcease, but she
imagined that her debts were insurmountable, despite $57,000
worth of securities she carried in her voluminous skirts. And she
sometimes insisted people were trying to poison her. She hurried
back to Chicago because she was convinced that the life of her son
Robert was in danger. He was perfectly well, but she was not. She
took to running out into the corridor of her hotel at night, screaming that she was being murdered. Robert, distraught by her behavior, reluctantly decided upon a hearing to determine her sanity.
On May 18, 1875, one of her doctors declared in writing: "I
hereby certify that I have examined Mrs. Mary Lincoln—widow—
and that I am of the opinion that she is insane and a fit subject for
hospital treatment."

The following day, a jury of twelve men heard testimony in her
case and agreed she was insane. She was placed in an institution
in Batavia, Illinois, where she stayed for three months. At the end
of that time, she was permitted to live with her sister, Mrs. Ninian

Edwards, in Springfield. By June of the following year, in 1876, she was once again declared competent to handle her own affairs, and she was released from the jurisdiction of the state. She went off to Europe again, because she said she would be "much less unhappy in the midst of strangers." She wandered to Germany, France, and Italy, always living cheaply, always unknown and unheralded. After an accident in Pau, France, where she fell from a stepladder, she returned to the United States in 1880.

On July 16, 1882, at the home of her sister in Springfield, Mary Todd Lincoln died at the age of sixty-three. Like much of her life, death had not been pleasant. She had been in pain, covered with boils, and at the end she was almost completely paralyzed and blind, as she believed, "from constant weeping." Even with all her evident ills, Robert continued to maintain that much of her suffering was imaginary; and, Mary, with all her mother's love, defended his right to criticize her. An autopsy revealed, however, that she had been suffering from "cerebral disease," which she had had for years. Robert and the others were far from being totally right.

Mary was buried in Springfield's Oak Ridge Cemetery, beside the bodies of her husband and children in the Lincoln Memorial Vault.

Newspaper reports announcing her death did not mention the nature of her illness or the problems that had plagued her through the final years of her life. A dispatch from Springfield on July 19 described Mary Lincoln's funeral services at the First Presbyterian Church in this way:

> The arrangements were simple, there was no attempt at display, and the minister attempted no eulogy, according to her expressed wish. The sermon was largely biographical and very interesting in historical reminiscence.

Eliza Johnson
1810–1876

Two and a half blocks from Ford's Theater, the Vice President of the United States, Andrew Johnson, was asleep in Washington's Kirkwood House when John Wilkes Booth fired a bullet into the head of Abraham Lincoln. Within a short time, the hotel was swarming with officials, friends, and the curious. The stunned Andrew Johnson, awakened from a sound sleep, knew that the totally unexpected had happened for the third time; the Vice President would soon have the enormous task of running the country.

The death of Abraham Lincoln the following morning brought grief and shock to millions, and anxiety to many others. Johnson's daughter, Mrs. Martha Patterson, wrote to her father that Mrs. Johnson, at home in Tennessee, was "almost deranged" from fear that he would be assassinated as well. But Eliza Johnson's fears were groundless; at 10 A.M. on the morning of April 15, 1865, in the parlor of the Kirkwood House, her husband was sworn in as the seventeenth President of the United States.

For Andrew Johnson, a tailor from Greeneville, Tennessee, and a lifelong Democrat, it was the culmination of an eventful career. His strong view against the extension of slavery, and his vocal opposition, to the secession of his own southern states made him, in Lincoln's view, the ideal man to balance the Republican ticket in 1864. With an antislavery, Jacksonian southerner as candidate for Vice President, Lincoln and the Republicans hoped to win the uncertain border states. They were right, for they scored an easy victory over General George McClellan and the Democrats, 2,213,635 votes to 1,805,237. Six weeks after the beginning of Lincoln's second term, Andrew Johnson, Democrat from Tennessee, inherited the highest office in the land by dispensation of the Republican party and the gun of a fanatic assassin.

In Nashville, Tennessee, Eliza McCardle Johnson prepared for the journey that would take her to Washington as the new First Lady. Like her husband, she had begun her life in poverty. Now, at the age of fifty-four, she was too ill to enjoy or savor the honors that suddenly fell upon her, but she did not fear them, as had others before her.

The "plain people" of eastern Tennessee lived in the mountains or in small towns nestling in the foothills. They existed as best they could, extracting a meager sustenance from the inhospitable ground, or working in the towns for their more successful and aristocratic neighbors. John McCardle, a Scotch-Irish shoemaker, and one of the plain people, settled in Greeneville with his young wife, Sarah Phillips. The McCardles had one child, a daughter Eliza, born on October 4, 1810, in Leesburg, Tennessee, a hamlet some twenty miles to the northeast of Greeneville.

John McCardle was neither successful nor long-lived. He died when Eliza was a child, and he left his widow and small daughter to fend for themselves. Greeneville, a town of seven hundred people, offered little opportunity for a penniless widow. But Mrs.

McCardle managed to support herself and her daughter by weaving; Eliza contributed her share by helping her mother make crazy quilts and rough sandals with cloth uppers. By the time Eliza was sixteen, she had received a basic education, perhaps with the help of her mother, or perhaps through the kindness of those in town who had their own libraries.

On a mild Saturday afternoon in September of 1826, a group of three people, together with a rickety wooden cart drawn by a blind old pony, came down from the Great Smoky Mountains into Greeneville. The pony was led by a sturdy young man of eighteen; beside him trudged his stepfather, and in the cart behind, which contained all their worldly goods, rode his weary mother. A curious crowd watched their tired and dusty entrance into the town.

Among those watching was sixteen-year-old Eliza McCardle. The young man asked her if she knew of an empty house or cabin where they might stay; she directed him to the local storekeeper. And so it was that Andrew Johnson, born in Raleigh, North Carolina, and Eliza McCardle, born in Leesburg, Tennessee, met in the town of Greeneville. There is a story, unconfirmed yet persistent, that Eliza was teased about this dusty and travel-worn young man who had spoken to her, and she replied, with her saucy Scotch-Irish haughtiness, "He's all right, I might marry him some day."

The newcomers stayed in Greeneville only for a short time. Andrew, a tailor, could find no work there, for the town had a tailor; he and his mother and stepfather moved on to Rutledge about forty miles away, but six months later they returned to Greeneville. Andrew had been lured back by news that the local tailor had gone and by memory of the friendly girl with the hazel eyes, light brown hair, and tall, shapely figure. Andrew went into business for himself, and once his trade was established, he courted the girl he had not forgotten. On May 5, 1827, Andrew Johnson, not yet nineteen, and Eliza McCardle, not yet seventeen, were married by Mordecai Lincoln, a distant relative of Abraham Lincoln.

Andrew and Eliza Johnson moved into a two-room frame and

board house on the main street of the town. In the front room, Andrew had his shop; the back room was their home. Andrew, stocky, about five feet ten inches, had a strong square face, intense dark eyes, and a rich, modulated voice. He had never been to school; he could, in fact, barely read and could not write his name, yet he spoke with the assurance of an orator.

When Andrew was three, his father died; at the age of fourteen, Andrew was apprenticed to a tailor. Tailoring was the only trade he knew, and now he used his sure fingers to support his family. Andrew was expert at his trade, and his wife was frugal. They needed little to live on; money came in steadily. With Eliza's help, he learned to write; he hired a man to read to him for fifty cents a day while he industriously worked with his needle and thread and scissors.

Eliza early recognized that her young and persevering husband was beyond the ordinary. He had a capacity for leadership that others acknowledged and obeyed. She worked with him to improve his education, and she urged him to join a debating society at Greeneville College, about four miles from town.

Andrew Johnson was a working man, and he spoke for all the working men in Greeneville. In 1828, barely two years after he had arrived, they elected him as their town alderman, much to the astonishment of the aristocratic gentry. But Eliza was not astonished then, or ever in her lifetime. She regarded Andrew's success with a certainty born of confidence.

The Johnsons had five children in all. Four were born within a space of six years: Martha on October 25, 1828; Charles on February 19, 1830; Mary on May 8, 1832; and Robert on February 22, 1834. At his birth, Eliza was not yet twenty-four. There would be no more children for many years.

In 1831, Andrew and Eliza bought a brick house on Water Street, for a sum slightly under $1,000. Johnson also bought a white clapboard building, which he moved to his own lot. He nailed a wooden sign over the entrance: "A. Johnson, Tailor." The sign remained there through his entire life. In less than three years, the illiterate, penniless Andy Johnson had become an affluent and respected member of the community.

Johnson's growing prominence in the town won him the mayoralty of Greeneville; he served until 1833. His tailoring shop grew as well, and before long he had a number of assistants. Eliza, a shrewd manager, proficient housekeeper, and devoted wife and mother, concentrated on the affairs of her family and home. The snobbishness of the "better element" in the town did not disturb Eliza as much as it did her husband. He angrily exclaimed that they were "a cheap, purse-proud set . . . not half as good as the man who earns his bread by the sweat of his brow!" Eliza may have agreed, but she calmly went about the business of being the wife of Greeneville's brightest political hope. The social life did not interest her, and if the purse-proud aristocrats persisted in snubbing her family, she had too much pride and common sense to be hurt by their vanity.

In 1835, Andrew Johnson jumped from the insularity of local politics into the mainstream of government—he was elected in that year to the Tennessee legislature. Eliza remained at home, "caring for the children and practicing the economy"; the family fortunes steadily improved under her prudent supervision. Johnson bought a farm and the first of eight slaves he and Eliza were eventually to own.

Eliza carefully guided her children in their instruction and homework, as she had done with her husband years before. But there were no frills in their academic and social education; for Eliza it was enough that they be well adjusted. Ironically, she succeeded with her daughters, but not so with her two older sons, for they became alcoholics.

By 1842, Johnson had served in both houses of the Tennessee legislature, and he was ready for the national scene. He ran for Congress in the fall of 1842, and was elected representative from the First Congressional District of Tennessee. The leaders of the Democratic party in Tennessee had been appalled at the thought of a tailor in Congress, but the mountain people and the working man stood solidly behind him, their voices determined and unwavering, and the Democratic leaders grudgingly surrendered. Johnson served in Congress for ten years. At the time of his first election, he was thirty-four and Eliza was thirty-two.

With the tailor shop humming under the management of Lewis Self and the family finances now grown to $50,000, the Johnsons bought a larger house in 1851. A sizable brick building on Main Street, it had become available for purchase when the original owner found he could not complete it. In January of 1852, the family moved in. Four months later, the second daughter, Mary, was married to Daniel Stover.

In October of 1853, Johnson was elected governor of Tennessee. Eliza had hoped to move with him to the new state capital in Nashville, but it wasn't possible. She had not been well for some years, and it was thought best that she stay in Greeneville.

Eliza's mother died in April, 1854; four months later, her fifth and last child, Andrew, Jr., was born on August 5. Eliza, now forty-four, became weaker after his birth. She had "phthisis, or slow consumption," a disease that was to leave her a semi-invalid for the rest of her life. And sadly, little Andy had apparently inherited his mother's infirmity, as had his older brother Robert, who drank too much and suffered hemorrhaging of the lungs.

Martha, who had married Judge David Patterson in 1855 and now lived outside of Greeneville, came to her mother's house as often as possible to help with the chores. And Eliza, when she was well, fussed over little Andy, as did his father.

Johnson served two terms as governor; he was elected to the United States Senate in 1857. Once again, he and Eliza were parted, but she did make one trip to Washington with him, in the fall of 1860. With the outbreak of the Civil War in April of 1861, Eliza and Johnson returned to East Tennessee, even though his life had been threatened by southern sympathizers and extremists if he came back to his home state. In his Senate speeches, Johnson had made very clear that he strongly opposed secession and would do all in his power to maintain the solidarity of the Union. Southern slave-owners openly voiced their hatred of him. To them, he was the worst kind of traitor, a turncoat who betrayed his own people.

In 1862, with Middle and West Tennessee, including Nashville, controlled by General Grant's Union forces, and with East Tennessee in the hands of the Confederates, Johnson went back to Washington to plead for help for the staunchly pro-Union and beleaguered mountain people of East Tennessee. Johnson's family were somewhere behind enemy lines; his son-in-law, Dan Stover, was leading a band of guerrilla fighters known as "the Bridge-Burners" (so-named for their skill in burning railroad bridges). Eliza was staying at the Stover farm in nearby Carter County. Her house in Greeneville had been confiscated, and her safety constantly threatened. Johnson made an impassioned appeal to the sympathy of the northern senators: "My wife and children have been turned into the street, and my house has been turned into a barrack, and for what? Because I stand by the Constitution. . . . This is my offense. . . ."

One who listened, and heard, was Abraham Lincoln. He asked Andrew Johnson to serve as military governor of Tennessee, and he urged immediate relief of East Tennessee, but the Confederate troops stubbornly resisted, and Eliza still remained behind enemy lines. On April 24, 1862, the commanding officer of the Confederate forces for East Tennessee, General Kirby E. Smith, gave Eliza and her family thirty-six hours to leave his jurisdiction. She was much too ill to comply; somehow, the stress of war postponed her departure. Meanwhile, an anxious Andrew Johnson telegraphed repeatedly for word about them, only to receive the discouraging reply: "No news from home."

In September, Eliza, as worried about her husband as he was about her, requested permission to pass through the Confederate lines to join Mr. Johnson in Nashville. Permission was granted, and she set out with her children and grandchildren, escorted by Dan Stover. After a humiliating and frustrating journey, during which they were shunted back and forth from one town to another and harassed by rebel soldiers who bore no love either for the wife of the traitor Andrew Johnson or his family, they arrived in Nashville on October 13, 1862. Eliza had not seen her husband for almost a year, nor had he ever had definite word of her and the children. It was a glorious reunion, as recorded in the diary of a Nashville citizen: "Even the Governor's Roman firmness was overcome, and he wept tears of thankfulness at this merciful deliverance of his beloved ones from the hands of their unpitying persecutors."

In April of 1863, their oldest son, Charles, was thrown from a horse and killed. He was thirty-three. Robert, twenty-nine, was showing no signs of reforming; he continued to drink. Andy, aged nine, apparently had tuberculosis. Later in the year, Eliza's son-in-law, Dan Stover, who had so faithfully fought for the Union, died of the same disease.

The assassination of Abraham Lincoln dramatically changed Eliza's life. The Confederate forces had long before withdrawn from Tennessee, and Eliza had returned to her home in Greeneville, where she intended to live quietly, even though her husband had been elected Vice President. But now she would have to live in Washington. She arrived there on August 6, 1865. The disease that was slowly killing her prevented her active participation in the social life of the White House; her daughter Martha Patterson was hostess for her. Eliza selected a small room for herself, in an upstairs corner of the mansion overlooking the front lawn; here she spent her days, knitting, reading, chatting with her family and her friends.

Civil War deprivations and disorderly looting after the death of Lincoln had left the White House in a shambles. With the help of $30,000 appropriated by Congress, Martha worked diligently to restore the mansion to its former elegance and splendor. By the end of 1866, the work was completed, and beginning with New Year's Day, January 1, 1867, the Johnsons held a series of receptions and levees. To the delight of Washington society, the White House was festive once again.

Eliza, unfortunately, was rarely well enough to come downstairs. In the four years she lived in the Executive Mansion, she made only two public appearances, once at a reception for Queen Emma, the thirty-year-old widow of King Kamehameha IV of the Sandwich

Isles (Hawaii), and the second time for her husband's sixtieth birthday celebration, on December 29, 1867.

Politically, the years of 1867 and 1868 were not kind to the Johnsons. Reconstruction of the shattered southern states was going badly, and in February, 1868, there began a struggle between Congress and the President that would give Eliza months of aggravation and worry. In a trial that lasted until May 26, Congress attempted to remove President Johnson from office because it believed he was usurping their powers. By a vote of 35 to 19 (which fell one vote short of the required two-thirds), the Congress failed in its attempt. Johnson's stubborn resistance reaffirmed the separate authority of the Executive; never again has this vital presidential principle been challenged or questioned in similar depth.

When the acquittal was announced, a White House aide ran all the way from the Senate chambers to the Executive Mansion to relay the news to the waiting President, and he then hurried upstairs to Eliza's room. The aide, Colonel W. H. Crook, describes the scene:

"He's acquitted!" I cried; "the President is acquitted!"

The frail little lady . . . rose from her chair and in both her emaciated hands took my right hand. Tears were in her eyes . . . as she said: "I knew he'd be acquitted; I knew it. . . . Thank you for coming to tell me."

I shall never forget the picture of that feeble, wasted little woman standing so proudly and assuring me so positively that she had never doubted for one instant that her beloved husband would be proved innocent. . . .

At the end of Johnson's single term, in March of 1869, the family returned to Greeneville. Six weeks later, thirty-five-year-old Robert, "his own worst enemy," died of a far too strenuous life. Eliza tenaciously clung to life for seven more years. She died in Greeneville on January 15, 1876, at the age of sixty-five, only six months after her husband had died of a stroke on July 31, 1875. They were both buried in the Andrew Johnson National

Cemetery in Greeneville, on a knoll Johnson himself had selected. Their sickly son, Andrew, Jr., outlived them only by three years.

There is no record of Eliza's last words or thoughts, but she must have remembered the homage paid to her late husband by the people of East Tennessee a short time before. Johnson's body had lain in state for three days; on August 3, 1875, thousands of mourners, who had flocked into Greeneville from the mountains and villages, solemnly marched behind a troop of Masonic Knights Templar to the peaceful and secluded hilltop where Johnson was to be buried.

The final prayer was read by U. A. Rouser, a mechanic, one of those Johnson had represented so faithfully through a long life of service. The body had been wrapped in a flag of the United States, containing all thirty-seven stars, with the head cushioned on his well-worn and often-read copy of the Constitution, for Andrew Johnson had once declared, "I desire no better winding sheet than the Stars and Stripes, and no softer pillow than the Constitution of my country."

Julia Grant
1826–1902

After the bloody Battle of Shiloh, which began on a Sunday morning in April of 1862, there was a public outcry for removal of the Union general, Ulysses S. Grant. Loss of life on both sides had been heavy and ghastly. Grant was called a butcher, and a drunkard. Lincoln gravely listened to the charges. His answer was simple: "I can't spare this man—he fights."

General Ulysses S. Grant, plucked from the abyss of anonymity by the Civil War, was indeed a man who fought. Perhaps he had been drinking while his troops were taking a fearful beating at Shiloh Church on the Tennessee River. But the next day, he pressed the attack and forced the Confederates into retreat. It was a tremendous victory for the Union, and sorely needed. There would be many more such victories, all of them at a terrifying human loss. Grant himself was aware of the horrible toll, but he felt the war would be shortened by his tactics, and in the long run, lives would be saved. No one can say whether his theory was correct, but the ultimate triumph was his. The glory of Shiloh, Vicksburg, and Appomattox was still aflame in 1869 when he became the eighteenth President of the United States at the age of forty-six.

But peacetime treated him badly. One of the worst Presidents ever to serve, he was helpless in the face of powerful opposing forces who wrecked the dream of Reconstruction. Gullible, naive, he trusted the wrong people, and saw his two terms as President rocked by scandals and corruption. It would have served his reputation far more if he had remained a triumphant general.

His First Lady, Julia Dent Grant, shared his glory and his defeats. She struggled with him through the crushing twin burdens of poverty and obscurity; she was at his side on many of his battlefields; she refused to be daunted by the scandals that would have shattered a lesser woman. Julia Grant, one of the better-known First Ladies, made no notable contributions, but she was Mrs. Ulysses S. Grant. We cannot remember one without the other.

Five miles to the west of St. Louis, Colonel Frederick Dent and his family lived on a thousand-acre farm known as "White Haven." Dent, who originally came from Maryland and was married to Ellen Wrenshall, brought thirty slaves with him to the Missouri Territory and a plantation philosophy he steadfastly maintained throughout his entire life. Julia, the fifth of the Dent children and the first of four daughters, was born at "White Haven" on January 26, 1826.

Frontier schooling was sporadic, and formal education, for those who could afford it, started late and ended early. After a haphazard attendance at a log cabin school near "White Haven," Julia, at the age of ten, was sent to a private school in St. Louis where the students were allowed to select the studies that interested them the most. Julia devoted herself "to history, mythology and the things I happened to like. I had a sweet little voice and I took both instrumental and vocal lessons." She neglected to add that she was proficient as well in sketching and in the domestic arts, which she and her sisters learned from their diligent and thrifty mother.

By the summer of 1843, when Julia was seventeen, she completed her schooling and returned to "White Haven" in February of the following year. A short and lively girl with dark brown hair and brown eyes that unfortunately crossed, Julia was neither beautiful nor unattractive. She was a bit plumper than she should have been, but for a young and recent graduate from the Military Academy at West Point, Lieutenant Ulysses S. Grant, her figure was perfect.

Grant, who had graduated twenty-first in a class of thirty-nine, had been a classmate of Julia's brother and was now stationed at Jefferson Barracks in St. Louis. He met Julia on a visit to "White Haven." Five feet eight inches in height, he was a thin, serious young man, clean-shaven, with blue eyes and reddish hair, and a clear complexion that reminded Julia of "porcelain."

For Grant, it was love at first sight, as he admitted many years later; for Julia, her love for the "darling little lieutenant" was longer in developing, but at the end of three months, she knew she wanted to marry him. On a late spring day in May of 1844, when the rivers and streams in Missouri were flooding as a result of heavy rains, Grant and Julia began an informal engagement that was to last four years. Carl Sandburg, in *Abraham Lincoln, The War Years,* describes the scene: "They were buggy-driving across a flooded bridge when she cried, 'I'm going to cling to you no matter what happens,' and safely over, he asked, 'How would you like to cling to me for the rest of your life?' "

Her answer was "yes," but her father's opposition put an end to her hopes for an immediate marriage. A Regular Army man, in the eyes of Colonel Dent, could never support his daughter in the proper manner. In 1845, Julia's father did give his approval, but trouble with Mexico over the annexation of Texas meant further postponement of their plans, for Grant was assigned to the army of Zachary Taylor. The Mexican War was to keep Grant and Julia separated until July of 1848; they were married a month later, on August 22, in her father's St. Louis home. Julia was twenty-two and Grant was twenty-six. Grant's parents, Jesse and Hannah Grant, who lived in Ohio, refused to come to the wedding. Stubbornly antislavery, they were horrified that their son had married into a slave-owning family.

After a honeymoon trip to Ohio, where Grant and Julia visited his parents, they returned to St. Louis, and from there went immediately to Sackett's Harbor, New York, a former naval station on Lake Ontario near Watertown, where Grant was to be stationed. They spent the bleak winter of 1848–49 on the post, in bare quarters not designed for homemaking. For the first time, Julia had no slaves to attend her, but she managed nicely, with the help of her mother's early training.

Julia was faced with another problem. Grant was a heavy drinker; his intemperance sometimes reached an extreme level. She persuaded him to join an anti-alcohol group named Rising Sun Division No. 210 of the Sons of Temperance Lodges in Watertown; he became its presiding officer, and often could be seen sturdily marching at the head of a temperance parade. It was a minimal gesture, for he later returned to his old ways.

From Sackett's Harbor, the Grants went to Detroit, where they were to remain for two years. In the spring of 1850, Julia hurried to St. Louis, where her first child, a son named for her father, was born on May 30, in the home of Colonel Dent.

When she became pregnant for the second time, Julia went to Bethel, Ohio, to have her child at the home of Grant's parents. On July 22, 1852, her second son, Ulysses Simpson, was born (because of his birth in the Buckeye State of Ohio, he would later be known as "Buck").

Grant was transferred to the Pacific Coast. Now that he was separated from Julia and the children by half a continent, he fretted under the dull routine of the cheerless frontier outposts and took to drinking again, as heavily as before. By the spring of 1854, his commanding officer gave him the choice of reforming or resigning. Grant chose to resign, and he returned to "White Haven."

Grant and Julia had often talked about farming, and now decided they must give it a try. They settled on a sixty-acre tract Colonel Dent had given them as a wedding present. Rough and uncultivated, it presented a challenge to the Grants, but they were happy to face it. Julia's brother Louis had permitted them the use of his cottage, "Wish-ton-Wish," (an Indian name meaning "whippoorwill"), while he went to California to try his luck in the Far West. And it was here at Louis's pleasant cottage, standing in a grove of trees, that Julia's only daughter, Nellie, was born on July 4, 1855.

Julia and Grant now went to work on a house of their own. Working from a design sketched by Julia, Grant cleared an area in a stand of oaks and cut and scraped the logs for their house. They were living on $50 a month that Grant earned by hauling and selling firewood in St. Louis. Their neighbors and neighbors' slaves helped with the raising of their house, and "Hardscrabble" was ready for occupancy. Grant gave the name to their new log cabin as a wry observation on the life he and Julia undoubtedly faced.

The cabin was prophetically named, for the next few years were difficult. The Grants survived only because of Julia's frugality and the bounty of the land. Grant was not a successful farmer, nor did real estate, which he later tried in St. Louis, prove to his liking. But no matter how badly things were going, plump little Julia remained cheerful and optimistic, finding great joy in her children and in the love of her husband. Her fourth and last child, Jesse Root Grant, named for her father-in-law, was born in St. Louis on February 6, 1858.

In April of 1860, the Grants moved to Galena, Illinois, where Grant joined the family tanning and leather business. Like his other ventures, Galena was a trap, and Grant impressed no one with his skills as a businessman. But far-off gunfire at Fort Sumter, South Carolina, in April of 1861, transformed the world for them. The business failure would soon become the military genius of the age.

With Julia's encouragement, Grant volunteered his services to the Union Army. In June of 1861, Governor Yates of Illinois commissioned him a colonel in command of the Twenty-First Regiment of the Illinois Volunteers. Two months later, Grant became a brigadier-general, and the long years of obscurity were over. Julia and Grant accepted his sudden fame as if it had always been their due, with a calm simplicity and quiet assurance. Julia's father, pro-South, had attempted in vain to induce Grant to join the Confederates. From that moment, Dent and the Grants were to remain politically opposed, but Grant always treated his father-in-law with deference. Nor was opposition confined to the Dents. An elderly sister of Grant's father owned a plantation and slaves in Virginia. She passionately declared, "If you are with the accursed Lincolnites, the ties of consanguinity shall be forever severed."

For most families, the years of the Civil War meant the rending heartbreak of long separation. Julia and her children were more fortunate; they were often with Grant during many of his engagements, sometimes within sound of heavy gunfire. Julia took a casually healthy attitude towards her children; she permitted her oldest son, Fred, only thirteen, to ride out with his father to the edge of actual combat. During one skirmish, Fred received a slight wound on his leg. It may seem strange that Grant would permit his family to share his dangers, but others, notably General William Tecumseh Sherman, did the same, and perhaps the congeniality of family life lessened their tensions and sharpened their military facility, for both Grant and Sherman succeeded where many other Union generals failed.

With the surrender of Confederate General Robert E. Lee at Appomattox Court House, Virginia, on April 9, 1865, the long and bitter struggle was over, and Grant, who had been a failure at the age of thirty-two, was now, at forty-three, hailed as the greatest man in the country next only to Lincoln himself. The luster of his name shone more brightly than ever in May of 1868, when the Republican party, meeting in Chicago, nominated him unanimously on the first ballot as their candidate for President. He accepted the nomination with a simple statement that became a victorious slogan for the Republicans: "Let us have peace."

Julia's eight years as First Lady began in a most inauspicious manner. The Inaugural Ball, on the night of March 4, 1869, was held in the north wing of the newly completed Treasury Building. As usual, there was a tremendous crush of expensively gowned women and handsomely outfitted men. The new First Lady wore a gown of heavy white satin trimmed with pointe lace. But most of the guests paid scant attention to the First Lady; they were too busy gasping for breath in the construction dust that filled the stifling air. Many women fainted. Few of the crowd ever got to the supper tables. There was much confusion with the checking of wraps; more than one illustrious guest lost a valued coat or headgear, including the noted newspaperman Horace Greeley, who stalked out minus his white beaver. Julia, reveling in the glory of her husband's triumph, was radiantly impervious to the confusion and disorder.

Fortunately, Julia's succeeding receptions and levees all came off splendidly. Washington society enjoyed her parties, particularly her formal dinners at which as many as twenty-nine courses, prepared by an Italian steward named Melah, were served at costs ranging up to $2,000. It must be noted that when the wines were poured, Grant's glass was usually turned down.

The first of a series of state receptions took place in January of 1870 when the Grants entertained Prince Arthur of England. In the fall of 1871, Grand Duke Alexis of Russia was their guest; in March of 1872, the Japanese Ambassador Iwakaura; in December of 1874, King David Kalakaua, then ruler of the Sandwich Isles (his reception was reported to have cost $25,000, appropriated by Congress); and Dom Pedro II, Emperor of Brazil, in May of 1876. But the one social event that neither the public nor the Grants themselves would ever forget occurred on May 21, 1874, when seventeen-year-old Nellie Grant was married in a lavish White House wedding to Algernon Charles Frederick Sar-

toris, nephew of the famous English actress Fannie Kemble. Grant
and Julia did not approve of Sartoris and they thought Nellie too
young to marry. When they finally did give their consent, it was
not entirely without misgiving, for during the ceremony, Julia had
tears in her eyes, and after the ceremony, Grant was found sobbing
in Nellie's room.

Like her husband, Julia believed in people and instinctively liked
anyone who was nice to her and her family. She and Grant accepted many gifts during their stay at the White House; they did
not seem to realize that some of the gifts carried strings and required a return favor. And they were the subject of much criticism
because of the many relatives Grant appointed to government
jobs; like John and Abigail Adams, Julia and Ulysses Grant were
staunch supporters of nepotism. But public rebuke went further.
The Grant administrations were satiated with scandals; a number
of Grant associates and appointees were involved in the worst kind
of corruption, generated by high living and enormously expensive
appetites. But Julia and Grant were personally above suspicion,
although they had shown extremely bad judgment in their choice
of friends.

When Grant's second term ended, Julia and Grant took a trip
around the world that lasted two years and brought them fame and
adulation in major capitals of Europe, Asia, and Africa. They returned to the United States in the fall of 1879 and settled in New
York with the help of influential banker friends. Their world trip
had left them almost penniless, but the generosity of others made
it possible for them to buy a four-story mansion on New York's
East Sixty-Sixth Street.

From that point, life should have treated them kindly, but it did
not, and Julia was once again called on to bolster the family with
her usual good cheer. As had happened too often, Julia and Grant
were victims of their gullibility and their naive trust in people.
Grant had lent his name and prestige to the new brokerage firm
of Grant and Ward; Grant's young partner, Frederick Ward,
swindled the firm of all its assets and the Grants were bankrupt.

In 1885, Mark Twain, representing a publishing house, came to their rescue with a generous contract for Grant's *Memoirs*. Under the extremely liberal royalty terms, Grant's estate eventually re-received $450,000 for the two volumes he wrote.

But the writing was far more difficult than Mark Twain had anticipated, for Grant by then was a dying man. He had cancer of the tongue and throat; it was a painful illness, sometimes causing him unbearable anguish, and yet he dictated at a rapid pace, keeping one step ahead of death, until the disease had so consumed his tongue and throat he could no longer speak, and he then scribbled his notes whenever the intense pain permitted. He completed his second volume barely one week before he died, on July 23, 1885, at the age of sixty-three.

Those last months of Grant's life were perhaps the most difficult Julia had ever endured, for she forced herself to be cheerful. Grant knew he was dying, but she would not permit talk of death in his presence. She was determined to be the ever-optimistic Julia he had always known, and she played her role to the end.

She herself lived for seventeen more years. Her sons made excellent marriages, and she had many grandchildren. She loved them all, as she had so dearly loved her own children; fortunately, they all survived her. Although many of her old friends had gone, she found others to replace them. One was Varina Davis, who had come to New York to live after the death of Jefferson Davis in 1889. She and Julia saw much of each other, and it seemed fitting that the widows of two of the dominant characters in the immense tragedy that had been the Civil War should become the closest of friends in their final years.

Julia died in Washington, D.C., on December 14, 1902, when she was not quite seventy-seven. She was interred next to her husband's remains in the magnificent marble edifice known to tourists the world over as Grant's Tomb. Situated on a peaceful grassy hill on Riverside Drive in New York City, it overlooks the Hudson River.

At General Grant's funeral, the eulogy, delivered by the Reverend John Philip Newman, could well have been spoken seventeen years later, at Julia's own funeral, for these were some of Dr. Newman's words:

> He, the Doric column to sustain; she, the Corinthian column to beautify. He, the oak to support; she, the ivy to entwine. . . . She shared his trials and his triumphs, his sorrows and his joys, his toils and his rewards. . . . Lovely and pleasant in their lives, and in their death they shall not be divided. Side by side they shall sleep in the same tomb, and she shall share with him whatever homage future ages pay at his national shrine.

Lucy Hayes
1831–1889

The year 1876 marked two extraordinary events in the history of the United States. It was the centennial of the country's birth and the year that a presidential election did not elect a President. The major candidates were two governors: Republican Rutherford B. Hayes of Ohio and Democrat Samuel J. Tilden of New York. With the scandals of Grant's Republican administration still reverberating, Hayes was given little chance. But the overconfident Democrats made one basic error: they forgot that the Republicans could be as calculating as they themselves had been.

In the election of November 1876, Tilden received 4,300,590 popular votes to 4,036,298 for Hayes. Of the electoral votes, Tilden had 184 (only one short of the required majority of 185) while Hayes had 166. The nineteen electoral votes of three southern states, Florida, Louisiana, and South Carolina, were in dispute, with Republicans and Democrats presenting opposition slates of electors for certification. The Democrats clearly had the majority in each state, but it had been achieved through violence, intimidation, and murder. Many recently freed slaves were too terrified to vote (if they had voted, most of them would have chosen the Republican party). The Ku Klux Klan and the poor whites were conducting an unparalleled reign of terror. The Republicans, for their part, refused to accept the Democratic majorities, although many of their own votes were fraudulent, with numerous cases of multiple voting.

For the first time in its history, the country did not have a new President. The deadlock continued for months. Finally, in March of 1877, only three days before the scheduled Inauguration, an electoral commission consisting of eight Republicans and seven Democrats voted along strictly partisan lines, with all Republicans for Hayes and the Democrats for their man. The result, announced on March 2, gave Hayes the additional votes he needed, and he became the nineteenth President by an electoral count of 185 to 184. He had lost the popular vote by 300,000.

It was a tainted victory, but Hayes became a more than adequate President, despite the bitterness of the Democrats and the handicap of a sardonic nickname, "Rutherfraud" B. Hayes. He and his wife, Lucy Webb Hayes, were unassuming and pleasant; their four years in the Executive Mansion were quiet and unpretentious. But Mrs. Hayes, at least, became a permanent part of White House lore. Because of her refusal to serve alcoholic drinks, she was called "Lemonade Lucy," often derisively. It was an odd appellation, for she was the ideal First Lady, a charming, handsome, and intelligent woman.

At twenty-five, Rutherford Birchard Hayes was a coy romantic who archly wrote to an adoring sister that he intended to "get me a wifey." When he first met Lucy Webb in July of 1847, she was sixteen, and he thought of her as "a mere child." Lucy, a demure and lovely young lady with black hair and deeply dark eyes, had been chosen for him by his mother. Hayes, whose thoughts were constantly on marriage, had no interest in Lucy, for he considered her too young. His own experience had been more confined to daydreaming than doing, yet in contrast to the sixteen-year-old Lucy, twenty-five-year-old Hayes viewed himself as knowledgeable and knowing in the matter of love.

For her part, Lucy was favorably impressed with the well-mannered Rutherford, and she would not have objected if he had pressed his attentions upon her, but there was an older girl named Helen Kelley who interested him far more. The incident with the glamorous and exciting Miss Kelley eventually came to nothing, and he turned, in time, to courtship of the gentle and uncomplicated Lucy.

Lucy Webb was born in Chillicothe, Ohio, on August 28, 1831. Through her mother, Maria Cook, and her father, James Webb, Lucy traced her ancestry back to seven active participants in the American Revolution. Her father's family had settled on Ohio land they had received from a grateful government for their services in the Revolution. During the course of their stay in the West, the Webbs had accumulated property and slaves. Lucy's father, a doctor, abhorred the custom of slavery; at his first opportunity, in 1833, when Lucy was two, he traveled to Kentucky to arrange for the freeing of his slaves. He intended to send them to Liberia, but before he could complete his arrangements, he was stricken with cholera and died. His wife was left with Lucy and two older sons.

Mrs. Webb herself gave unconditional freedom to the slaves, for she insisted that before she would sell them, "I will take in washing to support my family." Lucy's own strong antislavery views were influenced by her mother's convictions.

Chillicothe, established in 1796, had been the first state capital for Ohio. When Lucy reached the proper school age, there were a number of private schools in the town devoted exclusively to the education of the boys and girls of the more prominent families. One of these schools was conducted by the elderly Miss Baskerville, who had become a tradition in Chillicothe. Like the other girls in Miss Baskerville's charge, Lucy was imbued with the correct religious precepts and characteristics of virtuous deportment.

By the time Lucy was ready for higher education, she impressed her elders with her "devotion to religion" and her politeness in dealing with older people. Rutherford's mother, Sophia Hayes, herself a widow of many years, was particularly taken with this latter characteristic of Lucy's.

Lucy and Rutherford met in Delaware, Ohio, where Lucy's mother had moved so that her two sons could attend college there. Lucy continued her education with occasional instruction from some of the professors at Delaware's Ohio Wesleyan University; in the fall of 1847, the Webbs moved to Cincinnati, and Lucy, who had just turned sixteen, entered the Wesleyan Women's College. When she graduated with honors three years later, she had won "the respect and approval of her teachers . . . [and] the affection and confidence of her schoolmates." She had enjoyed "all proper amusements like a bright, healthy, happy schoolgirl." (Lucy Hayes was the first First Lady to have a college education.)

Rutherford Hayes, between his ineffective moonings over other young ladies, had sometimes dropped in at Wesleyan to visit with Lucy. He had started a law practice in Cincinnati, and though he had not yet threatened the more solidly entrenched attorneys, he had a respectable income, and a growing reputation. In his relations with women, he was hampered by a pervasive attachment for his sister, Fanny, two years older. His father had died before he had been born, as had the first three of his mother's children. After the death of her husband, and still suffering from the shock of so quickly losing her first three children, Rutherford's mother, Sophia Hayes, had lavished all of her affection on Rutherford; in time, however, her only surviving daughter, Fanny, replaced her as the dominant feminine figure in Rutherford's life. Fanny fussed and fluttered over Rutherford as if he had been her own son; it was this intense affection and bond between brother and sister that hindered him in his search for meaningful love. It was not until June of 1851, when he was twenty-eight, that he took the first positive steps to emancipation. On a sudden impulse, he proposed to Lucy, for he had decided, as he had noted in his diary the previous month, "By George! I am in love with her!" She accepted his proposal with the confession that she liked him "very well."

Lucy and Rutherford were married on December 30, 1852, at the home of her mother in Cincinnati. Curiously, his mother did not attend, although his sister did. (Despite his marriage and his new responsibilities, Hayes did not completely free himself of his deep tie to Fanny until her death in 1856.) At the time of their marriage, Lucy was twenty-one and Rutherford was thirty.

Not quite eleven months later, their first child, Richard Austin, was born on November 4, 1853. Through the next twenty years, Lucy was to have seven more children. Her last, a son, was born on August 1, 1873, when she was almost forty-two. Of her eight children, seven were boys and one, her sixth-born, Fanny, was her only daughter. Three of her sons, Joseph Thompson, Scott Russell, and the last-born, Manning Force, lived less than two years each. They died of unspecified causes, although of the first one to die (Little Jody, as Lucy had adoringly called him), Hayes noted in his diary: "Teething, dysentery, and brain affected." The other five children, all of whom made successful marriages, outlived both their parents.

In the beginning, Lucy and Rutherford lived in her mother's house, but after the arrival of their first son in 1853 they moved to their own home. Mrs. Webb, who had never remarried, came with them; she was not an interfering mother-in-law, but appears rather to have been a settling influence on Rutherford. Her presence added to his performance as a responsible head of a household, which he had never been with his mother and sister and bachelor uncle, Sardis Birchard, who had always been his surrogate father.

There was another influence that had an even greater impact upon him, and that was Lucy's advanced opposition to slavery. Subtly but decisively, her thinking on the subject drew him to a position closer to hers. In 1856, with the new Republican party on the scene for the first time, he cut the Gordian knot of political ambiguity represented by the moribund Whigs, and he joined the Republicans. (It should also be noted that 1856 was the year his sister Fanny died.) The new party, although not yet totally committed to the outright abolition of slavery, was nevertheless opposed to that "peculiar institution," as was Lucy, and Rutherford's membership signified a radical step for him.

Rutherford's growth was paralleled by Lucy's. She was mother, housewife, and mistress of a respectable, three-story home. Despite her multiple responsibilities, she began to take an active interest in charitable affairs, and she gave much of her time to working with hospitals and the poor.

The outbreak of the Civil War brought an eventful change to the Hayes household, for Rutherford decided that he must enlist at once; Lucy did not attempt to dissuade him. In June, Governor Dennison commissioned him a major in the Twenty-Third Ohio Regiment. Despite a complete lack of training and with no knowledge whatever of military fundamentals, Hayes started at the top, thanks to his political contacts and his growing prominence as a lawyer in Cincinnati. Within six months he was promoted to lieutenant-colonel.

At the beginning, the war was a great lark to Hayes. He relished the dream of winning glory on the battlefield. For Lucy, the Civil War was like a personal vendetta against "the slave power." She enjoyed reading her husband's accounts of his soldiering, and one of her regrets was that she had not been at Fort Sumter "with a garrison of women." But in time, reality for both of them intruded, and what had been "great fun" for Hayes turned into a grim matter of flesh and blood and death. The war became far more personal in September of 1862, when Hayes was struck by a musketball on the left arm just above the elbow. He fell to the ground, weak and nauseated; he thought he was to be abandoned by his troops, and called to them: "Hallo, Twenty-Third men! Are you going to leave your colonel here for the enemy!" Fortunately they did not, and Lucy came as soon as she could to nurse him back to fighting trim.

Lucy's arrival in the combat zone brought her face to face with the horrors of war, and she was shaken by what she saw. On September 26, Hayes wrote to his uncle, Sardis Birchard: "Lucy is here. . . . She visits the wounded and comes back in tears; then we take a little refreshment and get over it."

Lucy's next visit to Hayes took place in January of 1863, when she and their two oldest sons joined him and the rest of the Twenty-Third at their camp in West Virginia. She stayed for two months, and spent much of her time working and visiting with the wounded in the camp hospital. There were to be other visits to her husband, and during each Lucy continued her custom of comforting the wounded soldiers. Years later, the grateful men of the Twenty-Third remembered her thoughtfulness and consideration with a memorial gift on her silver wedding anniversary.

The end of the war found Hayes a brevet major-general and a congressman elected *in absentia.* He served in Washington until 1867, when he was elected governor of Ohio, and he moved, with his family, to the state capital at Columbus.

As the governor's lady, Lucy was in the public eye more than ever, and she devoted herself with increasing energy and concern to the poor. One of her favorite projects was the new Home for Soldiers' Orphans at Xenia. She "ransacked the city of Columbus for money, books, gifts, etc. etc. . . ." and when the Ohio legislature hesitated over its adoption of the home, Lucy "exerted all her influence with her friends, especially in the Senate." She was rewarded with an affirmative vote by a majority of exactly one, and the State of Ohio officially undertook support of the Orphans' Home due largely to Lucy's persistence.

Hayes served as governor for two successive terms; in 1872 he made an unsuccessful attempt for election to Congress, and he was then elected to a third term as governor of Ohio in the fall of 1875. He served for a period of only fourteen months, for he, Lucy, and the family left Ohio on Thursday, March 1, 1877, to travel to Washington in the event the special electoral commission declared him to be the nineteenth President. He was officially so declared on Friday, March 2, while he and Lucy were still en route. Because presidential inaugurations could not take place on a Sunday, Hayes was actually sworn in as Chief Executive on Saturday, March 3, when he took the oath of office in the Red Room of the White House. He thus became the first President to accept the oath of office in the White House itself.

The entrance of Lucy Hayes on the national scene as the new First Lady marked an abrupt change in the social outlook of the entire country. The opulence of the Grant administrations gave way to the staid simplicity of Lucy Webb Hayes. She was editorially praised for her quiet dignity and her ladylike lack of ostentation. The Philadelphia *Times* damned the Grant years for their "reckless extravagance . . . thousands of dollars have frequently been spent on a single toilet. . . . Much of the corruption which disgraced the late Administration arose from the desire that wives and daughters might be gorgeously arrayed on state occasions." But Lucy Hayes, said the editor, "deserves the thanks of every true woman for the stand which she has taken against extravagance in dress." Lucy, no matter the occasion, always wore a high-necked dress, with a minimum of ornamentation. With her "singularly gentle and winning face," she doomed, for the next four years, the décolletage and bare arms that had been so popular at the White House before her.

If Lucy's simplicity of dress startled Washington society, they were shocked by her ban on alcoholic drinks at the Executive Mansion. A lifelong believer in temperance, and a devout member of the Methodist Episcopal Church, Lucy had never permitted alcohol in any form in her home; since the White House was now her home, she saw no reason to change her way of living, despite the outraged cries of the capital's social leaders and despite the derisive "Lemonade Lucy" designation. But she had far more support than criticism; the Women's Christian Temperance Union, in particular, hastened to praise her. In gratitude for her ban against alcohol, the WCTU commissioned a full-length portrait of her in a ruby velvet gown. The painting, by Daniel Huntington, a celebrated American artist, hangs in the White House collection.

Receptions at the White House were as well attended as ever, in spite of Lucy's alcoholic proscription. An early guest was Helen Herron, daughter of close friends from Cincinnati. (Miss Herron herself later became mistress of the Executive Mansion as the wife of William Howard Taft, the twenty-seventh President.) Lucy's most notable contribution to White House tradition was the Easter egg-rolling. For many years, the children of Washington had been permitted to roll their eggs on the grounds of the Capitol building; on Easter Monday of 1878, a few grumpy Congressmen objected, and the children were chased away, whereupon Lucy promptly invited them to use the White House lawns. Every First Lady since then has repeated the invitation.

On December 30, 1877, President and Mrs. Hayes celebrated their silver anniversary. In the first such ceremony ever seen in the White House, they repeated the wedding that had taken place in Ohio twenty-five years before, with as many of the same guests as they could assemble. Lucy wore her wedding gown of figured white satin; unfortunately, as her husband noted in his diary, Lucy was "large but not unwieldy," and the seams had to be let out.

Hayes declined a second term, and in 1881, he and Lucy retired to "Spiegel Grove," the beautifully wooded estate in Fremont, Ohio, they had inherited from his uncle, Sardis Birchard. (The name had a German derivation, for Birchard had imagined the pools on the estate "reflecting like mirrors"—the German word for mirror is *Spiegel*.) As she had during her years as the governor's wife and as the First Lady, Lucy spent her retirement in charitable work. She assumed the national presidency of the Home Missionary Society of the Methodist Episcopal Church, and served in that office for a number of years.

On June 21, 1889, on a Friday afternoon of a lovely summer day, Lucy Hayes suffered a stroke as she sat in her room, serenely sewing and looking out at her children playing tennis on the lawn. She lingered for three more days, sometimes conscious, sometimes not, but never saying another word. Early on Tuesday morning, on June 25, 1889, the end came for her, with "all her family watching in silent anguish as her gentle spirit took its flight." She was two months short of fifty-eight. Hayes wrote this about her in his diary:

> Lucy Hayes is approaching the beautiful and happy ending of a beautiful, honored and happy life. . . . Without pain, without the usual suffering, she has been permitted to come to the gates of the great change which leads to the life where pain and suffering are unknown. . . . She is in heaven. She is where all the best of earth have gone.

Three and a half years later, on January 17, 1893, Hayes died at the age of seventy years. Lucy and Hayes were both buried in the Spiegel Grove State Park in Fremont, Ohio.

Lucretia Garfield
1832–1918

Ingenuity and greed, with a healthy assist from an abundance of natural resources, teamed together in the 1870s and 1880s to create a time of zestful growth and expansion in the United States. But there were cracks in the magnificent façade. Exploited labor began to stir. And the brotherhood that flowered from sea to shining sea blossomed for the white man only. Still, the United States was growing too rapidly for anyone to stand in its way.

By 1880, the Republicans, under Rutherford B. Hayes, had restored stability; the business panic of the 1870s had yielded to peaceful plenty, and the incumbent Republicans were sure they could not lose the coming presidential election. Fearing public reaction to a third term, their quadrennial convention rejected the strong comeback bid of Ulysses S. Grant and chose, instead, on the thirty-sixth ballot, James A. Garfield of Ohio, a long-time congressman and Civil War general. Hailed as a dark horse, Gar-

180

field, from the beginning of the convention, had worked carefully and diligently for his own nomination, awaiting only the proper moment to break through the expected deadlock. According to a contemporary observer, Garfield was the "consummate politician of the convention . . . the wise man of the hour."

Despite forebodings of the disgruntled Grant supporters, the Republican ticket was victorious. Garfield received 4,454,416 votes to 4,444,952 for the Democrat, Winfield Scott Hancock of Pennsylvania. Garfield's popular vote margin was barely 9,500, though he safely won the electorial votes, 214 to 155, to become the twentieth President of the United States.

Who was Garfield? What kind of President was he? Or would have been? History will never know, for he did not live long enough to tell us. Nor do we know what kind of First Lady Lucretia Rudolph Garfield would have been. She and her husband have been almost forgotten, except for the unusual circumstances of his death. In a sense, they too were beyond the ordinary, and deserve far more from posterity than they have received.

Intellectually gifted, well read, the Garfields were unlike the run-of-the-mill, commonplace political couple so often seen in Washington and other governmental centers in the nineteenth century. Lucretia removed herself from the inbred world of the socially ambitious, although in the years she lived in the federal capital as the wife of a congressman, she did as much entertaining as her husband's modest salary would permit. Never rich, the Garfields stayed within their means; they were respected by their associates for their genuine hospitality and taste. When Lucretia entered the White House as its new mistress, it was said that she was considered "a homebody . . . a lady whose refinements, attainments and fine character the people will like."

Lucretia Rudolph was born in the village of Hiram, in Ohio's Western Reserve, on April 19, 1832. In the sparsely settled Western Reserve there were many religious sects opposed to the ownership of slaves. One of the early settlers was Zebulon Rudolph, who was married to Arabella Mason. Rudolph, of German descent, was said to be related to a soldier who had gone to France, where he became the Duke of Elchingen, better known as Napoleon's brilliant Marshall Ney. Mrs. Rudolph, on her mother's side, was descended from the Revolutionary War hero, General Nathanael Greene.

Zebulon Rudolph had a large farm in Cuyahoga County and a large family. A member of the Disciples of Christ, Rudolph was one of the organizers of the Western Reserve Eclectic Institute in Hiram. Both Mr. and Mrs. Rudolph were strong believers in education, as well as proper religious indoctrination. Lucretia was given every opportunity for schooling; one of the schools she attended was Geauga Seminary, in the neighboring village of Chester. In 1849, when she was seventeen, she met another student at Geauga, a young man of eighteen named James Garfield.

Garfield, who lived in nearby Orange, was a tall, well-built young man with blue eyes and a ruddy complexion. His father had died at the age of thirty-three, when James was eighteen months old. Mrs. Garfield, determined to keep her family together, worked the farm her husband had left until her children were old enough to help. There was never any money for extras; education was a hardship, but she somehow found enough for James, and sent him off to Geauga.

His interest in Lucretia was perfunctory. A slender girl with brown hair and brown eyes, Lucretia was rather plain, with a smallish face, a wide mouth, and prominent forehead. At Geauga she attended some lectures and met Garfield there. She impressed him with her quiet and studious manner, but there is no evidence that his feelings were romantic. They did have, however, a common thirst for knowledge and a love of the classics; they both excelled in the study of Latin.

In the fall of 1851, Lucretia was enrolled at the Western Reserve Eclectic Institute in Hiram, the school her father had helped to organize. She had not seen Garfield since he had left Geauga in 1850, but she met him again at the Institute, for he had come there as a teacher. They now saw more of each other than they had at Geauga, for James was her Latin teacher. He was a student

182

as well, and he apparently spent much time with Almeda A. Booth, nine years his senior. Miss Booth, who had "resolved forever to maintain her 'maiden widowhood,' " helped him with his own study of Latin and Greek, and undoubtedly helped him as a teacher.

Whatever his relationship with Almeda Booth may have been, it did not stand in the way of his growing attachment for Lucretia. "Crete," as James called her, did not object to his interest; by 1854, when he was ready to enter Williams College in Massachusetts, Jim and Crete came to an understanding. Within two years, he would graduate from Williams, and return to Hiram. Lucretia agreed to wait for him, but rather than remain dependent upon her parents she took a teaching job in Cleveland. From there she went to Bayou, Ohio, a "very insignificant village," where she taught painting and drawing. She boarded with the Pratt family; in later years, Mr. A. M. Pratt described her in these words: "She [was] graceful, sweet, amiable, retiring, with a disposition as lovely as a star-lit sky."

James returned to Hiram in 1856, and joined the faculty of the Western Reserve Eclectic Institute as professor of ancient languages. His salary was a small one, and he and Lucretia decided to await a more auspicious moment. The following year, at the age of twenty-six, Garfield was appointed president of the institute. He now chose to concentrate upon a career in education, although he did some preaching as well. A salary increase permitted him to make systematic savings; within another year, he and Crete were able to marry. The marriage took place on November 11, 1858. They had met nine years before.

Lucretia and Garfield moved into a small cottage on the edge of the village green across from the campus. This was to be Lucretia's Ohio home for the next nineteen years, and it was here that the first three of her seven children were born—on July 3, 1860, Eliza Arabella; on October 11, 1863, Harry Augustus; and on October 17, 1865, James Rudolph.

In 1861, as had Grant and Hayes before him, Garfield enlisted for service with the Union Army during the Civil War. His college degree, plus his recent entry into politics as a Republican member of the Ohio state senate, earned him a commission as a lieutenant-colonel. Within six months, he rose to the rank of brigadier-general; in February of 1863, he was appointed General Rosecrans' chief of staff. Like Hayes, Garfield had no prior military knowledge or training before the Civil War; his religious beliefs, in fact, were strongly antiwar, as were Lucretia's. The Disciples of Christ, the sect to which they both belonged, was dedicated to peace. But Garfield and Lucretia were strongly opposed to slavery, and any means of destroying it was justified in their eyes. As Garfield wrote to a friend: "[We] believe that the sin of slavery is one of which it may be said that without the shedding of blood there is no remission."

Lucretia did not have a chance to join her husband at his encampments, as had Mrs. Grant and Mrs. Hayes. But James did return to Hiram in August of 1862, when he suffered a relapse of the malaria that had been plaguing him for many years. He stayed in Hiram for about six months, and then reported to General Rosecrans in February of 1863. In December of that year he resigned his commission to take a seat in Congress as representative from the Nineteenth District of Ohio. He arrived in Hiram in time to attend the funeral of his first-born, Eliza Arabella, who died on December 3, 1863, at the age of three and a half. Stricken as Lucretia was at the death of her daughter (her second-born, Harry Augustus, was not yet two months old), she had the strength to be a source of comfort to her husband, who had seen much of suffering and death on the battlefields, but had felt none as keenly as this. He told his dearest friend: "I am grieved and broken in spirit . . . but I can endure almost anything so long as this brave little woman is left me."

Garfield's stay in Hiram was all too short, since he had to report to Washington for the congressional session that had begun on December 7. It was the first of many sessions, for he served as a congressman for seventeen years. During much of that time, Lucretia and the children were with him in Washington. Of her last four children, two were born in Washington—Mary (known as "Molly") on January 16, 1867, and Abram, on November 21,

1872—and two were born in Hiram—Irvin McDowell, on August 3, 1870, and Edward, on December 25, 1874. The last one, Edward, lived less than two years; he died on October 25, 1876. The five surviving children all lived well into the twentieth century. Abram Garfield did not die until 1958, when he was eighty-six.

In Washington, Lucretia made little impact upon society; she spent a great deal of time at the Congressional Library, selecting books to read while caring for her children. She and Garfield became active in the Washington Literary Society; Garfield served one year as its president. The group often met at their home (for some time, the Garfields had lived in boarding houses while staying in Washington, but they eventually saved enough to buy a house).

Lucretia decided she ought to teach Latin to her sons, but after many years away from it, she was afraid she had grown rusty. Garfield gave her a copy of Caesar's *Commentaries*. To her delight, she found she could still do an adequate translation, even from so difficult and advanced a book; she did teach her sons, and, unquestionably, was the best Latin instructor they would ever have.

In 1877, the Garfields moved from Hiram to Mentor, Ohio, some twenty-five miles from Cleveland. At Mentor, on property covering 160 acres, they built a spacious two-and-a-half-story house designed by Lucretia, and given the name of "Lawnfield." It was a far more fitting residence for the family of Ohio's most distinguished congressman than their small cottage in Hiram.

The nomination of Garfield as the Republican presidential candidate in 1880 was a complete surprise to Lucretia; a bystander reported there were tears in her eyes when she received the telegram announcing her husband's nomination. In response to a question asking whether she wasn't glad and proud, she quickly answered: "Oh, yes; but it is a terrible responsibility to come to him and to me." During the hectic months preceding the election, when her home was constantly filled with party aides, representatives of the press, friends, casual visitors, well-wishers, hangers-on, she retained her poise and dignity. This remarkable ability to remain calm and possessed under the most trying of conditions impressed the correspondents who interviewed her. But she insisted that the privacy of her family was inviolate; she would not permit photographs of her to be taken or used, although she relented at last and sat for one official photograph.

After her husband's election, she faced her new life in the White House with the same even-tempered reserve that had characterized her at Mentor. Leaders of Washington society expected four years of relatively unexciting social activity in the Executive Mansion, but they could once again look forward to the benefits of some alcoholic beverages, for Lucretia was not the strict prohibitionist Lucy Hayes had been.

Lucretia and her eighty-year-old mother-in-law, Eliza Ballou Garfield, who had always lived with them, were both present at Garfield's Inauguration. Much to the surprise of the onlookers, the new President, after taking the oath and kissing the Bible, exuberantly kissed his mother and wife, in that order. It was the first time a new President had so publicly displayed his love and affection for the two women dearest to him. At the Inaugural Ball that night, Lucretia revealed a quiet simplicity of taste and elegance. She wore a "handsome dress of heliotrope satin, trimmed with rich lace, a bunch of pansies in her corsage, and no jewelry."

Socially, in the few weeks she had as mistress of the Executive Mansion, Lucretia performed adequately. On the political level, she exerted a behind-the-scenes' influence that was recognized by governmental leaders and her husband alike. When James G. Blaine was appointed to the Garfield cabinet as Secretary of State, his letter of acceptance to President Garfield included these words: "I wish you would say to Mrs. Garfield that the knowledge that she desires me in your Cabinet is more valuable to me than even the desire of the [President] himself."

Unlike her predecessors, Lucretia did not plan to refurnish the White House to please her own tastes only. She and Garfield decided to redo the Executive Mansion in an historically constructive manner, based upon previous administrations. They did some research at the Library of Congress, but their plans had to be postponed, for Lucretia became ill. The political world, with its conniving and scheming and freely flung abuse, distressed her. Coupled with a severe attack of malaria, endemic to swampy Washington, she found she could no longer function as hostess of the White House. She was taken to recuperate at the soothing and cooler seashore at Elberon, New Jersey.

On July 2, .1881, President Garfield left the White House to travel by train to Elberon, where he was to join his wife and family. As he passed through the ladies' waiting room of Washington's Pennsylvania Station, amiably chatting with Secretary of State Blaine, a crazed assassin named Charles Guiteau leaped toward the President with a wild cry and shot him twice, once in the arm and the second shot in the spine. Guiteau, undoubtedly insane, had no other motive than imagined wrongdoing on Garfield's part. (After a bizarre and lengthy trial, Guiteau was hanged in June of 1882.)

Garfield's wounds were not immediately fatal. He lingered for over two months, while the whole world anxiously hung on every medical bulletin. Through the long ordeal, Lucretia maintained her composure. She presented a picture of calm and magnificent self-control that evoked the admiration of the entire world. At last, in Elberon, New Jersey, where he had been taken for a few moments of comfort away from the overwhelming heat and humidity of Washington, James A. Garfield died of his wounds, complicated by blood poisoning, on September 19, 1881, at 10:35 P.M. He was not yet fifty. He was buried two days later in Lake View Cemetery, in Cleveland, Ohio.

The public did not forget Lucretia with the burial of her husband. A public drive for funds, conducted by financier Cyrus W. Field of New York (who himself made a generous subscription), raised over $350,000 for the Garfield family. Lucretia used some of the money for college educations for her children, and donated $10,000 to a university in Kansas that took the name of her husband.

For a time, Lucretia traveled abroad with her only daughter, Molly, and then lived quietly in Bournemouth, England, where she attempted to escape the glare of publicity. But she preferred her native land, and returned to Mentor, Ohio. On June 14, 1888, at "Lawnfield," two of her children were married in a double ceremony—Molly to Joseph Stanley-Brown, and Harry Augustus to Belle Mason.

Lucretia's children did much to replace the loss of her husband. Abram became a successful architect; Harry and James were law partners. Harry later became a professor at Princeton under Woodrow Wilson, and president of his father's and his own alma mater, Williams College. James was Theodore Roosevelt's Secretary of the Interior.

Lucretia survived her husband by more than thirty-six years. During that time, she lived simply, in the relative anonymity of her private life. She died at her winter home in South Pasadena, California, on March 14, 1918, at the age of eighty-five. She was buried in Lake View Cemetery, next to her husband, in Cleveland.

Ellen Arthur
1837–1880

American democracy has too often relied upon accident, yet remarkably it has come through unscathed. The country is never prepared for the sudden death of a President and, worse, the direct line of succession sometimes falls upon a man not one single voter would willingly choose for his Chief Executive, as happened in 1881.

The Republican party, meeting at Chicago's Exposition Hall in June of 1880, found itself split between two factions. Senator Roscoe Conkling of New York refused to support James A. Garfield, the convention's choice for President. In his derisive estimation, Garfield, whom he called the "trickster of Mentor," could never win. He ordered his followers to reject the nomination for Vice President if it were offered to them.

The first choice of the convention leaders, Levi P. Morton, dutifully complied with Conkling's instructions, but the second choice, Chester A. Arthur, did not. Defying his party boss's fiat with the humble declaration: "The office of Vice President is a greater honor than I ever dreamed of attaining," he promptly accepted. By a double accident of defiance and death, Chester Alan Arthur became the twenty-first President of the United States when he took the oath of office at 1:30 A.M. on September 20, 1881, in his home in New York City, three hours after James Garfield died.

Arthur's succession to the Executive chair was incredible in other respects, for he had never been elected to a public office prior to the Vice-Presidency. He had, in fact, been removed by President Hayes from the only appointive position he had ever held. It is difficult to imagine a man less qualified for the Presidency than Chester Alan Arthur, yet he was not a bad Chief Executive. He acted independently of party pressure, remained free of scandal and corruption, and administered in a capable if uninspired fashion.

Chester A. Arthur was the fourth Vice President to succeed to the Presidency upon the death of the President; he was also the fourth widower to enter the White House. His wife of twenty years, Ellen Herndon Arthur, had died not quite two years before at the age of forty-two. Ellen Arthur was a lovely woman with a social background that would have suited her exactly if she had lived to become the First Lady. Politics did not interest her; society did. Washington's social leaders would have welcomed her.

An overnight success and a sudden hero have one capacity in common—each can move the American people to an excess of sentimentality, occasionally accompanied by a maudlin outpouring of generosity. Such was the case with Lieutenant William Lewis Herndon, a naval officer in command of a passenger and mail ship, the *Central America,* plying the coastal waters of the Atlantic between New York and Panama. (Herndon was on leave at the time from the United States Navy, a common practice that permitted officers to assume commercial commands.)

Lieutenant Herndon, who had won honors and fame by exploring the wild Amazon River in 1853, was destined to play a

190

far more fateful role. On September 11, 1857, the *Central America,* fully loaded, ran into a severe tropical storm off Cape Hatteras. Despite a serious leak, it remained afloat until its 450 passengers and crew of 100 were removed the next day by a brig that had come to its rescue. Its captain, Lieutenant Herndon, waited on board while all the others were taken off his sinking ship. His exhausted crew rowed back for him, but there was not enough time to save him. Fearing his men would be swamped, he ordered them to pull away. Reluctantly, they obeyed their captain's last order and pulled away just in time. They watched in horror as "Dressed in full uniform, standing on the bridge, with indomitable gallantry he went down to death with his ship."

A grateful country did not forget his courage. At Annapolis, a monument was erected in his memory, and Congress, by special legislation, had a medal struck in his honor. Nor was that all. The people of New York, to commemorate the lieutenant's unselfish bravery, gave a fine townhouse on Manhattan's West Twenty-First Street to Herndon's widow and daughter. Mrs. Frances Hansbrough Herndon and Ellen Lewis Herndon, who was then twenty, moved in early in 1858.

Ellen Lewis Herndon was born in Culpepper Court House near Fredericksburg, Virginia, on August 30, 1837. Besides her father, there were other distinguished navy men in her family. An uncle, Lieutenant Matthew Fontaine Maury, became head of the United States Naval Observatory at Washington, and achieved a transitory fame as an oceanographer.

The Herndons were among the more prominent families of Fredericksburg. Ellen, a vivacious young lady with a lovely soprano voice, had all the benefits of gracious southern tradition and training. While her father was not personally wealthy, the antecedents of the Virginia Herndons and Maurys guaranteed Ellen's social success. When she was sixteen, she and her cousins were taken on a tour of Europe by her uncle, Lieutenant Matthew Maury, who was attending a naval conference at Brussels.

Ellen first met Chester A. Arthur in New York, after the death of her father, when she and her mother had moved into the house on West Twenty-First Street. Arthur, son of a Baptist clergyman of upstate New York, had achieved a modest success as a lawyer in New York City. Tall and ample, Arthur was a well-read man who exuded both dignity and good cheer. He was living at the Bancroft House, a residential hotel on Lower Broadway, not far from the Herndons'. Arthur was friendly with another Bancroft House resident, Dabney Herndon, Ellen's cousin. It was Dabney who introduced them.

Ellen and her mother were as popular in New York as they had been in Virginia; they did not penetrate the sanctified portals of New York's ultra wealthy and self-proclaimed aristocracy, but they were accepted by the genteel and more democratic well-to-do, some of whom could lay claim to far more authentically aristocratic ancestry than many of the newly rich. For Chester A. Arthur, the social level on which the Herndons moved was more than enough, and his relationship with Ellen did him no harm.

Acquaintance evolved into friendship, love, and finally marriage. Ellen and Chester Arthur were married in New York's Calvary Church, on October 25, 1859, when Ellen was twenty-two and Arthur twenty-nine. After a honeymoon of two weeks, they moved into her house to live with her mother.

Arthur, making his way steadily upward, had decided upon politics as a secondary career, and had become active in the New York Republican organization. He did not seek public office, but was content to be a minor power behind the scenes.

On December 10, 1860, Ellen gave birth to their first child, a son whom they named after her famous and heroic father, William Lewis Herndon. From the beginning, Ellen hovered over the boy and carefully tried to protect him from disease. During the summer, she went with him to the cooler and quieter areas of New Jersey.

Chester Arthur, in the meantime, had joined the New York state militia; it was a natural move for an ambitious young politician. Governor Edwin D. Morgan placed Arthur on his military staff as engineer-in-chief. When the Civil War broke out, Arthur was appointed assistant quartermaster-general of New York; in April of 1862, Governor Morgan commissioned him full quarter-master with a rank of brigadier-general. Fortunately for Ellen's peace of mind, Arthur was not involved in active warfare, although, in 1862, he was sent to Virginia to supervise the needs of New York troops.

The Civil War brought anguish of a different sort for Ellen. Like Mary Lincoln, she had many relatives in the South. But unlike Mrs. Lincoln, who had to prove her loyalty to the Union through President Lincoln's public assertion of her allegiance, Ellen Arthur did not have to disavow her implied support of the Confederacy. Her husband was prominent in political circles, and she therefore could not openly speak her mind, but she had only to keep her thoughts to herself. To Arthur's friends and associates, she was mute on the subject of the war; they asked for no further proof of her loyalty.

Ellen did not actively support the South, yet she could not help but be concerned about her family in Virginia, all of whom were fighting for the Confederate states. Her cousin, Dabney Herndon, had been captured by northern troops in April of 1862; when General Arthur went to Virginia on his supervisory mission, his rank helped him to effect a transfer of prisoners, and Dabney was permitted to return to his regiment. (Dabney was captured again the following year, and again Arthur secured his release.)

On January 1, 1863, a Democratic governor, Horatio Seymour, replaced Republican Edwin Morgan. With Governor Seymour's Inauguration, Chester Arthur's commission as quartermaster-general of New York was revoked, and for him the Civil War came to an early end; he returned to the practice of law.

Six months later, Ellen suffered a loss even more acute than the dramatic passing of her father, for it involved the death of her two-year-old son. Billy died on July 7, 1863, in Englewood, New Jersey, "from convulsions, brought on by some affection of the brain." As Arthur reported it to his brother, "Nell [was] broken hearted . . . her heart was wrapped up in her dear boy."

One year later, her second son, named Chester Alan for his father, was born in New York on July 25, 1864. And finally, a daughter, named for her, was born on November 21, 1871. (Son and daughter survived both parents. They lived into the twentieth century, with the daughter dying first, in 1915. The son, Chester Alan, Jr., was married three times, and devoted more time to playing polo than to earning a living. He died in Colorado Springs at the age of seventy-three.)

The early years after the war found Arthur's practice flourishing. In 1867, the Arthurs were prosperous enough to move into their own house, a fine structure on Lexington Avenue, in New York's exclusive Gramercy Park. Ellen did a great deal of entertaining; she became active in the newly organized Mendelssohn Glee Club as a featured soloist.

The Mendelssohn Glee Club occupied much of Ellen's time. An accomplished singer, she had no desire to perform professionally, yet music was important to her, and the glee club gave her an opportunity to appear in public. Organized in 1867 with an original roster of twenty-four talented amateurs under the leadership of a dynamic young conductor named Joseph Mosenthal, the glee club was a serious musical organization that later accepted professionals. Shortly after its inception, it began an annual summer custom of nautical outings to West Point and Coney Island, with much informal singing. There can be no doubt that Ellen thoroughly enjoyed these day-long excursions by boat.

Rehearsals, too, proved to be a joy, despite the work. After rehearsals, the male singers went to the homes of the ladies to stand on the curbs outside and lift their voices in serenade. One of the favorite objects of their serenading was Ellen; often the men would stand in the bitter cold, gallantly singing away. Arthur, disregarding the lateness of hour, would invite them in for proper refreshments to dissipate the chill in their bones.

On May 14, 1867, a "Private Concert of the Mendelssohn Glee Club" was performed at Dodworth's Hall, near Grace

Church, on New York's lower Broadway. Appearing as a "Principal Soloist" was "Mrs. Chester A. Arthur, Soprano." In Part I of the program, she sang Donizetti's "La Mere et l'Enfant"; in Part II, she joined a Quartette for Female Voices in Rossini's "La Charite"; and she was then the soprano voice in a trio composed of herself and the Messrs. Bush and Howland—they did the "Ave Verum" from Kreutzer's "Night in Granada." On January 24, 1868, Ellen was once again a principal soloist; she sang the "Cavatina" from Donizetti's "La Favorita," and then led the entire club in Hiller's "O World, Thou Art Wondrous Fair."

Ellen devoted as much time as she could to the Mendelssohn Glee Club, and later to charitable organizations. Her public appearances did much to advance her husband's career. She went to Albany to sing in a benefit concert for the Child's Hospital. A local newspaper reported that "her voice and manner won the praises of those who heard her."

By the end of 1871, when her daughter was born, Ellen began to limit her work with the glee club. In that same year, Arthur was appointed by President Grant as Collector of the Port of New York, a juicy political plum. When Rutherford Hayes succeeded to the Presidency in 1877, he sought the ouster of Arthur as part of his campaign to reform the spoils system. Arthur resisted, but had to capitulate in the end, and accepted his suspension from office in July of 1878.

For Ellen, as well, the year 1878 was momentous and painful. In April her mother died in France; the sad and fatiguing task of bringing her body back to the United States was left to Ellen. The long journey across the Atlantic depressed her to the point of continual melancholy from which she never really recovered.

In January of 1880, when Arthur was in Albany on Republican party work, Ellen fell ill. As reported by the *Albany Argus* five days later, her illness "at first was supposed to be a comparatively harmless attack of pneumonia." By early the next day, Sunday morning, it was evident that Ellen was seriously ill, and Arthur was called to hurry home. Because of the Sabbath, the only available transportation was a milk train. Arthur arrived in New York at midnight, to find Ellen "beyond hope of recovery." She died of pneumonia twenty-four hours later, on January 12, 1880, at the age of forty-two.

The Mendelssohn Glee Club, in gratitude for the many years she had devoted to them, sang at her funeral services at the Church of Heavenly Rest, on New York's Fifth Avenue. The state legislature passed a resolution in her memory:

> Resolved, that we have learned with deep regret of the sudden and untimely death of Ellen Lewis Herndon, wife of Chester A. Arthur, of the city of New York, and that we extend to her bereaved husband and family our sincere sympathy in their great affliction.
>
> Resolved, that a committee of eight be appointed by the chairman to attend the funeral ceremonies at Albany.

When Ellen's body arrived in Albany at 2:50 on the afternoon of Thursday, January 15, the committee of eight, together with Governor Cornell and members of his staff, were waiting at the station. They all joined the funeral cortege, which proceeded by sleigh to the Rural Cemetery, where Ellen was buried in the Arthur family plot.

Chester Arthur did not remarry. When he became President after the death of James Garfield, he dedicated a window in Washington's St. John's Church in Ellen's honor. He kept Ellen's room intact at their Lexington Avenue home (as Andrew Jackson had done for Rachel).

Six years and ten months after Ellen's death, Chester A. Arthur died in New York City of Bright's Disease, a kidney ailment, complicated by apoplexy and good living. Fifty-six at his death, Arthur had consumed too much "fine wines and terrapin and other rich food." After he left office, he was neglected by the public, but suitable homage was paid to him at his funeral by President Cleveland, former President Hayes, and other dignitaries. Chester Alan Arthur was buried in Albany's Rural Cemetery, in the family plot next to Ellen.

Frances Cleveland
1864–1947

Presidential election campaigns are neither models of propriety nor temperate courtesy. Name-calling, mud-slinging, invective, and imputation have been part of the pattern since the American press first discovered it had a voice. The campaign of 1828, between Andrew Jackson and John Quincy Adams, was one of the worst, but the presidential election of 1884, between the Democrat, Grover Cleveland, and the Republican, James G. Blaine, reached a new high for low tactics.

Both candidates, it developed, were vulnerable to charges of improper conduct, the one in private life and the other in public office. Edwin L. Godkin, editor of *The Nation,* contended that Blaine, as Secretary of State, had "wallowed in spoils like a rhinoceros in an African pool."

As for Cleveland, reform mayor of Buffalo and reform governor of New York, his political background was untainted; he swept into the Democratic nomination on the second ballot, to the consternation of New York's machine, Tammany Hall, whose "henchmen paced the lobbies raging like lions." They would soon have more reason to rage, for within ten days of Cleveland's nomination a storm of unheralded magnitude burst about the Democrats and their candidate. A Buffalo newspaper revealed that Cleveland, in 1874, had accepted responsibility for the welfare of a boy born to an unwed mother.

Cleveland did not deny the charges, although he admitted only the *possibility* of parentage "out-of-wedlock," since several of his married friends had also been involved. His very honesty saved the day for him. When all results of the election were in, Cleveland was the twenty-second President of the United States by a popular vote of 4,874,986 to 4,851,981 (a bare margin of 23,000) and a safer electoral margin of 219 to 182. Rather than James G. Blaine, who had been "delinquent in office but blameless in private life," the people preferred Grover Cleveland, the man who had been "a model in official integrity but culpable in his personal relations."

Grover Cleveland's personal relations were vastly improved in 1886, when he married twenty-one-year-old Frances Folsom. Cleveland, who had entered the White House a bachelor, with an image tarnished but not irrevocably destroyed, left it happily married, the picture of a contented and peaceful family man, due in large measure to the beautiful girl who became his wife. Frances Folsom Cleveland, the youngest of all First Ladies, graceful and charming, brought a youthful elegance to the White House.

Buffalo in the 1860s presented two faces to its inhabitants: half of it a conservative New England fusion of culture and commerce, and the other half a rowdy mixture of saloons and factory smoke, underscored by endless streams of freight carried on the Erie Canal and the Great Lakes. It was a city of contrasts and a city of opportunity for ambitious men.

Two young lawyers, whose lives were to become fatefully entwined, found themselves in Buffalo during this period. One of them was Grover Cleveland, a confirmed bachelor, already turning to fat from too much beer and not enough exercise, and the other was Oscar Folsom, married to Emma Cornelia Harmon. Folsom, a gregarious, cheerful chap who preferred fast trotters to ponderous lawbooks, became one of Cleveland's closest friends and, later, his law partner. On July 21, 1864, Folsom sent word to his good friend that Mrs. Folsom had given birth to a daughter, and Cleveland promptly came to see the newly born infant. It was the first and only instance of an adult future President meeting his future wife when she was still an infant. Cleveland, at the time, was twenty-seven. (When his sisters once asked why he hadn't married, he replied, without then realizing how prophetic his words would be: "I'm only waiting for my wife to grow up.")

Frances, the Folsoms' only child, was constantly fussed over by her indulgent, adoring father and his equally indulgent and adoring friends. (Cleveland bought her first baby carriage.) To Frances, Cleveland became almost an uncle; she saw him frequently during her childhood years, when he was a casual visitor to the Folsom house. From the beginning, Cleveland called her Frank, and he watched her grow from a lively and friendly child to a beautiful young lady. Frances received her education in Buffalo public schools; after graduation from high school she attended Wells College in Aurora, New York, not far from Buffalo.

On July 23, 1875, Oscar Folsom was thrown from his carriage and instantly killed. Because Folsom died without a will, Cleveland was appointed administrator of his estate and acted as guardian to Frances who was then eleven. Cleveland thus played a most important role in Frances' life, and she regarded him as more than a friend or legal protector.

During Frances' years of growing to maturity, Cleveland's career brought him steadily to the top of the political ladder. In 1871, when Frances was seven, he became sheriff of Erie County and served in that office for three years; in 1882, he was elected mayor of Buffalo on a reform ticket; the following year, again on a reform ticket, he was elected governor of New York; and the year after that, in July of 1884, when Frances was a few days short of twenty, he was nominated by the Democratic party to be their candidate for President. Cleveland, whom Frances had known for her entire life, had come a great distance from the day of her birth twenty years before. (Like many other young men of his day, Cleveland, who never attended college, became a lawyer by clerking in a law office and studying law on his own, with the help of his employers and associates.)

Cleveland's entrance into the White House in 1885 brought a recurring flood of rumor and matchmaking, both covert and open. He was fat, coarse, often rude (he was known to brush right by White House guests without even a bare nod), yet he was the most eligible man in the country, and one woman after another was linked with his name. Cleveland either took no notice of the rumors, or laughed them off. In one instance, when Mrs. Oscar Folsom was persistently mentioned as a possible mate for the bachelor President, Cleveland grumbled that people were marrying him off to old women (Mrs. Folsom, as it happened, was younger than he). But all rumor and guessing came to an end on May 28, 1886, when the White House staff announced that the President and his former ward, Frances Folsom, were engaged to marry.

The engagement, according to Cleveland's spinster sister, who had been acting as his White House hostess, had been "probable" for at least two years, "agreed upon" for one, and kept secret all that time. Although Frances had not seen a great deal of Cleveland during her college years, they did correspond, and boxes of roses arrived regularly for her from the governor's mansion in Albany, and later from Washington. In 1885, Frances and Cleveland did have some time together, when she and her mother spent ten days at the White House.

In the spring of 1886, Frances and Mrs. Folsom traveled through Europe; upon their return to New York on May 27, they were met at the ship by Cleveland's aide, Colonel Daniel Lamont, who whisked them away from eager reporters. The engagement was announced the following night, and the entire country went wild with the news. Bands and orchestras everywhere played Gilbert and Sullivan's phenomenally popular song from *The Mikado,* "He's Going to Marry Yum-Yum," and it was reported that the gruff bachelor Cleveland actually blushed upon hearing the tune. (Frances was indeed a Yum-Yum; tall and graceful, with a figure of willowy perfection, she was a dark-eyed, brown-haired beauty who moved the normally impervious press to rapturous adulation.)

The wedding, which took place on June 2, 1886, was the first and only marriage of a President in the White House itself (John Tyler married Julia Gardiner at a church in New York). The Cleveland–Folsom wedding was the most widely publicized social event of 1886. Only forty selected guests were invited, but each detail of the affair was meticulously reported by a news-hungry press and devoured by an avid public. The ceremony, conducted in the Blue Room, began at exactly 7 P.M., when the President and his future bride stepped into the magnificently flowered room to the music of John Philip Sousa's Marine Band. At that precise moment, churchbells all over the city of Washington pealed in merry triumph, and the navy yard cannon boomed a salute. The twenty-one-year-old bride, "blushing like the morn beneath her misty veil," and the forty-nine-year-old groom repeated their vows from which the word "obey" had been omitted at Cleveland's own request. In the toast that followed, the happy young bride, like Lucy Hayes a firm believer in temperance, drank Appollinaris mineral water.

A short honeymoon at Deer Park, in Maryland's Cumberland Mountains, was, grimly, a forerunner of the glare of publicity that was to surround Frances Cleveland. The press, employing telescopes, spyglasses, and inside informers, reported everything they could see or learn, and their eager readers devoured the tiniest detail, down to such foolish headlines as "MRS. CLEVELAND FISHES." When the honeymoon couple came back to Washington, it was more of the same; for the rest of that summer of 1886, the

Clevelands did manage a semblance of privacy in a country house he had purchased in the Georgetown area, not far from the capital. But Frances was not forgotten; she was idolized everywhere. Women the country over copied her hair style. Her name was used in questionable advertising; in one ad, it was claimed that her wonderfully clear complexion had resulted from regular use of arsenic.

In the fall, the Clevelands returned to a refurbished White House, and Frances began her formal entertaining shortly after the beginning of the year, in January of 1887. She was an immediate success. Thousands of people came to her public receptions, some of which she held on Thursday evenings and Saturday afternoons, so that working women could come to see her. At one such public affair, nine thousand people obediently trooped through the White House receiving line just to shake her hand and to see her sparkling smile, which never faltered through the interminable hours. At the end, both of her arms had to be vigorously massaged (the left hand suffered sympathy pains).

The election of 1888 did not have the vilification of the preceding one, but it was bad enough. Cleveland was accused of beating his wife, a charge that Frances and Cleveland tried to ignore. Frances' mother was angered into calling it "a foolish campaign story without a shadow of foundation. . . ." But the rumors persisted, and at last Frances herself was forced to issue a denial to the "wicked and heartless lies. I can only wish the women of our country no better blessing than that their homes and their lives be as happy, and that their husbands may be as kind and attentive, as considerate and affectionate as mine." Cleveland, in writing to a friend, said this of Frances: "I am sure of one thing. I have in her something better than the presidency for life—though the Republican party and papers do say I beat and abuse her."

To counter the image created by this story (some of his opponents began to refer to Cleveland as "the beast of Buffalo"), Frances' picture was used on her husband's election posters. Despite this tactic, which was the first time a President's wife had become part of a campaign, Cleveland lost the Presidency to Benjamin Harrison, and Frances had to make extensive preparations for their departure from Washington.

When the Clevelands were ready to leave the White House in March of 1889, Frances warned the staff to take good care of the mansion, for "we are coming back just four years from today." They did return, in March of 1893. During the intervening four years they lived in New York City, in a house on Madison Avenue. Cleveland practiced law and quietly laid plans for his renomination in 1892, while Frances went about the business of being a housewife and mother. On October 3, 1891, her first child, a daughter, was born. Named Ruth, the baby was to become the darling of the country just as her mother had been.

The election of 1892, which once again found Cleveland and Benjamin Harrison as the principal contenders, was far different from the previous one in 1888. Labor, smarting under the repressive whiphand of huge employers like Carnegie Steel, turned away from the Republicans; so did many of the ordinary citizens, who were not pleased by Harrison's predilection for granting unwarranted pensions to Civil War veterans. The result was a turnabout, and Grover Cleveland's return to the White House in March of 1893 as the twenty-fourth President with Adlai E. Stevenson as his Vice-President. Cleveland thus became the only President ever to serve nonconsecutive terms. (For the puzzled school child, Cleveland's two terms are counted individually; he is both the twenty-second President and the twenty-fourth. All other Presidents serving more than one term are counted only once.)

The return of the Clevelands to the Executive Mansion signaled a spurt of opulent entertaining. The Pension Building, completed only a few years before, was again the scene of the Inaugural Ball (it had been used for Cleveland's first Inaugural, when he was still a bachelor). The thousands who came to see the President and the First Lady found a radiant Frances; she wore a gown of heavy white satin with an empire front, tightly fitted back, crystal beads, and embroidery. Diamonds completed her dazzling costume. One of the more popular guests was the eighteen-year-old Kaiulani, a lovely Hawaiian princess.

On the twenty-fourth of May, 1893, the Clevelands held a State dinner in honor of the Princess Infanta Eulalie, aunt of the seven-year-old king of Spain. Frances herself created the floral arrangements; she had long been interested in flowers, and spent many hours in the White House conservatory. Her decorations for the Princess Eulalie reflected the Spanish national colors, red and yellow.

Major official entertainment for the balance of 1893 was interrupted by the arrival of a sister for little Ruth. Esther was born in the White House on September 9, 1893. (Esther was the only child of a President actually to be born within the White House itself.) On July 7, 1895, Esther and Ruth were joined by sister Marion, who was born at the Clevelands' summer residence in Buzzards Bay, Massachusetts (on Cape Cod). Frances' growing family meant less time for her to devote to social activities, although she continued with the established receptions and the formal dinners required by protocol and tradition.

The completion of Cleveland's second term, in March of 1897, was the occasion for a tearful good-bye from the departing mistress of the White House and the staff who had served her faithfully and willingly. Frances' loyal aides and servants decorated the State Dining Room table with her favorite flowers, pansies and jonquils.

From Washington, the Clevelands moved to Princeton, New Jersey, where the retired President became a trustee of the university and occasional lecturer (Woodrow Wilson was a member of the faculty). Their new home, "Westland," was a large colonial mansion of stone and stucco. Princeton was a charming, isolated village; occasionally, Frances and Cleveland journeyed into New York to visit with friends and to see a play.

On October 28, 1897, Frances gave birth to a son, Richard Folsom, and not quite four years later, on July 18, 1903, her second son, Francis Grover, was born. He was her last child; at the time of his birth, she was thirty-nine, and Cleveland was sixty-six.

In January of 1904, their daughter Ruth suddenly developed what was thought to be tonsillitis. Four days later, the doctors knew it was diphtheria, and on the fifth day, January 7, 1904, Ruth died at the age of twelve. It wasn't until the spring that Frances and Cleveland could talk dispassionately about her; he wrote to his sister that "there has been given to both Frank and me such confident faith that it is well with her, and such a feeling that we are the only losers. . . ."

Five years later, on June 24, 1908, when he was seventy-one, Grover Cleveland died in Princeton from a variety of ailments, complicated by a failing heart. He and Frances had been married for exactly twenty-two years and twenty-two days.

Frances stayed on in Princeton after Cleveland's death. In 1913, when she was forty-nine, she married Thomas Jex Preston, Jr., professor of archaeology at Wells College, her alma mater. Professor Preston later joined the faculty at Princeton. (Frances survived Cleveland by forty years; her four remaining children all survived her.)

Before her second marriage, and for many years after, Frances interested herself in charitable work and women's organizations. She was active in the Women's University Club, and during World War I she headed the National Security League's Speakers' Bureau. In 1922, she became national chairman of the endowment fund for Wells College.

Her most notable contribution resulted from her long-time presidency of the Needlework Guild of America, a nationwide organization composed of women accomplished at the art of needlework, or simply interested in it. One of its important functions was distribution to the destitute and needy of clothing either made by its members or bought for that purpose. In 1936, at the height of the worst financial depression in modern times, the Needlework Guild, under the tireless leadership of Frances Cleveland Preston, a gifted needleworker in her own right, distributed 1,836,000 garments.

FRANCES CLEVELAND

When Frances was eighty-three, she went to Baltimore to help celebrate the fiftieth birthday of her lawyer son, Richard Folsom Cleveland. Without warning, for she had not been ill, she died in her sleep that night, on October 29, 1947. Although death came to her as Mrs. Thomas Preston, she was buried in Princeton next to her first husband, Grover Cleveland, for the country and the world remembered her as a First Lady.

Caroline Harrison

1832–1892

Fraud and corruption permeated the American political scene for much of the nineteenth century. It was not uncommon for votes to be bought, for men to vote more than once, and for non-existent voters to be registered. On occasion big money played important roles in the selection of a national candidate. Generous financial support from the new industrial and mercantile giants, who hated and feared Grover Cleveland's reform-minded policies, substantially contributed to his defeat in the presidential election of 1888. His Republican opponent, Benjamin Harrison, became the twenty-third President of the United States with an electoral total of 233 to Cleveland's 168, although Cleveland had a margin of 100,000 popular votes.

Benjamin Harrison's election must be ranked a political oddity, for he was never a popular figure, despite his illustrious name. An austere, distant man, he commanded no burning loyalties, yet he did have enough support to win. When he heard the results of the election, he exclaimed: "Providence has given us the victory!" One of his party aides dryly remarked in answer that "Providence hadn't a damn thing to do with it."

Measured on a presidential scale, Benjamin Harrison would be close to the bottom. Not so his First Lady. Caroline Lavinia Scott Harrison was one of the most creative and accomplished women ever to serve as mistress of the White House. She was also, according to Frank G. Carpenter, Washington correspondent for the *Cleveland Leader*, "the best housekeeper [the] Pennsylvania Avenue mansion has yet known." A modest and hard-working First Lady, Caroline Harrison has been overshadowed by the more spectacular of the presidential wives, but the warmth, friendliness, and easy dignity she brought to her position should accord her a memorable place in the continuing story of the White House.

Benjamin Harrison first met Caroline Lavinia Scott in 1848, at Walnut Hills, Ohio, a village a few miles from Cincinnati. Benjamin, at the time, was fourteen, and Caroline was fifteen. He had been born on August 20, 1833, at the North Bend, Ohio, farm of his grandfather, William Henry Harrison; Caroline had been born on October 1, 1832, in Oxford, Ohio, where her father, the Reverend John Witherspoon Scott, had been a minister and educator. Caroline's mother was the former Mary Potts Neal of Pennsylvania.

There were three children in the Scott family, two daughters and a son, with Caroline the middle child. They were all well schooled, for their father was a pioneer in the education of women, and considered one of the three "most illustrious educators of the early West," along with Robert Hamilton Bishop and William Holmes McGuffey, author of the renowned *Readers*. Scott had begun his career at Miami University in Oxford, Ohio, in 1828; in 1848, he was teaching at Farmers' College, where Benjamin had enrolled as a freshman. The following year, Scott moved his family back to Oxford, and established The Oxford Female Institute. Ben remained in Walnut Hills to complete his studies at Farmers' College.

For the year or so they had known each other, Ben and Carrie were no more than children, but old enough to believe they were in love. A serious young man, Ben was short and blond, with bright blue eyes; fortunately, Caroline was shorter than he, and though she was not beautiful, he found her "charming and loveable, petite and a little plump, with soft brown eyes and a wealth of beautiful brown hair." By October of 1850, their separation came to an end. Ben completed his studies at Farmers' College and enrolled at Miami University in Oxford. Caroline's presence in the Ohio college town undoubtedly influenced his choice of school, for his father had expected him to attend either Harvard or Yale.

Ben and Carrie saw much of each other during the next two years. As students they were diligent and determined to learn, yet they had time for gay and innocent diversion. Accomplished in painting and music, Carrie strangely did not care for housekeeping and was careless about her dress. A notation in a Harrison scrapbook commented: "Her petticoat had a way of slipping its moorings . . . and peeping from beneath her skirt." (In later life, she would overcome these failings.)

When Ben graduated from Miami in June of 1852, he and Carrie were definitely in love; they became secretly engaged, although Ben's poverty prevented actual marriage plans. Eager to earn a living, Ben decided to be a lawyer rather than a minister, which his teachers expected of him. He went off to Cincinnati for study of the law and clerking in an attorney's office, while Carrie stayed behind in Oxford to complete her own education and to teach music and sewing to younger students. By August of 1853, Benjamin and Caroline decided they could no longer wait and set an October date for marriage.

For Ben, however, there were still moments of indecision. He was troubled by his lack of money; his dearest friend, John Anderson, often cautioned him by letter to tread slowly. Anderson wrote that he was "under the impression that you are far from able to support Carrie as you will." Ben, admitting Anderson's premise, nevertheless did determine to go ahead as he and Carrie had planned. He was afraid to wait, in fear that something might happen to Carrie. He might "amass a fortune, secure world-wide fame," as he wrote to Anderson, and "come laden with yellow gold" to claim his bride, "but she is gone. . . . I wander to the quiet graveyard, where we have so often walked together, my heart leads me to a humble grave over whose brown clods the turf has already healed. . . . I drop a tear, and with that first gold that severed us for life I build a monument 'sacred to her memory' . . . and then, John . . . what then?"

Caroline Scott, nineteen days beyond her twenty-first birthday, and Benjamin Harrison, exactly two months beyond his twentieth, were married on October 20, 1853, at the home of her parents in Oxford, Ohio. Because Ben was underage, his father had to accompany him to the county seat for the marriage license. Tradition has it that Ben was embarrassed by his father's presence.

Carrie and Ben spent the first few months of their married life at the North Bend farm of his father, where Ben continued his law studies. He was admitted to the bar in 1854; he and Carrie then settled in Indianapolis, which had been deliberately chosen. His name in Indianapolis was "introduction enough," as his father pointed out—"the old men of Indiana . . . have become patriots of your grandfather and loved him as they loved no other public man." (William Henry Harrison, officially a resident of Ohio, had lived in Indiana for a number of years as its territorial governor.)

Success did not come quickly to Benjamin Harrison, for there were more lawyers than clients in the city of sixteen thousand. The first year was difficult. Ben had to augment his meager income with a job as court crier at a pay of $2.50 per day. In March of 1855, Carrie and Ben at last saw some hope of prosperity; William Wallace, a lawyer with an established practice and a craving for political office, asked Ben to become his partner so that he might be free to campaign. From that moment, Ben and Carrie would never again be poor.

For Carrie, the first year meant personal hardships. She had become pregnant, and had been ill during much of that time. She went back to Oxford, to have her child at the home of her parents; Russell was born in Oxford on August 12, 1854. There were two more children: a girl, Mary, born in Indianapolis on April 3, 1858, and a stillborn child, a daughter, in June of 1861. Russell and Mary (who became affectionately known as "Mamie") both lived well beyond their parents, and each had a happy and long marriage.

With Ben established in 1855, Carrie had time to devote to her own interests. First Presbyterian Church records characterize her during that period as "a power," with "artistic tastes." Creatively, she concentrated on needlework, with results impressive enough to be noted in the records. She was a leader among the younger women, who found her charming, gay, and friendly. Ben, in the meantime, joined the new Republican party, to the displeasure of his father, who had served in Congress as a Whig and was still loyal to the "cause of conservatism."

With the onset of the Civil War in April, 1861, Ben felt he ought to enlist, but after long discussions, he and Caroline agreed that his primary responsibility belonged to his family. By July of 1862, he could no longer ignore the call of his conscience and, at the age of twenty-eight, accepted a commission as a second lieutenant, in command of Company A of the Seventieth Regiment, Indiana Volunteers.

Despite his lack of military knowledge, Ben became a fighting soldier and able leader, and he was rewarded, in January of 1865, with a promotion to brigadier-general. Four months later, his military career came to a close and he returned to civilian life for good. Much to Carrie's relief, he had gone through every engagement without a scratch or serious illness.

When the Civil War ended, Caroline Harrison was thirty-two years old. She had seen her husband rise from an obscure young lawyer to a celebrated general within the space of eleven years. The next two decades would bring even more renown. Harrison's fame gradually spread beyond the boundaries of Indiana; in 1876 he was defeated when he ran for governor of his state, but in 1880 he was elected by the Indiana legislature to be a United States senator. Caroline continued her work with the First Presbyterian Church, devoting much of her time to the church's missionary society; but she did not neglect her primary skills in painting, music, and needle-work. As she had before her marriage, she taught these skills to the younger women, all of whom found that she "laughed readily . . . her gaiety and her intellectual gifts made her delightful."

In October of 1879, Caroline scored a personal social triumph when she entertained the visiting President Rutherford Hayes and First Lady Lucy Hayes at a lawn party. Her easy manner was a positive counterpoint to her husband's aloof shyness, for he never learned how to unbend publicly. He had become a potent politician in Indiana, yet few people cared for him. Caroline's friendliness did much to neutralize the damage he inflicted upon his career by his coldness.

When Caroline and Harrison went to Washington in 1881 after his election as senator, her warmth and charm continued to smooth the way for them, at her own receptions and others as well. With Caroline at his side, Harrison found these affairs "more a pleasure than a duty." But the first of a long series of illnesses began to plague her: In 1883, she was hospitalized in New York for many weeks as a result of surgery; in 1886, she suffered "a violent ill-ness" that Harrison attributed to lengthy work she had done on "tapestry painting." Caroline recovered nicely from each of her ailments, and by 1888, when the Republican convention met in Chicago's Civic Auditorium, she was content. Both of her children were happily married and her husband was considered a serious candidate for the presidential nomination.

Much of the sentiment at the Republican convention centered about James G. Blaine, who had lost to Grover Cleveland in 1884; Blaine, holidaying at the Scotland estate of steel magnate Andrew Carnegie, withdrew himself from serious contention. When the convention found itself deadlocked after five ballots, Blaine sent a code message, through Carnegie, that he wanted Harrison for the top spot, and Harrison was nominated on the eighth ballot.

One necessary device in the promotion of the Republican candi-date was an authorized biography. Chosen for this important task was General Lew Wallace, comrade-in-arms, brother of Harrison's first law partner, and author of the sensational best-seller, the historical novel *Ben Hur*. Wallace's selection as Harrison's official biographer elicited this classic pun from a mutual friend: "He did so well on *Ben Hur* we can trust him with *Ben Him*." The biography, sixty-five thousand words, was completed in a month, and contained only the barest mention of Caroline.

Harrison's election as a minority President brought the Harrison family into the White House in March of 1889. One significant change from the previous administration was immediately evident —the Harrisons filled the cramped Executive Mansion to overflowing with their children, grandchildren, Caroline's eighty-nine-year-old father, and her young widowed niece. The confusion was compounded by the presence of three Marys—the Harrisons' daughter (better known as "Mamie"), their daughter-in-law (whom they dubbed "May"), and Caroline's niece (nick-named "Mame").

One of Caroline's first tasks was the preparation of plans for the building of a new Executive Mansion. The White House had but five bedrooms and one bathroom; with so many Harrisons, Caroline rightly contended that conditions for the President's family were intolerable. She had three separate sets of plans drawn, two calling for drastic renovation of the Executive Mansion and the third envisioning a completely new structure totally removed from the site of the old. All three plans were rejected by Congress, but Caroline was appeased by an appropriation of $35,000 to redo and refurnish the White House. The venerable mansion was in a deplorable state; Caroline nevertheless made do with the available funds. The House was repainted, repapered, plumbing replaced, the old flooring removed (in some places five layers), chandeliers taken apart and scrubbed clean, and, most importantly, additional bathrooms provided. (Extermination of rodents and insects that had been allowed free rein through too many administrations was another necessary chore.)

The Executive Mansion saw a number of Caroline Harrison innovations. One was the first White House Christmas tree, put up in December of 1889. Another was the use of orchids for floral decorations at official receptions. Caroline counted a number of ancestors who had been active in the American Revolution; she was therefore chosen to be the first president-general of the Daughters of the American Revolution, and it was she who established the custom of orchid corsages for the DAR. Another noteworthy contribution was her collection of White House china. She herself designed the Harrison china, and had the old china from previous administrations gathered together for permanent display.

In May of 1891, the Edison Company installed electricity in the White House, but the Harrisons were so fearful of the new device they refused to touch the switches and would not turn their lights off and on. For a long time they slept either with all lights on or in total darkness.

On a personal level, Caroline made the same favorable impression upon Washington society as she had in Indianapolis. Her clothes were simple, yet tasteful, and American-made only. She was, always, a gracious hostess; the Harrison receptions were not the most exciting, but Washington found them enjoyable, and crowded. And many Washington ladies took advantage of classes in French instruction at the White House, and china-painting conducted by Caroline. The china was baked in her own kiln. Caroline painted numerous objects, including porcelain dishes, tiles, candlesticks, cheese covers, crackerboxes, flowerpot saucers, and milk pitchers. Much of her work was presented to church bazaars.

The Republican convention of 1892 renominated President Benjamin Harrison for a second term. But Caroline had become seriously ill, and Harrison did not campaign; out of respect for the First Lady's illness, Grover Cleveland, Harrison's Democratic opponent, gave up his own campaigning. Earlier that year, Caroline suffered heavy coughing spasms, accompanied by hemorrhaging. Confined to bed, she had grown steadily weaker, and at last, on October 25, 1892, at the age of sixty, she died of tuberculosis. Two days later her funeral cortege made its way through the streets of Washington to the depot, while thousands of people watched in respectful silence. Her body was taken by train to Indianapolis, where "a hundred carriages moved slowly in a five-mile procession" to the Crown Hill Cemetery for her burial in the Harrison family plot.

Benjamin Harrison survived her by eight years. He had re-married, on April 6, 1896, when he was sixty-two. His second wife was Caroline's niece, Mary Scott Lord Dimmick. Harrison died on March 13, 1901, the first President to die in the twentieth century. He was sixty-seven. He, too, was buried in the Crown Hill Cemetery.

Caroline Lavinia Scott Harrison had many friends and admirers throughout the entire country, but none were more loyal to her than those in Indiana. The noted Indiana poet, James Whitcomb Riley, spoke for all Hoosiers when he wrote these lines upon her death:

> Yet with the faith she knew
> We see her still
> Even as here she stood—
> All that was pure and good
> And sweet in womanhood—
> God's will her will.

Ida McKinley
1847–1907

In the hundred years between John Adams and William McKinley, the United States endured four major wars, violence and upheaval, hatred and destruction, and denial of basic human rights to many of its inhabitants. Yet, when the nineteenth century came to an exuberant close, America was one of the most powerful and magnificently flourishing countries in the world. In one hundred years, a small nation clinging tenaciously to the eastern seaboard had become the crowning gem of two oceans.

The last decade of the century brought many startling changes; the machine age had arrived. As for racial problems, they were annoyances to be swept under the rug; the ugly specter of Jim Crow haunted the black man only, who had no rights in any event.

When the two major parties met in solemn and boisterous convention in the summer of 1896 to choose their presidential candidates, they could not be concerned with racial repression or prejudicial legislation. There was a more important matter to settle—the election of a President.

The Republicans, meeting in St. Louis in June of 1896, selected William McKinley of Ohio on the first ballot. Three weeks later, the Democrats chose William Jennings Bryan of Nebraska. Despite a magic tongue, thirty-six-year-old Bryan, Populist crusader and darling of the silver-producing states, lost to the fifty-three-year-old McKinley by a popular vote of 7,104,779 to 6,502,925. McKinley became the twenty-fifth President of the United States by an electoral margin of 271 to 176.

A bland, friendly, strangely cheerful man, McKinley is remembered for two major events—the Spanish-American War and his assassination. But presidential lore dishonors him, for he possessed a characteristic no other President could ever claim—a completely unselfish devotion to the woman he married. The story of Ida McKinley, a frail invalid, is the story of her husband, for there has never been in public service a man so dedicated to the welfare of his wife.

Ida Saxton and William McKinley met in Canton, Ohio, in the summer of 1867. It was a casual meeting, at a picnic, and seems not to have impressed either. McKinley, born and raised in Niles, Ohio, had moved to Canton after the Civil War. He had served as a major, under the direct command of Rutherford B. Hayes. Ida, daughter of a wealthy Canton banker, was a willful, restless, and self-centered young lady who had received the benefits of an exclusive education at one of the best finishing schools.

Little is known of Ida's early years. She was born in Canton on June 8, 1847. Her parents were James Asbury Saxton and the former Catherine Dewalt. Ida had one sister, Pina (pronounced "Piney"), and a brother George. (George, who pursued a "shabby career as a Lothario," was murdered in 1898 by a disgruntled divorcée whom he would not marry. Despite her obvious guilt, a sympathetic jury refused to punish her for the killing of the "elderly libertine," and she was freed, to the cheers of the crowded courtroom.)

218

IDA McKINLEY

There is no record of Ida's preliminary schooling, but there can be no doubt that her well-to-do father saw to it that his children received the best possible education. When Ida was nineteen, she and Pina were sent to a finishing school for girls in Media, Pennsylvania. Ida may have been too old for Brooke Hall, but she enjoyed being there, for she remembered with fondness both the school and its head mistress, elderly Miss Eastman. In 1869, Ida and Pina went on an extended tour of Europe; when they returned to Canton, the restless Ida was put to work in her father's bank as a cashier. Her employment was most unusual, since women of that day simply were not trained for the commercial world, but Ida and Mr. Saxton had advanced ideas.

Ida's next meeting with William McKinley took place after she began working at the First National Bank. McKinley, an established attorney in Canton and prosecuting attorney for Stark County, was master of ceremonies at a lecture that featured the noted journalist, Horace Greeley. Ida was in the audience; she immediately liked Major McKinley's bearing and manner of speaking. She remembered their first meeting some two or so years before, and arranged another encounter that soon led to far more productive results. The impressionable William, thought to be still chaste at the age of twenty-seven, was an easy prey for the determined Ida, a small, slim beauty with dark eyes and dark hair framing a round lovely face alternating between serenity and discontent. He fell madly and completely in love with her, and remained so for the rest of his life.

The romance between Ida and the short major, who was barely above five foot six inches, was an immediate topic of conversation in Canton, particularly in view of Ida's jealousy and possessiveness. McKinley did not object to being wanted by the beautiful Miss Saxton; nor did her father resist, though McKinley was not wealthy. Ida and William were married on January 25, 1871, in Canton's new Presbyterian church. McKinley was four days short of his twenty-eighth birthday; the radiant bride, who wore a gown of ivory white satin trimmed in pointe lace, was twenty-three and a half.

219

Major and Mrs. McKinley, after a New York honeymoon, returned to Canton to live in a house on North Market Street, presented as a wedding gift by her father. A daughter, Catherine, was born on their first anniversary. Fourteen months later, a second daughter was born on March 31, 1873. But Ida's happiness was marred by the death of her mother a short time before.

The shock of her mother's passing, coupled with a difficult period of labor during the birth of her second child, deeply affected the high-strung Ida. She was seriously ill for a number of months. Convulsions demonstrated damage to the brain and continuing attacks indicated epilepsy. On August 22, 1873, another tragedy, though not unexpected, assaulted Ida's dangerously weakened nervous system. On that date, her second daughter, always a frail and sickly infant, died a scant five months after she had been born.

At the age of twenty-six, Ida McKinley became an hysterical semi-invalid requiring continual attention from her husband. When her health permitted, she hovered compulsively over her surviving daughter, golden-haired, bright little Katie. Katie knew her mother was ill. One day, when her uncle asked her to go for a walk with him, she solemnly replied, "No, I mustn't go out of the yard, or God'll punish mama some more." But Katie's obedient compliance with her mother's neurotic injunction did her no good, for she too died, at the age of three and a half, on July 25, 1875.

Katie's death destroyed forever any hope William may have had for Ida's recovery. She was now a hopeless epileptic, suffering frequent attacks accompanied by blinding headaches. McKinley, no longer the ebullient and cheerfully optimistic youth of six years before, was nevertheless considerate, understanding, and tactful.

When Ida was well enough to be with him, he supported her weight as they slowly walked together. He learned how to handle her epileptic spells, and to shield her gently from the shocked gaze of company. At the first hiss and sudden rigidity, he quickly threw a large handkerchief or napkin over her contorted face until the fit had passed. Friends and associates looked away, patiently; when Ida emerged, the covering on her face was removed and she picked up the thread of conversation as though nothing had happened. Through it all McKinley was mindful only of her. No matter how she pitied herself or how demanding she was, he gave her his total attention, never raising his voice in her presence, never berating her.

In 1876 William McKinley was elected to Congress; he and Ida moved to Washington in the spring of 1877. McKinley served as a congressman until 1891. During those years, Ida's health fluctuated in an irregular pattern, and much of McKinley's time was devoted to her. He was her constant companion. When he was not on the floor of the House, he sat with her, or took her for drives. He was alert to her every need and call. Often, when he was away from her, his manner would be distracted, as if half listening for her plaintive cry.

Ida was never alone. Although he could not really afford it, McKinley hired a maid to be with her. Families of other congressmen came to call, and McKinley's constituents from Ohio dropped in. Remembering the loss of her own, she was pathetically fond of children and eager to have them for company.

Through the years she crocheted, fiercely, and made thousands of bedroom slippers, which her maid mounted on cork soles and laced with satin ribbon. They were sent to friends and relatives who accepted them with more long-suffering patience than gratitude. Ida also made the black satin bow ties that became a McKinley trademark.

McKinley's service in the House of Representatives came to an end in 1891; later that year he was elected governor of Ohio, and he moved with Ida to the capital at Columbus. For the four years he served as governor, Ida seemed to improve, or rather her temperament was more composed, and she gave the appearance of recovery. The illusion, however, was real only to McKinley, who pounced upon every possible cure with alacrity and eagerness, even when suggested by the most obvious charlatan.

To McKinley, Ida was always "the most beautiful girl you ever saw"; visitors would see only a crippled woman with a taut skin aged by illness and self-pity. In McKinley's view, Ida was deserving of any position society chose to bestow upon her, and he spared no expense to bring about her ultimate recovery so that she would be ready for her responsibilities. But the recovery never came. Still, when the Republican convention of 1896 nominated her husband for President of the United States, Ida prepared herself to become the First Lady. It was what McKinley wanted, and what Ida herself, in the long years of her ordeal, had convinced herself she was capable of attaining.

The McKinleys arrived in Washington on March 2, 1897, two days before McKinley's Inauguration as the twenty-fifth President. In December, Ida had gone to Chicago to select her White House wardrobe, designed and executed by Marshall Field and Company. The many fittings and the badgering by press and public exhausted her; when she returned to Canton, she spent a bad winter. She nevertheless attended the Inaugural Ball on the evening of March 4, at the Pension Building, a huge barnlike structure.

As usual, the ball was too well attended; dancing was impossible because of the crowd, who willingly endured the crush for the privilege of looking at the new President and his First Lady. Ida did not disappoint them, although there had been some fear she would not attend. She did arrive, in a beautiful blue and silver gown, and an evening wrap of lavender silk trimmed in white Alaskan fox. She was pale and weak, and had to lean on her husband's arm, but she managed to endure the arduous ritual for part of the evening. During the grand promenade, always the highlight of the Inaugural Ball, Ida had a sudden seizure and had to be hurried away, to the puzzlement and consternation of the celebrants. McKinley took her home and helped her into bed, and then went to sleep himself, while the noisy ball continued without them.

The McKinley White House years were neither exceptional nor notable. Ida's inability to function as mistress threw responsibility for maintenance of the mansion upon the staff, for McKinley took no interest in the housekeeping affairs. But most of the help were conscientious and loyal. They were especially fond of the President, who never failed to greet even the lowliest of clerks with a cheerful wave and happy smile.

Ida's insistence upon performing her duties as the President's hostess placed a great strain upon all who were close to her. There was constant worry that she would suffer one of her attacks. Yet, strangely, there were long periods when she was relatively well, well enough, in fact, to preside over pleasant gatherings. She had musicales, with the famous violin-cellist Leo Stern as soloist; she invited a hundred alumnae from Brooke Hall to the White House for luncheon, and it was a most delightful affair. But these moments were interludes only; for the better part of her stay in the White House, Ida was a trial to everyone.

The country at large knew nothing of Ida's infirmity. To the average citizen she was simply "delicate," an invalid who languished in martyred silence, enduring the cruelty of an unexplained malady. The truth about her condition was the best-kept secret in Washington, for those who knew, and they were many, refused to put a name to her illness, as did McKinley.

The Spanish-American War, the shortest in America's history and one of the most unnecessary and unjustified (despite the mysterious sinking of the *Maine*), temporarily deflated McKinley's good humor. Goaded by an imperialistic and clamorous press and by a new set of young war hawks, including Henry Cabot Lodge of Massachusetts, McKinley waged his war against Spain at a cost of $50 million and five thousand four hundred American lives, most of whom were victims of tropical disease. But the country objected neither to the casualties nor the expense; all in all, it had been a "bully" adventure.

With the successful conclusion of hostilities against Spain and the acquisition of new territories to administer, the United States emerged as an unquestioned world power. In November of 1900, the people demonstrated their affection for the affable McKinley by reelecting him to a second term, this time with Theodore Roosevelt as his Vice President (McKinley's first Vice President had been Garret Augustus Hobart of New Jersey). Ten months later, Mc-

Kinley and Ida went to Buffalo to visit the Pan-American Exposition. While Ida was resting at the home of friends, McKinley was shot twice by a discontended "anarchist." The shooting took place in the exposition's crowded Temple of Music, at four minutes past seven on the evening of September 6, 1901.

The assassin, Leon Csolgosz, was immediately captured. As the President fell, clutching his abdomen, he gasped, "My wife . . . be careful how you tell her—oh, be careful."

McKinley lived for eight more days. During that time, Ida astonished everyone by exhibiting a self-control no one had previously suspected. Privately, however, she was stricken almost beyond consolation, as she confided to her diary. Her scrawl, childishly painful, spoke of her wish to die: "I do not want to live if I can go with My Precious to Heaven Above where all is love there will be no sorrowing there."

She was with McKinley until the end. Just before he died, he put his arm around her, and smiled, as he so often had. For others, his last words had been, "Good-bye all—good-bye all. It is God's way. His will, not ours, be done." But for Ida, there were the whispered words of their favorite hymn, "Nearer, my God to Thee, nearer to Thee."

McKinley died on September 14, 1901, at the age of fifty-eight. He was buried in a tomb near the Westlawn Cemetery in Canton, Ohio.

For the six remaining years of her life, Ida lived quietly on Canton's North Market Street, in the small house her father had given her as a wedding present. They were lonely years, and to friends who sometimes came to visit, she still spoke of her wish to die. H. H. Kohlsaat, a newspaper publisher and editor, and long an associate of McKinley's, wrote about a meeting with her two or three years after McKinley died:

> Although it was a warm spring day, she sat in a chair over a register from which the heat poured, a frail figure in a plain black gown. . . . Over and over she moaned, "Why

should I linger? Please, God, if it is Thy will, let me go. I want to be with him. I am so tired."

Ida McKinley died on May 26, 1907, not quite sixty. Many government officials, including President Theodore Roosevelt, attended her funeral. One of the hymns she requested was "Nearer, my God, to Thee." She was buried next to her husband and the two baby daughters who had died more than thirty years before.

Edith Roosevelt
1861–1948

On Friday the thirteenth day of September, 1901, Theodore Roosevelt, forty-two-year-old Vice President of the United States, was characteristically enjoying himself in the mountains of New York. Assured that the gravely injured McKinley would recover from the gunshot wounds the crazed Csolgosz had inflicted upon the President, Roosevelt had taken his family for a holiday in the Adirondacks.

At eleven that evening, he was awakened from a sound sleep by an urgent message from Buffalo. McKinley was dying, and the Vice President must leave immediately; there would be a special train waiting for him at North Creek, the nearest railroad station, thirty-five miles away.

Using three separate teams of horses, Roosevelt and his driver hurtled through the Adirondack darkness on a buckboard, down dangerously rutted mountain roads, often skirting a precipitate drop. Roosevelt arrived at North Creek at five-thirty in the morning, to learn that McKinley had died some three hours before. He sent a telegram to his waiting wife: "President McKinley died at 2:15 this morning. Theodore Roosevelt."

How had it happened? How was it that this young, intensely vigorous man whom McKinley's close friend and adviser, Mark Hanna, had characterized as a "damn cowboy" was now the President? Roosevelt had achieved world-wide fame in the brief encounter we call the Spanish-American War. He had led his Rough Riders up San Juan Hill, his teeth flashing, his saber rattling, every nerve and fiber alive with the excitement and pleasure of battle. Back in New York after the war, the ready-made hero was a shoo-in for the governorship of his state and served for two years. But he was too eager a reformer for the party bosses; against his will, they maneuvered his nomination for Vice President to run with McKinley in the election of 1900.

The ticket of friendly Bill McKinley and dashing Teddy Roosevelt was an easy victor over the Democrats. The Republican party bosses had buried the rambunctious Roosevelt in the Vice-Presidency—a certain dead end for overzealous politicians. But Mark Hanna was furious; he stormed at his friends: "Don't any of you realize there's only one life between this madman and the White House?"

Hanna fretted needlessly. Theodore Roosevelt became a forceful President. Cheerfully aggressive, decisively moral, and never a man of moderation, he led the United States onto the field of global diplomacy as a recognized world power. A firm and spirited leader, eternally convinced of the rightness of everything he did, Roosevelt broadened the Presidency to the position of independence and authority it has enjoyed ever since.

Edith Kermit Carow Roosevelt, who was neither his first nor his greatest love, knew his faults and his virtues. She understood him, and she did her best to influence him when she thought he was wrong. She sometimes succeeded. She was a gracious and considerate First Lady who was exactly the right kind of wife for the energetic and enthusiastic twenty-sixth President of the United States.

Theodore Roosevelt and Edith Kermit Carow met when she was a baby and he was about three years old. Edith, the older of two daughters, was born on August 6, 1861, in Norwich, Connecticut; she was brought to New York shortly after. Her parents, Charles and Gertrude Tyler Carow, owned a house on Union Square, next to Theodore's grandparents. Theodore's younger sister, Corinne, was born six weeks after Edith; the two girls virtually grew up together.

Edith and Theodore had much in common. Both were voracious readers. Edith's father was a member of the New York Society Library, New York's oldest circulation library. In one period of twenty-eight months, the Carows borrowed 648 books. Theodore, too, loved to read. And he shared a love of nature and wild things with her. As Edith and Theodore grew older, it seemed right for them to be together, though he was three years her senior.

In 1869, when he was eleven, Theodore and his family were traveling through Europe. Theodore did not care for the trip at all; in November, he found more reason to prefer the familiar scenes of New York, as he confided to his diary: "In the evening Mama showed me the portrait of Eidieth Carow and her face stired up in me homesickness and longings for the past which will come again never, alack never."

He did of course see her after their return, but as the years slipped by and he prepared for college, they had a quarrel, never explained, and a coolness developed between them. He went off to Harvard and she enrolled at Miss Comstock's private school for girls on New York's West Fortieth Street. She was a puzzle to her classmates, who could not understand why she preferred a book to their silly chatter.

In October of 1878, Theodore fell madly in love with seventeen-year-old Alice Hathaway Lee of Boston. They were married in

228

Brookline, Massachusetts, in October of 1880. Edith's reaction to news of Theodore's first marriage has never been revealed, for she never spoke of it, nor apparently did he want to know.

Three and a half years later, on February 12, 1884, Roosevelt's first daughter, Alice, was born in his mother's house. His daughter's birth was the prelude to a horrible double tragedy. Early in the morning of February 14, Valentine's Day, his mother died of typhoid fever; a few hours later, his wife died of Bright's Disease plus the complication of childbirth. Death came to both in the same house where the infant, Alice, had been born. Roosevelt's mother was forty-nine, and his wife was twenty-two.

For at least a year Roosevelt refused to think of marriage again, and took no interest in other women. He avoided Edith and she avoided him. In the fall of 1885, they accidentally met at his sister's home, and from that moment, his spirit revived.

Never the winsome beauty that Alice Lee had been, the brown-haired Edith had a patrician quality that lifted the plainness of her face above the ordinary. Reared in luxury, she knew the value of money. Her family had been wealthy for some generations. French Huguenots on her father's side, the family name, originally Quereau, had been Anglicized to Carow by her grandfather at the beginning of the nineteenth century.

Soon after Edith started seeing Theodore again, her father died; the money he left, Mrs. Carow felt, would go further in Europe, so she and her two daughters sailed to England. By now, Roosevelt had decided to marry Edith; she, of course, was willing, and had been for a number of years. He sailed to England to join them; he and Edith were married in London on December 2, 1886, at St. George's Church in Hanover Square. Edith was twenty-five, and Roosevelt was twenty-eight.

After a European honeymoon, Edith and Theodore Roosevelt returned to the United States. Edith was now faced with the problem of raising Alice Lee's child and living in Alice Lee's house. During his first marriage, Roosevelt had decided to build a large three-story home in Oyster Bay, on New York's Long Island.

229

Though Alice died before the house was even started, he went ahead with it after her death, and planned to call it "Leeholm," in her honor. When he brought his second wife back from Europe, the Oyster Bay residence was given the name of "Sagamore Hill," after a local Indian chief. (The word "Sagamore" is a corruption of "sang'man," an Abnaki tribal designation for chief or ruler.)

Edith plunged into her new role as wife and mistress of a huge house with an orderly zest. Theodore was happy to leave the supervision of "Sagamore" to her; he was too busy with his political career. The twenty-six-room house bustled with constant activity; there was a never-ending stream of relatives, friends, associates, and reporters, and Edith sometimes found herself sighing for a bit of solitude. But "Sagamore," like its master, had a vitality of its own, and Edith could no more stop the ebb and flow than she could stop the sun from rising.

As with the house, the family finances were left solely in her care. Edith constantly deplored the high cost of living, yet she managed to retain a farmer, a gardener, a coachman, a cook, a waitress, a nurse, a maid, a chambermaid, a laundress, and a furnaceman. For all this help, she paid $210 a month. As her family grew, she learned to practice simple economies; one example was the purchase of a "beautiful dinner gown" for "$188.00 reduced from $325.00."

Little Alice, now in Edith's care, was three and a half when Edith's first child, Theodore, Jr., was born in Oyster Bay on September 13, 1887. He was followed by Kermit, on October 10, 1889, and Edith's only daughter, Ethel, on August 13, 1891. Edith's last two children, Archie and Quentin, were born in Washington, Archie on April 9, 1894, and Quentin on November 19, 1897.

Marriage to a man like Theodore Roosevelt was a complex matter. Edith was expected to run his bustling household with a sure hand, and had to be as well a sportswoman, a naturalist, a zookeeper, a part-time doctor, and an amateur psychiatrist. Fortunately, she loved the outdoors and outdoor activity as much as

230

her husband and her active children. Nor did she object to the multitudinous creatures in their menagerie. The children had ponies, dogs, guinea pigs, flying squirrels, rabbits, snakes, lizards, frogs, white mice, and any variety of wild beast they could safely bring into the house.

Edith looked upon her husband as another child; a close friend once said of him: "One thing you must always remember about Roosevelt is that he is about seven years old." But Edith did not indulge Theodore. One day, when working on his barn, he received a nasty cut on the forehead; he hurried back to the house, blood pouring from his wound. With no sign of panic, Edith said, "I wish you'd do your bleeding in the bathroom. You're spoiling every rug in the house."

When Roosevelt became the twenty-sixth President of the United States in September of 1901, Edith and the children were in the Adirondacks. She had to find her own way back to Oyster Bay, supervise the immense job of packing, and move her noisy family and all their belongings from "Sagamore" to the White House. Washington was no novelty to her, for she had been there before, the last time in 1897 and 1898, when Roosevelt was Assistant Secretary of the Navy in McKinley's cabinet.

Edith's first official act as the new First Lady took place at the Washington services for the assassinated McKinley. She and Theodore were staying with his sister, Mrs. William Sheffield Cowles, at the Cowles home at 1733 N Street. They were to stay with Commander and Mrs. Cowles until the White House was ready for them. Edith later described that day as "one of the saddest things" she had ever known.

But sorrow and confusion must give way to the practical matters of living; with the arrival of the long line of vans bearing their household goods, Edith's chores as mistress of the Executive Mansion began in earnest. The White House was soon buzzing, for the lively Roosevelts had taken over, lock, stock, and every visible nook, not to mention nooks previously invisible.

Socially, the seven and a half years the Roosevelts spent in the White House cannot be classed among the more distinguished or exciting that Washington had known. The President and the First Lady did their share of entertaining, but they often preferred an informal family evening. The Executive Mansion, however, never lacked for guests, particularly at noontime, when as many as twenty friends and casual visitors would be invited to join the President and the First Lady for lunch.

Edith instituted a number of changes in the social routine. She had no wish to shake hands with thousands of strangers during the course of a tiring public reception, so she adopted the habit of appearing with a bouquet of flowers in her arms. The First Lady's weekly levees, which began with Martha Washington and continued under each administration, were changed by Edith to musicales. At one such musicale, the famous Polish pianist, Ignace Jan Paderewski, was the featured artist.

The newspapers of the country were delighted with the presidential family, for the Roosevelts, by the very nature of their perpetual activity, provided a ceaseless fund of stories. The pranks of the youngsters and Alice's lively adventures proved a particular joy to the press. When a friend suggested to the President that he ought to take a firmer hand with his precocious debutante daughter, who had her coming-out party in 1902, Roosevelt replied: "I can do one of two things. I can be President of the United States or I can control Alice. I cannot possibly do both."

The outstanding social event of the Roosevelt White House years occurred on February 17, 1906, when the twenty-two-year-old Alice married Nicholas Longworth, balding, thirty-six-year-old Congressman from Ohio. For the newspapers, Alice's wedding at the profusely floral Executive Mansion was the spectacle of the new century. There were, according to varying versions, "seven hundred," "a thousand," or exactly 680 guests. One of them was Nellie Grant Sartoris, who had been married in the same East Room thirty-two years before.

When Edith and her family first moved into the White House, she found the venerable structure totally inadequate and lacking in living quarters. Other First Ladies before her had had the same complaint, but she persevered. Congress listened, and promptly appropriated $475,445 for restoration and new furnishings. Based upon the original plans of a century before, this first major renovation of the Executive Mansion gave Edith the living room she needed.

Roosevelt left the White House on a wave of adulation and popular approval unmatched since the days of Andrew Jackson. For Edith, these early years after Washington were happy, but the presidential election of 1912 brought moments of despair. Roosevelt, running as the candidate of the newly formed Progressive party, badly split the Republican vote; his hand-picked successor of 1908, William Howard Taft, came in a poor third, even though he was the incumbent President. The Democrat, Woodrow Wilson, won over Taft and Roosevelt both. Public enthusiasm for Roosevelt faded to a whimper; his political star, for the moment, flickered to a point of extinction.

For Edith, Roosevelt's defeat brought some compensation; he was home, and they could enjoy the serenity of middle age. Their children were married or in school, and "Sagamore" sometimes seemed empty without them, but they returned often enough to restore the old vitality and life to the large house.

On January 6, 1919, at the age of sixty, Theodore Roosevelt's boundless energy at last ran dry. He had been suffering from inflammatory rheumatism and had been in and out of hospitals, but this week in January he was back at "Sagamore." Edith wrote of him to her oldest son: "As it got dusk he watched the dancing flames and spoke of the happiness of being home, and made little plans for me." But time had run out for the man who never quite grew up; by five o'clock the next morning he was dead, of a blood clot in his coronary artery. He was buried in Young's Memorial Cemetery, near his beloved "Sagamore."

The two major wars of the twentieth century were far more personal for Edith than any war had been for other First Ladies.

Yet the sorrow they brought her she bore "with the dauntless courage she always shows in hours of great trial," as Roosevelt had once written of her. In World War I, Quentin, who had enlisted as a flyer, was shot down during a dogfight over France on July 14, 1918. He was not yet twenty-one. In World War II, at the age of fifty-three, Major Kermit Roosevelt died of natural causes on June 4, 1943, while on active duty in Alaska. And on July 12, 1944, General Theodore Roosevelt, Jr., died in Normandy at the age of fifty-six, of a heart attack and exhaustion. Edith's other children, Ethel and Archie, both survived her.

Edith lived almost thirty years after the death of her husband. They were full years, for she refused to be defeated by grief. She traveled extensively, often to places no woman of her age or breeding had ever seen. Her journeys took her around the world, to Siberia, to the Kaietuer Falls in the wild interior of British Guiana, to Yucatan's Uxmal, to South America's Iguazu Falls. Her odyssey began when she was fifty-eight, and she made her last major voyage when she was seventy-seven, aboard the liner *Vulcania*.

With all her travels, Edith found time for charitable work, and for the Republican party, to which she remained intensely loyal. She actively opposed Franklin Delano Roosevelt, a long-time Democrat. She frostily referred to him as the "distant cousin of my husband."

During the forties, Edith lived in retirement at "Sagamore," with books her constant companions. Some years before, in 1935, she had broken her hip, and though she had recovered, she was never the same. Advancing age did not help; by late spring of 1948, it was apparent she was seriously ill. Her only daughter, Ethel, wife of Dr. Richard Derby, Edith's personal physician, was with her constantly. On September 29, 1948, Dr. Derby and Ethel spent the night at her bedside. She died the following day, September 30, at the age of eighty-seven.

Edith had once said: "Nothing would please me more than that when I die they put this inscription on my tombstone, 'Everything she did was for the happiness of others.' " But she was buried next to Theodore under a simple headstone that bears only their names, the dates of their births, and the dates of their deaths.

Two years after Edith died, "Sagamore Hill" was purchased by the Theodore Roosevelt Association. In 1963, thirteen years later, the association presented "Sagamore" to the American people, to be administered by the Park Service of the Department of the Interior as a national shrine.

Helen Taft
1861–1943

Stretching tenuously for 1,152 miles in the far-off Pacific, the Philippine Islands suddenly impinged themselves upon the consciousness and conscience of the United States at the end of the Spanish-American War. Few people had ever heard of this distant archipelago, comprising some seven thousand one hundred islands, most of them less than a mile square. But there were those, Theodore Roosevelt and others, who insisted that the Philippines, lying southwest of Japan, due east of Indo-China and ten thousand miles from the American heartland, had to play an integral part in the emerging foreign policy of the United States.

Others, including President McKinley, were not so sure. Goaded by traditional American morality and cries of imperialism, McKinley hesitated and sought divine direction in prayer. In the end, guided by a voice, unseen, unheard, but not unheeded, McKinley announced in favor of annexation of the Philippines. It was our sacred duty, he proclaimed, "to educate the Filipinos, and uplift and civilize and Christianize them." Whether this is what the Filipinos wanted was apparently not to the point. By a generous payment of $20 million to Spain, which had ruled over them for three hundred years, the Philippine Islands officially came under American domination in December of 1898.

Awareness of the Philippines brought another name before the public. William Howard Taft of Ohio, appointed first governor-general of the Pacific archipelago, became a national figure. His four years of service in the Philippine Islands and his subsequent post as Secretary of War in President Roosevelt's Cabinet enhanced his image and prestige, and when Roosevelt chose him to be his successor in 1908, Taft was an easy victor, rolling up a comfortable margin of 7,678,908 to 6,409,104 for Democrat William Jennings Bryan, running for the third time.

Taft was a somewhat reluctant twenty-seventh President. He preferred the Supreme Court, but ran for the Presidency because of his wife. Helen Herron Taft seized every opportunity to push her husband along the path to the White House. Much smaller and far more petite than her oversized husband, at 340 pounds the biggest President ever to serve, Helen Taft made up in ambition what she lacked in stature. She knew what she wanted, and that was the Presidency.

Helen Herron Taft saw her well-planned strategy bear triumphant fruit on March 4, 1909, when William Howard Taft rode to the White House through the snow-covered streets of Washington with his First Lady seated in the carriage beside him. No other presidential wife had ever done that. But Taft's triumph belonged to her, and she had every right to be there.

The Tafts and the Herrons were long-time residents of Cincinnati, "Queen City of the West." Alphonso Taft and Judge John Williamson Herron were "warm friends and had practiced law at the same bar for more than forty years." Their wives, Louise

Maria Torrey Taft and Harriet Collins Herron, knew each other well enough to exchange visits. A Taft daughter, Fanny, and one of the six Herron girls, Maria, were schoolmates. Yet with all this interweaving of Tafts and Herrons, Will and Helen did not meet until she was eighteen, and he was twenty-two. The size of their families may have been partially responsible, for the Tafts had ten children and the Herrons eleven. Helen, oldest of the daughters, was born in Cincinnati on June 2, 1861.

In her long and detailed autobiography, *Recollections of Full Years,* Helen Taft devotes almost no space to her childhood. She speaks of girlhood days spent "placidly in Miss Nourse's school," known in Cincinnati as "The Nursery," which all the Herron girls attended. One of her first passions was music, and she faithfully practiced on the family piano "with such persistence that I wonder the whole neighborhood did not rebel."

A major event of importance occurred for Helen, known to all as "Nellie," when she was seventeen—she was invited to the White House by Lucy Hayes. Nellie's father had once been a law partner with Rutherford Hayes; Nellie's youngest sister, born during the Hayes administration, was named Lucy in honor of Mrs. Hayes. Nellie's stay at the White House sparked the ambition that was to color much of her adult life.

Nellie and Will Taft met at a bobsledding party in Mt. Auburn, a Cincinnati suburb where the Tafts lived. Nellie, gray-eyed, brown-haired, with a small waist and "petite" figure, was a serious and demure young lady who did not greatly impress the large Mr. Taft, whose five-foot-eleven-inch frame already carried well over 220 pounds. They met frequently after that first fun-filled coasting party on a winter's night, according to her own account, but apparently the meetings were not quite that frequent. The following July she wrote to a friend from the summer spa where she was vacationing:

"Who do you think arrived and stayed until Tuesday but that adorable Will Taft . . . it was such a splendid opportunity to make an impression . . . but alas! he strikes me with awe, and I could not make any more out of it."

Will's interest in Nell languished for the next two years; she herself found no one man to suit her. She was, as she admitted, "very exacting, and at the same time unwilling to make the least advance, so what wonder that I am not always satisfied." A close friend of Will's and a Yale classmate, Howard Hollister, courted her in a haphazardly serious manner, but nothing came of it. She and Will did see each other at a salon that she and several other young ladies had organized for the purposes of engaging in "brilliant discussion of topics intellectual and economic," and, coincidentally, to attract eligible young men.

Undecided what to do with her life, Nellie began teaching at private schools, first at Madame Fredin's, next at a school known as White and Sykes, and finally at her own school, Miss Nourse's. In 1882, Will decided that Nell might after all be the right girl for him; he enjoyed her salon, where, he reported, "the lamps and gas are only lit for the sake of conventionality. The phosphorus that scintillates from the brain of each member," he went on, was sufficient illumination.

Nell did not return his interest, despite Valentine verse like the following that she dashed off in a romantic moment:

> St. Valentine the good!
> Now cheer & cheer him still
> For giving Will to Nellie
> And giving Nellie to Will.

Will, however, was persistent, and she did at last accept his proposal in June of 1885. They were married a year later, on June 19, 1886, at the home of her parents in Cincinnati. Nellie was twenty-five and Will was not quite twenty-nine. They had met more than seven years before.

Their European honeymoon lasted one hundred days, and was the beginning of a long life of travel for both Tafts. By nature and training, Nellie was a thrifty young lady; their first voyage across the Atlantic was made on a third-rate ship, the *City of Chester,* but the entire trip eventually cost $1,000.

239

When Will and Nellie Taft returned to Cincinnati, they moved into their own home, dubbed the "Quarry," because of its location on the site of an old quarry in East Walnut Hills. Within a short time, Will was appointed to the Superior Court of Ohio to fill a temporary vacancy. He was later elected to a full five-year term. Will was delighted; he had always dreamed of the bench. To have reached it at the age of twenty-nine was indeed a sweet victory. Nellie did not relish his first taste of success as did he; she feared he would bury himself for good in the sedateness of the judiciary, but made no attempt to influence his decision at that time.

Nellie soon found herself with more pressing demands. The first of her three children, Robert Alphonso, was born in Cincinnati on September 8, 1889. Not quite two years later, on August 1, 1891, Nellie had her second child and only daughter, Helen Herron; and finally, on September 20, 1897, her third and last child, Charles Phelps, was born. (Robert served as a senator from Ohio and himself attempted to reach the Presidency. Charles, too, became active in politics, as mayor of Cincinnati, and during World War II with the Department of State.)

In 1890, to Nellie's delight, President Harrison appointed Taft Solicitor General of the United States, a position that required them to move to the federal capital. In Nellie's view, Washington offered far more opportunity for her capable young husband than Ohio ever could. And she still remembered, vividly, the impressions the exciting capital had made upon her when she visited the White House some years before.

Nellie enjoyed Washington, even with two babies to look after, but her pleasure was short-lived; in 1892 Harrison appointed Taft to the Federal Circuit Court in Ohio. Acceptance meant returning to Cincinnati and a return for her husband to what she feared would be "a groove for the rest of his life." Again Taft accepted a position she did not want him to have. He served as circuit judge for eight years.

They were eight years that Nellie described as "tranquil," and perhaps "too settled." Yet she managed to keep occupied. Her love of music led her to the establishment of the Cincinnati Symphony Orchestra. Funds of course were needed; many of her friends and relatives rallied to the cause, and the orchestra shortly became a successful venture. Oddly, Nellie had stopped playing the piano, even though she had enjoyed it before her marriage. Her son Robert later said that he "could not remember ever having heard her play."

In January, 1900, President McKinley sent a telegram to Taft. "I would like to see you in Washington on important business within the next few days. On Thursday if possible." When Taft arrived at the White House, he learned that the President wanted him to head a commission for the establishment of a civil government in the Philippine Islands. Taft said he needed a week to talk it over with his wife and family. Nellie, who saw the move as a positive step toward her eventual goal, was quick to urge acceptance, as did members of his family. On the seventeenth of April, 1900, the five Tafts, Will, Nellie, and the three children, together with forty others, left San Francisco on the United States Army transport *Hancock* bound for distant and mysterious Manila.

Taft thought his mission might take no more than nine months; they stayed four years. On July 4, 1901, McKinley appointed him the first civil governor-general of the Islands, to replace the military governor, General Arthur MacArthur (his son was the famous general of World War II, Douglas MacArthur). The Tafts moved into Manila's Malacañan Palace; with her usual ingenuity and natural thrift, Nellie made attractive use of native adornments such as bolos, hats, and spears for wall decorations in the palace.

Soon after Theodore Roosevelt became President, he offered Taft a seat on the Supreme Court. Much to Nellie's relief, Taft refused, for he had now become attached to his "little brown brothers," a term he himself originated. (Taft, genial and friendly, meant well in so describing the Filipinos, but in the end his phrase became patronizing and insulting.) Also, Taft was convinced that more work had to be done in the Philippines, and he was needed to complete the job. Roosevelt, after once more urging the vacated

Supreme Court seat upon him, at last agreed to let him stay where he was. Finally, in 1904, Roosevelt appointed Taft as the new Secretary of War in his Cabinet, and Taft could no longer refuse; he consoled himself with the thought that, as Secretary of War, he would still have supervision of the Philippines.

For Nellie, this new appointment was exactly what she wanted. She found it a far more pleasant prospect than the Supreme Court, "because it was in line with the kind of work I wanted my husband to do, the kind of career I wanted for him and expected him to have."

Taft's new position entailed a great deal of traveling; his huge bulk constantly running for trains offered a source of continual amusement to newspaper cartoonists. Unwittingly, these satirical artists helped the Secretary of War to the White House, for their gentle poking of fun at the good-natured Taft made him a familiar figure to anyone who read a newspaper.

Taft's Inauguration on March 4, 1909, seemed an omen of bad luck, for the worst snowstorm in years struck the capital. To the incoming President, the blizzard was to the point, for he reportedly remarked: "I always said it would be a cold day when I got to be President of the United States." To Nellie, the weather was no worse than Roosevelt's visible cooling of his former enthusiasm for her husband; somewhere along the way, Roosevelt had decided that Taft was ready to betray his principles. This conviction was strengthened by Taft's conservatism during the next four years and led, in part, to Roosevelt's entry in the election of 1912 as a third-party candidate against his old friend. Nellie never quite forgave Roosevelt, and her attitude toward him, dating from Taft's Inauguration, was less than friendly.

Nellie's Inaugural ride at the side of her husband was not her only show of independence. She intruded upon many of Taft's conferences, often taking part in important discussions, apparently with his consent, for he accepted her presence and her remarks without rebuke. The extent of her participation was reported by Captain Archie Butt, President Taft's aide, in a scene he witnessed.

Mrs. Taft, angry with her husband for being too good-natured and easy-going with his subordinates, snapped at him: "Will, you approve everything—everything everybody brings to you!" "Well, my dear," the President replied, with a smile, "you disapprove everything, so we are even up."

Nellie Taft's active insinuation in governmental affairs did not last long; on May 17, two and a half months after her husband's Inauguration, she suffered a stroke that left her seriously ill for a number of months. She lost her power of speech entirely and had to practice long hours, with Taft's help, to learn to speak again. She made a complete recovery, except for a slight speech obstruction.

Four of her sisters and her daughter filled in for her as official White House hostess during her illness. By 1910, Nellie was well enough to resume her duties as First Lady.

The social highlight of the Tafts' four years in the White House was their silver wedding anniversary, celebrated in the Executive Mansion on June 19, 1911. Unlike the much smaller and almost private silver wedding of Lucy and Rutherford Hayes that also took place at the White House, the Tafts' twenty-fifth was a huge affair. According to Captain Butt, almost eight thousand invitations were sent out; actually, there were three thousand four hundred guests, still a sizable number for an anniversary celebration. Silver gifts by the truckload arrived at the White House, much to the discomfort of the Tafts, who nevertheless accepted them. (The House of Representatives presented them with a $1,700 solid silver service, and the Senate gave them compote dishes.)

Taft's administration did not make an indelible impression upon history, but the Taft years were notable in at least three respects: Taft and Nellie were the first presidential couple to use an automobile and the last to have a cow, and Taft was the first President to receive an annual salary of $75,000 a year. (Politically, the Taft administration must be credited with the final consolidation of the continental United States. On February 14, 1912, Arizona was admitted into the Union as the forty-eighth state.)

Taft's retirement from the Presidency was not a happy moment for Nellie. She was convinced that Roosevelt's intrusion in the election of 1912 had brought about her husband's defeat; when she left the White House on March 4, 1913, after the Inauguration of Woodrow Wilson, she hurried away without saying good-bye to any of the staff.

The Tafts had planned to return to Cincinnati, but instead moved to New Haven, Connecticut, where the former President was to become Kent Professor of Law at Yale University. If this were not precisely what Nellie may have wished, she managed to adapt to the "simpler routine of private life" in the college town. The Tafts lived in New Haven for eight years; during that time all three of their children married, and their daughter, Helen, beginning a distinguished career in education, became dean of Pennsylvania's Bryn Mawr.

On June 30, 1921, the dream of a lifetime at last came true for William Howard Taft. On that date, President Harding appointed him Chief Justice of the United States Supreme Court. The only man ever to serve both as President and Chief Justice, Taft was sixty-three when he finally reached the highest bench. Eight and a half years later, he was forced to resign because of ill health, and he died soon after, on March 8, 1930, at the age of seventy-two. At Nellie's specific request, Taft was buried in Arlington National Cemetery, the only President at that time to be buried there. Nellie felt that his distinguished service as Secretary of War in Theodore Roosevelt's cabinet had qualified her husband for this honor.

Nellie stayed on in Washington after Taft's death. They had moved there in 1921, when he had been appointed to the Supreme Court. As in New Haven, she lived quietly; she no longer participated in politics, as she had when she had been the First Lady.

After an illness that lasted for a year, Nellie Taft died in Washington on May 22, 1943, ten days short of her eighty-third birthday. She too was buried in Arlington National Cemetery.

The role of Helen Herron Taft as First Lady is a difficult one to assess. Whatever her failures or successes, she has one notable

244

accomplishment to her credit: Remembering the beautiful cherry trees from her stay in the Orient, Nellie arranged to have three thousand of them brought to Washington. On March 27, 1912, she planted the first tree, and the second was planted by Viscountess Chinda, the wife of the Japanese ambassador. For millions of tourists and visitors to the nation's capital, the lovely cherry blossoms are a living memorial to Helen Taft.

Ellen Wilson
1860–1914

When Theodore Roosevelt announced in 1912, "My hat is in the ring," he split the Republican party as no party had been split since the destructive division of the northern and southern Democrats in 1860. He piously intoned to his frenzied followers, "We stand at Armageddon, and we battle for the Lord," as if writing the lyrics for a marching song. His third-party Progressives nominated him by acclaim, and thereby brought defeat to William Howard Taft, who probably would have been reelected with Roosevelt's support.

The Democrats, aware that the Republican split virtually guaranteed success for them in the coming presidential election, droned through forty-six ballots before they finally nominated Woodrow Wilson, a man with a "Presbyterian face," pince-nez glasses, and the casually removed posture of a professor emeritus. Wilson's only other try for public office had occurred just two years before, when he had been elected governor of New Jersey.

246

ELLEN WILSON

A leading educator, president of Princeton University, and advocate of reform, Wilson may have been too intellectual for the average American, but he nevertheless received enough of their votes to become the twenty-eighth President of the United States. Roosevelt, with 4,119,538, and Taft, with 3,484,980, between them had more than Wilson's 6,293,454, but Wilson's overwhelming electoral majority of 81.92 percent easily gave him the Presidency.

Idealist, conservative dreamer, twice-married Woodrow Wilson was far more fortunate in his wives than in many of his lofty ambitions. His first wife, Ellen Louise Axson Wilson, was a gentle southerner whose soft Georgia accent charmed the White House staff, accustomed for ten previous administrations to the far more direct and matter-of-fact speech of the North. Ellen Wilson lived only seventeen months after she came to Washington; she is barely mentioned in most White House narratives, yet for thirty-one years she was the single most important person in Wilson's life.

Woodrow Wilson and Ellen Louise Axson left an extraordinary legacy of fourteen hundred letters they wrote to each other over a period dating from 1883 until 1913. From the outset, Wilson's letters were ardent and open in declaration of his love; Ellen's were far more restrained. In time she overcame her modesty, and her own expressions of love, while never equaling his for fervor and romantic emotion, were warmly affirmative.

Ellen's first letter was a brief note in which she addressed him as "Mr. Wilson," and signed "Sincerely your friend, Ellen Axson." Five months later, she had unbent enough to end a long letter, "Ah, my darling, I have no words—will never find them—to tell you how much; nor how very happy it makes me to hear you say —and repeat it—that you love me. Whenever I read it . . . it gives me a new and distinct thrill of delight, Good night, dear love. Yours with all my heart, Ellie."

Ellen and Woodrow met in Rome, Georgia, when she was twenty-three and he was twenty-six. (He had seen her briefly many years before when she was a baby and his family had come to visit hers.) Ellen, the oldest of four children, was born in Savannah, Georgia, on May 15, 1860. Her father, the Reverend Samuel Edward Axson, was a Presbyterian minister, as was Woodrow's father, Joseph Ruggles Wilson.

Ellen's education, first in Savannah and later in Rome, where her father had been transferred, had the double advantage of the finest "traditions of the old South" and her father's country parsonage, in Wilson's words "the best of all schools—for manners, purity, and cultivation." Perhaps there was undue emphasis upon social graces and reverence for God and home, but Ellen's education academically and artistically was not entirely neglected. She attended Shorter College in Rome and became an accomplished painter.

In early 1883, Ellen's mother, the former Margaret Hoyt, died suddenly, in childbirth; the baby survived. Ellen, not yet twenty-three, now had two younger brothers and an infant sister to care for. It was a difficult task, for her father suffered a deep melancholia after the death of his wife. Ellen's load, however, was lightened when an aunt in Gainesville, some eighty miles away, took the baby girl.

Woodrow, at twenty-six not quite sure what his career was to be, was taking a brief fling at law. He and a partner had an office in Atlanta. One day in April of 1883, the tall, slender, scholarly Woodrow came to Rome on business. As the son of a minister, he dutifully attended church on the Sabbath, and it was there, some rows in front of him, that he saw a girl with a "tip-tilted little nose, a perfect complexion, a sweetly curved mouth and hair like burnished copper." Woodrow decided at once that he had to meet this attractive young lady. He did arrange to see her, and from the beginning, he was smitten. She was just as taken with him, but shyness and southern propriety would not permit her to display her feelings. By September, Woodrow found the courage to propose, and Ellen, without hesitation, "immediately and joyfully said 'Yes!' "

Their marriage encountered certain obstacles. For one, there

248

was the matter of Woodrow's schooling. He knew now he would never make a good lawyer, and he had given up his office in Atlanta. His goal was politics; even as a boy he had dreamed of being a "statesman." But Woodrow Wilson the scholar could not become a politician without the proper preparation. He entered Johns Hopkins University to study for a doctorate in political science.

A second, and perhaps more restrictive impediment was the declining health of Ellen's father. The Reverend Mr. Axson needed her more than ever to take care of him and to look after the two boys. While Woodrow went off to Baltimore to study at Johns Hopkins, Ellen stayed behind in Georgia to care for her family. Finally, on May 29, 1884, the Reverend Samuel Edward Axson died. Ellen was now free to think of herself; her older brother went off to college and her younger brother moved in with relatives. And Ellen did something she had thought about for years—she went to New York to study at the Art Students' League. Marriage plans were once again postponed.

In January of 1885, Wilson's career was stimulated by publication of his first book, *Congressional Government*. A success from the start (it eventually had over thirty editions), the book established its young author as a leading political scholar.

Armed with a promise of royalties from his book and an appointment as an assistant professor at Bryn Mawr, Wilson at last persuaded the hesitant Ellen to forego engagement for marriage. On June 24, 1885, Ellen Louise Axson, twenty-five, and Woodrow Wilson, twenty-eight, were married in her grandfather's house in Savannah, Georgia. The services were jointly read by her grandfather, the Reverend I. S. K. Axson, and by Woodrow's father, the Reverend Joseph R. Wilson. Ellen wore a traditional white veil over a simple white dress that she herself had made.

Over the years, Ellen's abilities as a homemaker and housekeeper were put to severe tests; no sooner were the Wilsons comfortably settled than off they would go to another city and another house. In September of 1885, they moved into two rooms of a small frame house on the edge of Bryn Mawr's campus. They stayed there for a year. In 1886, Woodrow received a doctorate from Johns Hopkins University; his Ph. D. brought him a full professorship at Bryn Mawr and an increase in pay to $1,800 a year. Woodrow and Ellen moved to a larger house. Woodrow's sisters eyed the move with some trepidation, for they regarded their artist sister-in-law as "proverbially inefficient," but the bustling Ellen surprised them. She managed her increased household chores with a control and facility that would have done honor to a frontier wife.

Ellen had other tasks facing her, for the first of her three daughters, Margaret, was born in Gainesville, Georgia, on April 30, 1886. From the beginning of their marriage, Ellen and Woodrow were determined never to be separated, but Ellen firmly announced she would not permit *her* child to be born "north of the Mason-Dixon line." She gave birth to Margaret in the Gainesville home of her aunt, Mrs. Louisa Hoyt Wade. Ellen's second daughter, Jessie, was born in the same house on August 28, 1887. Ellen compromised enough to have her third child, Eleanor, at Middletown, Connecticut, on October 16, 1889.

Despite their honeymoon-inspired vows never to separate, Ellen and Woodrow were often apart. Either he was off studying or lecturing, or she was away having her babies. Later, he took a number of vacations without her, and she had some holidays without him. Their frequent separations are astonishing, in view of the fervent love and intense longing they evidenced for each other in their many letters.

An accomplished writer and devotee of style, Wilson found numberless ways to declare his love. The following passage from a letter to Ellen is a vivid example: "I would a thousand times rather repay you a tythe of the happiness you have brought me than make my name immortal *without* serving you as the chief mission of my life. Ah, my little wife, do you know that my whole self has passed over into my allegiance for you?" Ellen, less gifted than her brilliant husband, was nevertheless as eloquent. In 1892, she ended a letter to him with these words: "You have been everything to me—you *are* everything. If I could but tell you how devotedly, absorbedly, passionately I love you in return for all this happiness."

In 1888, Ellen and Woodrow moved for a second time, to Middletown, Connecticut, where Wilson had been appointed a full professor at Wesleyan College. Their stay at Wesleyan lasted two years, as had their residence at Bryn Mawr. In 1890, he was given a full professorship in Jurisprudence and Political Economy at Princeton University; he was more than happy to accept the appointment, for it had been one of his ambitions to teach there ever since he had graduated from Princeton in 1879, when it was known as the College of New Jersey. Princeton was to be the Wilson home for twenty years.

The household that had started with two was now seven, including their three daughters, one of Ellen's brothers, and her young sister. Throughout their long stay in Princeton, the family would include many more—aunts, uncles, nephews, nieces, Woodrow's sisters and their husbands, many of whom lived with Woodrow and Ellen for extended periods. And finally, Woodrow's widower father moved in permanently in 1895. The house on Princeton's Library Place often bulged, but it was a happy, busy home. The Wilsons managed to remain ahead of insolvency by virtue of Ellen's strict regard for economy and Woodrow's affinity for work. Ellen made her own clothes and the children's; Woodrow wrote, lectured, taught.

Throughout their entire marriage, Wilson leaned heavily upon Ellen for advice. He was too often preoccupied with his work to make necessary decisions, and he disliked involvement in money matters. He discovered Ellen was far more shrewd and sagacious than her gentle southern manner indicated, and he soon permitted her to help him make his vital decisions. (In later years, he was to be cruelly criticized for this dependence upon her and other women.)

By 1895, Wilson's earnings as a professor, as a writer, and a lecturer, had increased. He and Ellen bought the lot next door, built a comfortable house of stucco, with seven bedrooms, and moved in the following year. Ellen saw to it that everything was in place in exactly one day (with the assistance of ten hired helpers). For Ellen the crowning touch was the hanging in Woodrow's study of crayon enlargements she herself had made of five men her husband admired: the American, Daniel Webster; the British statesman, William Gladstone; Walter Bagehot, an English economist and author; Edmund Burke, English essayist, author, and politician; and finally, Woodrow's father, the Reverend Joseph R. Wilson.

This house on Library Place meant more to Ellen than any other, but she had to give it up six years later. In 1902, Wilson was appointed president of Princeton, and once again the family moved, this time to "Prospect," the university president's gloomy, twenty-room manor. "Prospect" and its stately furnishings were far different from the cheerful house Ellen and Woodrow had built and loved, but Ellen lost no time in refurnishing and redecorating to her taste. Under her ministrations, "Prospect" was, at least, bright and livable.

Wilson's service as president of one of the most prestigious universities in the world brought him to the attention of the entire country. In 1910, the New Jersey Democrats turned to the scholar politician for salvation. They had been out of office far too long, and they searched for a miracle. The professorial Wilson gave it to them. In the gubernatorial election later that year, Wilson swept to victory with a plurality of 50,000 votes. Wilson became front-page news, and two years later he achieved the impossible—he defeated Theodore Roosevelt and William Howard Taft to become the twenty-eighth President of the United States.

When the Wilsons moved into the White House in March of 1913, they made it clear to Washington society that they were not interested in tradition. They preferred to live as they always had; they announced there would be no Inaugural Ball, although preparations had been made and money expended. The Wilsons spent Inauguration night as a quiet family evening, enjoying the delight of being the new First Family of the land, and retired at a reasonable hour.

A month later, President Wilson once again shocked Washington when he personally appeared before a special session of both houses of Congress to address them. No President since John Adams had done that, but Wilson's appearance and speech brought tumultuous cheers and applause. On the way back to the White House, Ellen proudly said, "That was the sort of thing Roosevelt would have loved to do, if only he'd thought of it." Wilson, pleased at the suggestion, answered with a laugh, "Yes, I think I put one over on Teddy." He undoubtedly did, for the custom he revived of appearing before Congress in person has been continued by every succeeding President.

With her variegated duties as the new First Lady, Ellen was constantly involved with supervision of the White House and with the usual receptions, musicales, and formal dinners, but she managed to find time for her painting. Now that her children were grown, she was free to devote at least a few hours to her art, and she set up a studio on the third floor. She donated many of her paintings to charity, and was gratified to see them bring excellent prices, even when they were sold anonymously.

Appalled by slum conditions she encountered in Washington, Ellen persuaded Wilson to appoint a commission to study the matter. As a result of her prompting, the commission prepared a bill for presentation to Congress for improvement of housing in the poorer sections of the capital.

The major social events of 1913 and 1914 were the White House weddings of two Wilson daughters. The first, on November 25, 1913, when Jessie married Francis Bowes Sayre, was a lavish affair; six months later, on May 7, 1914, Eleanor married William Gibbs McAdoo, Secretary of the Treasury in Wilson's cabinet. This second wedding, unlike the first, was small and almost private, in deference to Ellen's failing health.

Ellen had been ailing for some time; in the spring of 1914 the White House physician, Dr. Cary T. Grayson, knew she was desperately ill. In July, three specialists confirmed his fears—Ellen had Bright's Disease (an ailment of the kidneys, often fatal, and named for an English physician, who had first diagnosed it).

While Ellen lay dying in her White House bedroom, war broke out in Europe, but she did not hear of it, for Wilson had asked that she not be told. But she did know that Congress passed her slum clearance bill (when the Senate learned that she could not live, it hastily pushed her bill through passage; the legislation, unfortunately, was later declared unconstitutional).

Dr. Grayson attended Ellen constantly; during the weeks he was with her, he found that she was concerned not about herself but rather about her husband, as she had been all her life. On August 6, 1914, she whispered to Dr. Grayson, "Please take good care of Woodrow." She died a short time later, at the age of fifty-four.

President Wilson sat beside her body for two days, and then he took her to Rome, Georgia, for burial next to her mother and father in the cemetery on Myrtle Hill. She was buried beneath a great oak overlooking the Etowah River. Her final services were conducted in the same Presbyterian church where Wilson had first seen her thirty-one years before.

Edith Wilson
1872–1961

Six months after Ellen's death, Woodrow Wilson met a forty-two-year-old widow, Edith Bolling Galt. His immediate interest in her seemed outrageous to many, and curious to others. Popular opinion apparently expected a period of extended mourning, with no romantic attachments to mar his sorrow. But Wilson was a man who had always relied upon women. Constantly in their company, he had an unusual faculty for making them his close friends. It was not so much a matter of forgetting Ellen, but rather of needing Edith.

Mrs. Galt was a tall, beautiful woman, a bit perhaps on the plump side, with a round face and flawless skin. Mature, intelligent, and knowledgeable, Edith Galt met Woodrow Wilson at a necessary moment in his life. He became as devoted to her as he had been to Ellen; even beyond his devotion, he placed more trust in Edith than anyone else, woman or man.

On her paternal side, Edith Bolling Galt had the most unusual ancestry of any First Lady. She was a direct descendant of the American Indian princess, Pocahontas. Pocahontas married John Rolfe, an Englishman who had migrated to Virginia. In 1675, their granddaughter, Jane Rolfe, married the first Bolling to settle in the New World, and thus the long line of Virginia Bollings was established, leading in a straight line to Edith.

By the middle of the nineteenth century, the Bollings were prominent planters, slaveowners, and men of substance. But the coming of the Civil War physically destroyed the archaically tranquil life they had enjoyed. With his patrimony in ruins, William Bolling moved his wife (the former Sallie White), his invalid mother, and his two children to a large old house in Wytheville, Virginia. Over the years their family increased, and William and Sallie had, in all, eleven children, two of whom died in infancy. Their seventh child and fourth daughter, Edith, was born on October 15, 1872, at 9 A.M. Her father, by then a judge in the circuit court, impatiently awaited her arrival, though it meant delaying the opening of his courtroom. In later years he was fond of reminding her that she began her life by "keeping gentlemen waiting."

Schooling in that section of Virginia presented a problem to a judge with a large family and a modest income. For Edith, it meant education at home, taught by her father and her aging grandmother. Edith learned the first two "r's" from Grandmother Bolling and the third from her father. When Edith was fifteen, she had her first formal training, at Martha Washington College in Abingdon, Virginia. This school was chosen for her because it apparently had an excellent course in music, which Edith was "eager to learn." But the school director was an unregenerated miser and "the epitome of all that was narrow, cruel and bigoted," in Edith's own words. He starved the girls and gave them no heat, so that their fingers, when they tried to play the piano, were too stiff with cold to strike the keys.

By the following June, Edith had enough of Martha Washington College and its heartless headmaster; in the winter of 1879, when she was seventeen, she enrolled at Powell's School in Richmond.

With an entire student body of only thirty young ladies and a director who was "father, counsellor and comrade" to each of them, it was a happier experience. Regrettably, Judge Bolling was forced to withdraw her after one year, for he had three younger sons to educate; funds for Edith's schooling and theirs as well were simply not available. In all, Edith spent exactly two years in school, yet, because of the diligent training she received from her grandmother, she was a literate, well-educated woman.

In the winter of 1880, after Edith completed her formal schooling, she went to Washington, D.C., to visit her sister, who had married Alexander Hunter Galt. Through her brother-in-law, she met his cousin, Norman Galt, tall, dark, immaculate in his dress, and nine years her senior. Norman Galt came from a wealthy Washington family, who owned the finest and most exclusive jewelry store in the capital. The store was founded in 1802; one of its early customers was President Thomas Jefferson.

Norman Galt fell in love with the tall and slender Edith from the moment he first saw her. As Edith herself tells the story, she did not feel as strongly about him; four years later, worn down by his "patience and persistence," she did at last marry him. Within two years, she suffered a miscarriage and was never able, after that, to have children.

In 1908, Norman Galt died suddenly, after a short illness. Edith inherited his entire estate, including Galt's. She placed the management of the store in the hands of a trusted employee, Christian Bergheimer, and spent much of the next few years traveling abroad until the outbreak of war in 1914.

The death of Ellen Wilson in August of 1915 left the White House lonely and empty for the President. Two of his daughters were married and living in their own homes; his third daughter, Margaret, was away studying for a singing career. Wilson's young cousin, Helen Bones, stayed on at the Executive Mansion to look after him and act as his official hostess. But she, too, missed Ellen, and she often drifted aimlessly from one room to another.

The White House physician, Dr. Cary Grayson, prescribed exercise for the President, and social diversion for Helen. Grayson was courting a young lady named Alice Gertrude Gordon, known to all as Altrude. Altrude and Edith Bolling Galt were close friends. Dr. Grayson asked Edith to include Helen Bones in their circle; Edith and Helen went for drives and walks together. On a windy afternoon in March, Helen invited Mrs. Galt to visit the White House. When they came in, they were both disheveled and windblown, their walking shoes covered with mud. It was precisely the wrong moment to meet the President, or so it seemed to Mrs. Galt.

Two men, dressed in comfortable old golf clothes, clumped up the stairs. With their own boots trailing mud behind them, they reached the second floor in time to meet Helen and Mrs. Galt. One of the men was Dr. Grayson and the other was President Wilson. Far from being the disaster Edith had feared, this first meeting was a glorious triumph. The President promptly insisted that the windblown widow stay for tea.

For Wilson, that day was the beginning of his new love. With the help of his daughters, who approved wholeheartedly of his interest in Mrs. Galt, he arranged to see Edith as often as he dared. The meetings, most of which were quiet dinners at the White House, or drives to the country, were handled with propriety and care, but gossip was inevitable. Edith was not sure how she felt about the President, though she knew he was in love with her.

Some of Wilson's associates were alarmed at his new interest; it was far too soon after Ellen's death for him to remarry. The year 1915 was still a time of innocence; with a presidential election approaching, public opposition to an early remarriage might well prove disastrous. Eventually Edith knew she was in love with Wilson, but she, too, was concerned about the 1916 election, and she asked him to wait at least a year. Without setting a date for marriage, they became secretly engaged.

Two of Wilson's advisers, his son-in-law William McAdoo, and his friend and associate of many years, Colonel Edward M. House, heard of the secret engagement and warned against a public announcement, which they feared would revive an old scandal that Wilson thought had been forgotten. (Wilson's name had been linked with a divorcée he had met on a Bermuda vacation some years before.)

Faced with the prospect of malicious gossip that could only bring pain to Edith, Wilson sent word that he would not hold her to her promise. When Dr. Grayson brought the message to Edith, he reported that the President, as he told Grayson what to say, "went white to the lips and his hands shook."

For many hours Edith sat thinking about it. In the early hours of the morning, she made her decision and wrote to the President that she was "ready to follow the road 'where love leads.' This is my pledge, dearest one, I will stand by you—not for duty, not for pity, not for honour—but for love—trusting, protecting, comprehending love. And no matter whether the wine be bitter or sweet we will share it together and find happiness in the comradeship."

Edith Bolling Galt and Woodrow Wilson were married three months later, on December 18, 1915, in her home on Washington's Twentieth Street. It was a small wedding, confined to forty guests, but to the press of the country it was front-page news. (The feared scandal never did materialize, nor was there a general outcry from an outraged public. Most people, in fact, exhibited unrestrained delight when the engagement was officially announced in October.)

The war was still a European affair when Edith undertook her duties as First Lady after a short Virginia honeymoon. From her house on Twentieth Street she moved her piano, her rolltop desk, and her Wilcox & Gibbs sewing machine. At the time, the well-used sewing machine seemed like a quixotic and useless piece of furniture to bring to the White House, but time, sadly, was to prove Edith's wisdom in saving it.

It was apparent from the beginning that Edith would be far more than the mistress of the Executive Mansion. She was Wilson's confidante, private secretary, his ear and his heart. She helped him with his correspondence, his documents, and many of his decisions. He taught her the private code that was known only to him and his personal emissaries abroad. (Not even his Secretary of State, Robert Lansing, knew it.) Politically, Edith was never as astute as Wilson. When the suffragettes began their unflagging campaign for the vote, Edith caustically referred to them as "disgusting creatures," and dismissed their zeal as "unladylike."

The presidential election of 1916, between Wilson and Supreme Court Justice Charles Evans Hughes, was a classic cliffhanger. With the far western votes of California not yet counted, victory for the Republican Hughes seemed assured. He went to bed confident that he had won, and *The New York Times* flashed the word that Hughes was the next President. But when the California votes were finally tallied, it was found that Wilson had won that state by a mere 4,000 votes, enough to give him California's thirteen electoral votes and the Presidency. A reporter who tried to tell Mr. Hughes of this astounding development was coolly advised that "the President was asleep" and could not be disturbed. The reporter answered, "Tell him when he wakes up that he's no longer the President."

The Democratic slogan, "He kept us out of war," contributed largely to Wilson's victory. Within a few months, the slogan was forgotten; on April 6, 1917, at Wilson's request, Congress voted a declaration of war against Germany, to make "the world safe for democracy."

Edith's role as First Lady now took on broader public dimensions. To set an example for the women of the country, she curtailed White House entertainment, and instituted meatless Mondays, wheatless Tuesdays, and gasless Sundays. Her sewing machine was put busily back into service to turn out pajamas, surgical shirts, bandages, and other items for the Red Cross. As Edith later wrote of it, "the wheels of that machine seldom were idle." Another Wilson economy was a herd of sheep to crop the White House lawns, thereby freeing manpower for the greater effort. And Edith arranged for the idols of the silver screen, Mary Pickford, Doug Fairbanks, and Charlie Chaplin, to sell Liberty Bonds at gigantic rallies on the Treasury steps.

With the end of the war in November, 1918, Wilson prepared his famous Fourteen Points, embodying one of the most idealistic and tragically unattainable proposals ever offered by a world leader. The League of Nations, in Wilson's view, was the keystone of future global security, but there were many at home who did not agree. Edith accompanied Wilson to Paris and watched him waste away while he fought with the other Allies for a softening of their harsh surrender demands; for the most part he lost. But he did achieve a singular triumph when the Peace Conference approved the League. Of all the wives present for the conference, Edith was the only one permitted to watch him win his victory, when she was smuggled into an alcove of the French Foreign Office on the climactic day by no less a personage than Premier Clemenceau himself.

It was a different story when Edith and Wilson returned to the United States. Edith had to stand helplessly by while Wilson, ill and weary from his long struggle in Paris, drove himself to exhaustion in a vain attempt to move a hostile Senate from its refusal to sanction American membership in his League. Implacably, Senator Henry Cabot Lodge, together with the isolationist "Irreconcilables," Senators Borah, Hiram Johnson, LaFollette, and Reed, blocked him at every turn.

With his dreams for the world crumbling about him, Wilson was on the point of physical collapse. Despite Edith's protests, he made a tour of the country to plead his case before the people. The tour began on September 3, 1919, with speaking stops scheduled in major cities across the country; on September 26, the trip was hastily canceled when Wilson was too exhausted to continue. Edith and Wilson arrived back in Washington on September 28 to find the capital and the entire country buzzing with rumors and apprehension over the President's condition.

Four days later, on the morning of October 2, Dr. Grayson was hurriedly summoned by Edith to the President's suite. When the doctor emerged ten minutes later, he was shaken and mumbling to himself, "My God, the President is paralyzed!"

Thus began a period unique in American history. With the President helpless, Edith, Dr. Grayson, and Wilson's secretary, Joseph Tumulty, agreed that the world must not know the extent of his illness. They closed the White House gates, posted sentries, and released only enough information to appease the press. In an unprecedented move, Edith Wilson assumed active stewardship of the Presidency. Politely and firmly shunting Tumulty into the background, Edith alone decided whom to see, what papers and documents to discuss, what issues to consider. Presidential decisions were hers, though she always maintained that Wilson himself made the final determination; her role, she insisted, was simply to screen and select for the man who lay physically helpless but mentally alert. In her view, what she did was correct and necessary; some historians differ. And to Wilsonian critics, Edith was the "Presidentress" while the period of her stewardship was "Mrs. Wilson's Regency." Other critics were more acrimonious; they accused her of changing her title from "First Lady" to "Acting First Man."

The exact length of Edith's "Regency" has never been clearly established. Only Edith and Wilson knew and they never spoke about it beyond a claim by Edith that it was only six weeks; others say it was anywhere from six months to seventeen and a half months (the balance of Wilson's term). Whatever the time involved, there is no question that Edith conducted the affairs of the Presidency. Today, the twenty-fifth amendment, "Presidential Disability and Succession," makes such an eventuality impossible. Ratified by the required thirty-eight states on February 10, 1967, this amendment clearly defines when a President is unable to perform his duties and clearly defines who is to assume responsibility in his place.

Within a few weeks, Wilson recovered from the worst effects of his illness, although he was left partially paralyzed. He did return to active supervision of his office, but Edith watched him carefully and zealously; she permitted him to do only as much as she alone thought he could endure. Until the end of his term, affairs of state moved slowly, and sometimes not at all. Still, the government and the country survived.

Wilson was a weary and disillusioned man when he and Edith left the White House in March of 1921 to make way for their successors, President and Mrs. Warren G. Harding. James M. Cox of Ohio, Harding's Democratic opponent, had promised Wilson he would continue the fight for the League of Nations, but the voters repudiated Cox, Wilson, and the League. Wilson's hopes for the future of mankind were crushed by the largest plurality in history against his candidate and his program.

Edith and Wilson retired to a large brick house on Washington's S Street. Before leaving the White House, they agreed upon Washington for their retirement because the Library of Congress would be available for a major book Wilson planned to write, and because the federal capital was home to Edith.

Wilson never did write his book. On February 3, 1924, his weary body finally succumbed, and he died at eleven-fifteen on a Sunday morning, at the age of sixty-seven. He was buried in Washington, in the crypt of the not-yet-completed Cathedral of St. Peter and St. Paul (now known as the National Cathedral or Washington Cathedral).

Edith, fifty-one when Wilson died, stayed on at the house on S Street. For a year, she remained in seclusion; when she emerged at last, she indulged her love of travel, and over the years made many trips to Europe and Japan, and once around the world. Militantly Democratic, she worked for her husband's party and for his memory. She was one of the most active and devoted directors of the Woodrow Wilson Foundation. In 1939, she published a lengthy autobiography, *My Memoir,* which ended with Wilson's death. She began the book on August 14, 1927, and wrote the last word on Armistice Day, 1937. The book was written, she said, to reveal "the truth concerning personal matters which has been often distorted by the misinformed."

She remained active almost until the very end of her life, despite a heart ailment. At the age of eighty-eight, in frigid 16 degree temperature, she was a guest on the reviewing stand at the Inauguration of President John F. Kennedy. Another guest, former President Harry S. Truman, kissed her on the cheek.

A little less than ten months later, on December 28, 1961, Edith Wilson died of "hypertensive heart disease and congestive failure." She was eighty-nine. She was buried in the same Washington Cathedral where her husband's body lay, in a crypt one floor below his. Her home on S Street, where she had lived for almost thirty-eight years after Wilson's death, became a national museum.

Edith Wilson died on the 105th anniversary of her husband's birth. This curious coincidence has a poignancy beyond the usual, for though she had spent only eight years with Wilson, she spent many more working to maintain and further his ideals. Many of those ideals he had meant to embody in the book he intended writing after leaving the White House in 1921. He got no further than the dedication, which he himself had typed on his battered old typewriter. He wrote these words for Edith:

> To E. B. W. I dedicate this book because it is a book in which I have tried to interpret life, the life of a nation, and she has shown me the full meaning of life. Her heart is not only true but wise; her thoughts are not only free but touched with vision; she teaches and guides by being what she is; her unconscious interpretation of faith and duty makes all the way clear; her power to comprehend makes work and thought alike easier and more near to what it seeks. Woodrow Wilson.

Florence Harding
1860–1924

A fortuitous phrase, a smoke-filled room, and a constitutional amendment combined to shape a phenomenal triumph for Warren Gamaliel Harding of Ohio in the presidential election of 1920. In May of that year Senator Harding declared that what America needed was "not nostrums but normalcy." Out of these felicitous words, the Republicans framed a campaign slogan that helped to sweep the Ohio senator to the Presidency in November. "Return to normalcy" meant, in effect, rejection of Wilsonian internationalism. "America First" as a phrase had not yet reached its zenith; as an ideal it was all-pervasive.

In the first and most famous of the smoke-filled rooms, the Republican elders decided amongst themselves that Warren G. Harding was to be their party's candidate. And finally, the Nineteenth Amendment, granting the vote to women, became federal law on August 26, 1920. It is safe to assume that the ladies, voting

265

for the first time in a presidential election, cast their ballots in huge numbers for the jowly but still vibrantly attractive Harding with the black eyebrows and white hair. In a landslide victory, Harding became the twenty-ninth President of the United States with an impressive total of 16,153,115 votes against 9,133,092 for his Democratic opponent, the drab and uninteresting James M. Cox.

Harding did not live up to the trust and faith of those who overwhelmingly and exuberantly voted for him. Weak and indecisive, he brought his cronies, the infamous "Ohio Gang," to Washington. While he himself played poker, drank bootleg whiskey, and indulged in various indiscretions, he seemed unaware that his friends were plundering and pillaging at every opportunity. His First Lady, Florence Kling Harding, failed in her role as well, although perhaps her major sin was that she tried too hard. A woman who desperately wanted happiness but didn't know how to achieve it, Florence Harding's life was full of discontent. She gave love, and received almost none in return. Still, there are many who choose to portray her as a devoted wife and charming hostess. For them, mere presence in the White House guarantees investiture of grandeur. But it is a peculiar fact of history that retrospection has the power to modify; gospel therefore is not immutable.

When Florence Kling first saw Warren Harding, as he strolled down the main street of Marion, Ohio, he was twenty-five and she was thirty. Harding was a totally masculine man, admired by many women and himself loving none. He could not really have been interested in the thin, plain Florence, but once she decided she must have him, he stood no chance before her determined onslaught. With one disastrous marriage behind her, Florence was a restless woman who had spent her years fighting for the things she wanted most. By the time she was formally introduced to Warren Harding, in the parlor of his father's house, where she had come to teach piano to his sister, her goal was marriage to him.

Her eventual success was due as much to his weakness as to her persistence. Harding's father once dryly remarked that it was a good thing Warren had not been born a girl, otherwise he'd always be in a "family way," since he could never say no to anyone. Warren most certainly could not say no to Florence, although he could not have loved her, then or later. He may have brought some happiness to her, but she brought precious little to him.

Florence Kling was born in Marion on August 15, 1860. Her father, Amos Kling, was the town banker and leading citizen. Her mother was the former Louisa M. Bouton. Amos and Louisa Kling had two other children, both sons; Flossie and her brothers were never close.

The Kling household was quarrelsome and contentious; despite its opulence and deserved reputation as the largest and finest house in Marion, its richness was never matched in warmth. Amos Kling and his daughter were alike in stubborn and headstrong temperament. They clashed, constantly. But Kling sent her to the proper schools, and saw to it that she learned how to ride, for she was, after all, daughter of the town's most influential man. She was proficient at the piano, and Kling allowed her to attend Cincinnati's Conservatory of Music.

When Florence returned to Marion, a young woman interested in young men, she was no more ready to obey her father's restraints than she had been before. She often slipped away to the local roller skating rink; the boys who took her there would never have been accepted in her house, but there was no one on her own social level she cared to see, except for Henry DeWolfe (known as "Pete"). Pete occasionally went skating with her, and in time they began to see a great deal of each other. Pete, two years older, was a young man of little character, but Flossie saw something in him she wanted. In March of 1880, Florence and Pete eloped. Their friends were not surprised; Pete married her "because he had to." Six months later, a son was born.

The marriage was a disaster. Pete had never worked and he didn't want to. Amos Kling refused to help; he was furious at the runaway marriage and birth of their child. Flossie, just as stubborn, would not ask him for money; her mother, without Kling's knowledge, gave her a few dollars and clothing, and Pete's father paid their grocery bills. Pete took to drinking, and then, after two years of mutual misery, left her. (He turned up from time to time, through the years, and died finally at the age of thirty-five.)

Flossie divorced Pete in 1886. She allowed her father to adopt her son, Eugene Marshall, and she herself rented some rooms not far from where the Hardings lived. She supported herself by giving piano lessons for fifty cents an hour.

Florence and Harding met in 1890, when he was editor and publisher of the Marion *Star,* a struggling newspaper he had acquired with two friends for $300. His antecedents and his future were unlikely to generate rapture in the heart of Mr. Amos Kling. Warren's doctor father was a former veterinarian now treating humans, none too profitably, and his mother was a midwife. There had long been a rumor in town that the Harding blood was "tainted"; somewhere along the line, so the talk went, a "Negro" had slipped into the ancestral line. As for Warren's prospects, they appeared dim, indeed. Kling was outraged that his daughter planned to marry such a man, and he threatened to blow Harding's head off if he encountered him in public.

Amos Kling's threats did not prevent the marriage. It must have been clear to Harding that his future father-in-law's wealth would, in all probabilty, never be his, but Flossie's social position represented an eminence he had previously coveted without apparent hope. He and Florence were married in a new house that Harding built on Mount Vernon Avenue. The marriage took place on July 8, 1891; Florence was a month short of thirty-one and Warren not quite twenty-six. Amos Kling did not attend the wedding, although Flossie's mother slipped in unnoticed for the ceremony.

The Harding house was built to hold a family, but there never were children. Florence's son, Marshall DeWolfe, continued to live with his Kling grandparents. (As had his father, Marshall died a failure at the age of thirty-five; they were both buried in unmarked graves. Marshall left two children, a son and a daughter. Florence, who never exhibited overwhelming affection for her son, was, for the most part, indifferent to her grandchildren, particularly when her husband became a prominent figure in Ohio politics, and she had no wish to be known as a grandmother.)

Warren Harding, easy-going and affable, allowed his wife to be the dominant force in their household, and at the *Star* as well. At one point, with more malice than admiration, he referred to her as the "Duchess," and the name stuck. She called him "Wurr'n," in her flat, midwestern style, and made it sound like a command.

Life with the unfeminine, demanding Florence must have been trying for Harding; his health troubled him and he teetered more than once on the edge of a nervous breakdown. In 1894, Florence sent him to Battle Creek Sanatorium for a long rest. She herself was often tense and edgy, but she found a remedy for her nerves at the offices of the *Star*. She had long complained to "Wurr'n" that he was too lax; his newspaper lacked efficiency and system. While he was away at the Sanatorium his circulation manager quit. Florence took over; her stay, she thought, would be a short one. She later said that she "went down there intending to help out for a few days," and she "stayed fourteen years."

She did bring system to the *Star,* with the brisk, tight-lipped autocracy she had learned from her father. She organized the newsboys into a well-drilled unit; authority was hers, and woe to the lad who challenged it. She did not shrink from punishment, and at least once spanked one of the boys. She scrupulously counted the pennies, something Harding had never bothered with, and she herself scrubbed the floors.

One of her newsboys was Norman Thomas, the perennial Socialist candidate for President. He wrote this about her:

> Mrs. Harding in those days ran the show. She was a woman of very narrow mentality and range of interest or understanding, but of strong will and, within a certain area, of genuine kindliness. . . . Her husband was the front. He was, as you know, very affable; very much of a joiner. . . . He was always personally more popular than his wife, [but] it was she who was the real driving power in the success that the Marion *Star* was unquestionably making in its community.

There are those who dispute Norman Thomas' appraisal; they insist that Harding would have made a success of the *Star* without her. Harding nevertheless permitted her to assume supervision of the newspaper while he indulged his lifelong passion for politics. Harding was a born politician, blessed with innate affability, the profile of a matinee idol, and the smoothly golden voice of a trained orator. Basically platitudinous, his shallow speeches gave the effect of profundity, but he was destined to go far, as Florence always believed, and as Harry Daugherty came to believe. (Harry Daugherty, pronounced "Dokerty," carefully guided Harding's career from Ohio to the White House. When he first met Harding, he reportedly said about the tall, handsome man with the prematurely gray hair: "Gee, what a great-looking President he'd make!")

Florence watched Harding grow in popularity and political stature beginning with his first elective victory in 1895 as county auditor of Marion; four years later he was elected to the Ohio state senate, and served there until 1903. In 1904 he was lieutenant-governor of Ohio. With Daugherty's help, Florence recast Warren in a more suitable image; she found a fashionable tailor for him and taught him how to dress. She herself faded as he blossomed.

In 1905, she was seriously ill; one kidney was diseased and had to be removed; she was never really well from that day. Forty-five at the time, she had lost any physical attractiveness Harding may have seen in her. He found his pleasures elsewhere, as he had for years. Florence suspected, and did her best to keep him under the closest surveillance, but he frequently avoided her vigilant eye. There is evidence that he was carrying on with a married woman, wife of a close friend in Marion. Yet, in spite of this clandestine and all-consuming romance and his complete lack of physical love for Florence, he was deeply concerned when she was ill, and attended her with the greatest solicitude.

Harding's opportunity for country-wide exposure came in the election of 1914. This would be the first time that senators would be directly chosen by the electorate, as provided by the newly ratified Seventeenth Amendment (before then, senators had been appointed by state legislatures). On November 3, 1914, Harding became the junior senator from the State of Ohio with a resounding total of 526,115 votes to 423,748 for his Democratic opponent. Warren Gamaliel Harding of Ohio had arrived on the national scene; standing beside him was Florence Kling Harding, and behind him Harry Daugherty.

For the gregarious Harding, Washington was simply a more populous Marion. He played poker with the boys and met the right people. He and Florence saw much of the Ned McLeans and the Nicholas Longworths (Mrs. Longworth was the former Alice Roosevelt, and Mrs. McLean was Evalyn Walsh McLean, a beautiful and spoiled young woman whose immigrant father had made a fortune in gold mining—in her own right she was famous as owner of the fabled Hope Diamond). Despite her friendship with them, Alice Longworth was never too impressed with the Hardings; she disliked their small town gaucheries, and referred to Harding as a "slob." But a curious friendship developed between Florence and the much younger Evalyn McLean.

Florence did not adapt as readily to the social and political world of the capital as did her husband. There were many who snubbed her; she kept a list of them in a little red book, which she later referred to with grim satisfaction when she became the First Lady.

Daugherty's suggestion, in 1919, that Harding was ready for the Presidency, was met with reluctance on the part of Florence and Warren both. Harding was happy where he was, and Florence thought the Presidency might kill her husband, who had suffered through the years from intermittent illness. Daugherty, however, was a persevering salesman, and he did at last persuade them; Florence became an enthusiastic partner in his plan. She worked assiduously alongside Daugherty, and her husband's overwhelming victory in November of 1920 was proof enough that she had always been right about this handsome but superficial man she had married and carefully groomed, sometimes against his will.

The outgoing First Lady, Edith Wilson, did not consider Florence Harding an ideal successor. The sophisticated and self-possessed Mrs. Wilson looked with some distaste upon Mrs. Harding's rouged cheeks and stiffly marcelled hair, nor did she approve of the new First Lady's nervous, strident way of talking. But the

271

people loved Florence; she told them that she and the President were "plain folks," and the common man everywhere believed and shouted her praise.

During the war, and Wilson's long illness, the White House had been closed to the public. Florence opened the doors and invited everyone in. It was the people's house, she said, and they were welcome to visit there. Sometimes, with Ohio heartiness, she would come running down from the second floor to greet the tourists, who were delighted to find the First Lady as down-to-earth as they were.

Harding entertainment was continuous, if not always lavish. There was never a night without company of some kind; it seemed almost as if the Hardings could not bear to be alone with each other. As protocol demanded, they hosted state dinners and receptions; Florence became famous for her garden parties and for her willingness to meet anyone who took the trouble to come to see her. One society reporter wrote that Florence "has literally shaken hands with tens of thousands of persons, in a steady streaming line through the White House gates. . . . No President's wife in the memory of the Capital has displayed such endurance." On a more intimate level, there were the President's poker parties with his cronies; Prohibition or no, the President and his pals had an ample supply of good liquor, and the "Duchess" was permitted to mix and serve the drinks.

Despite the constant entertaining, Harding found time to dally with a young lady he had been seeing for several years. She was occasionally brought in secret to his White House office; Florence once almost discovered them in a flagrant circumstance, but the President's watchful aides hurried the young lady out a side door. After that, relations between the President and his First Lady degenerated to bitterness and bickering, sometimes within hearing of the household staff.

To make up in some measure for the lack of affection at her own hearth, Florence spent many hours in veterans' hospitals. Often ailing, ankles swollen, she tramped from one bed to another, bringing a friendly word and a cheerful smile to former soldiers who would never walk or see again. They loved her, as she was, with her rouged cheeks, marcelled hair, rimless glasses, and voice too shrill.

In September of 1922, White House entertainment came to an abrupt halt when Florence suddenly developed a serious occurrence of her old kidney trouble. With only one kidney, her survival seemed uncertain, but she passed through a critical period, and slowly began to mend.

There were other problems for her and Harding—scandal and corruption. Too many of his Ohio cronies were on the take, in large and greedy quantities. What would later be the notorious Teapot Dome investigation was already brewing; some of Harding's appointees committed suicide and others conveniently fled to Europe.

It is almost inconceivable that Harding knew nothing about all this graft, but he did not, nor did Florence. When he first began to hear about it, in 1923, he was angry, and frantic. Something had to be done to restore the confidence of the country and to revive his flagging image. With Florence accompanying him, he went on a far western trip. But he was exhausted from a bout of influenza he'd had in Washington; he developed pneumonia on the way from Alaska to California, and he was put to bed in San Francisco, a very sick man. Florence was with him constantly.

On August 2, 1923, while Florence was reading to him, Warren Harding died of a blood clot on the brain. He was fifty-seven. Because Florence would not permit an autopsy, rumors flew across the country that he had been poisoned, perhaps by her in revenge for his infidelities. Florence paid no attention to the wild talk. Though she herself was not well, she faced the squalid aftermath of Harding's death with a quiet strength and determination. When she returned to the White House with his body, one of the maids commented, "She has turned to ice." The description was accurate, but not justified.

Warren Harding was buried in the local cemetery in Marion, Ohio. Friends and interested citizens started a fund for a huge

Harding memorial. It was to be almost eight years before the memorial would be completed and dedicated.

Florence returned to Marion, but she had little time to enjoy her retirement as a former First Lady. Her one remaining kidney could not function well enough to keep her alive, and she herself died at the age of sixty-four, on November 21, 1924, a year and three months after the death of her husband. Her body was escorted to the cemetery by an honor guard of twenty-three, augmented by a hundred additional soldiers. When she was laid to rest in the gray vault next to her husband, the Columbus Republican Glee Club of forty male voices sang her favorite song, "The End of a Perfect Day." Florence and Warren Harding lay side by side, sharing an intimacy they had never known in life.

Grace Coolidge
1879–1957

On a sweltering night in August, 1923, Calvin Coolidge, Vice President of the United States, walked to the crossroads general store in Plymouth Notch, Vermont. With him were a local reporter and a congressman. "Hot night," the Vice President remarked, and the three men ordered a Moxie, a popular New England soft drink. Coolidge drained his glass; deliberately, without a further word, he opened an old-fashioned purse with a snap clasp, took out a five cent piece, placed it on the counter, returned up the dirt road to his father's farm, and went to sleep. Five and one-half hours later, Calvin Coolidge became the thirtieth President of the United States.

There were no telephones at the Coolidge homestead, nor was there electricity. When word of Harding's death was flashed across the country, a messenger had to be dispatched to the Coolidge farm to awaken the Vice President. Upon hearing the news, Coolidge carefully dressed in a black suit, while his father, Colonel John Coolidge, shaved in the kitchen and put on a fresh collar and tie. They gathered in the sitting room, and there, with a kerosene lamp for illumination, Colonel John Coolidge, a notary public, administered the presidential oath of office to his son while an ashen-faced Grace Coolidge and a half dozen others solemnly looked on at a moment unique in American history. At 2:47 A.M., August 3, 1923, the brief ceremony was over, and the new President climbed upstairs and went back to bed.

By nature and character, Silent Cal presented a startling contrast to the jovial Harding. To a country in the midst of a booming prosperity, Coolidge's Yankee taciturnity and Vermont twang were joyous material for good-natured jesting. No one cared that he spoke but rarely. The twenties were roaring along on all eight cylinders; the stock market was heading for the skies; there was money to throw away; and the lovable Will Rogers kidded every politician in sight, including the laconic President himself.

Calvin Coolidge, elected to a full term in 1924, was a man neutral in appearance, personality, and accomplishment. There is little to say about his administration; he was neither a bad President nor a good one. His First Lady, Grace Goodhue Coolidge, was a perfect example of the ancient truism that "opposites attract," for she was a lively and attractive woman. As charming as her husband was colorless, she brought a gentle warmth to the raucous twenties.

Evidence indicates that presidential couples normally meet in an orthodox and ordinary way. But the first glimpse that Grace Goodhue ever had of the man who was to be her husband must rank among the more baroque of presidential introductions. The historic incident took place in Northampton, Massachusetts, in 1903.

Grace, who was then twenty-four, was watering the flowers outside the school where she worked as a teacher. She looked up at a house across the way and saw a man shaving at an open window.

Grace tried not to stare, but the sight of him was ludicrous, for he was standing in his union suit, and he wore a hat. She burst into laughter; he turned, saw Grace looking up, wide-eyed, and calmly went back to his shaving, hat still on his head. When he was later introduced to her, Calvin Coolidge carefully explained that he had an unruly lock of hair that would only stay put with a hat jammed over his head. The explanation was completely logical and free of guile, as was Coolidge himself.

Northampton was Coolidge's adopted home; Grace intended to live there on a temporary basis only. They were both born in Vermont, Calvin in the hamlet of Plymouth Notch, and Grace in the city of Burlington, on Lake Champlain. Coolidge had moved to Northampton in 1895, after his graduation from Amherst College, a few miles away. A classmate had gotten him a clerking job in the law firm of Hammond and Field; in 1897 Coolidge was admitted to the Massachusetts bar, and by the time he met Grace he had his own law office on Main Street.

An only child, Grace was born on January 3, 1879 (she was six years younger than Coolidge, who had been born on July 4, 1872). Both of Grace's parents came of old New England families. Her mother, the former Lemira Barrett, originally lived in Nashua, New Hampshire; she moved to Burlington, where she met and married Andrew Issachar Goodhue, a steamboat inspector for the Champlain Transportation Company.

Grace's childhood was uneventful, except for some trouble with her spine; a regimen of vigorous exercising strengthened her back so that as an adult she experienced no sign of her early weakness. She started her schooling at the age of five, in a small brick schoolhouse where lessons were conducted by Miss Cornelia C. Underwood. From there, Grace went to Burlington High School. She graduated in 1897, when she was eighteen.

College was delayed for a year by poor health. In 1898, when she was nineteen, Grace enrolled at the University of Vermont. An average student academically, and far more active socially, she joined the Glee Club, performed in college plays, and helped to found the Vermont chapter of the Pi Beta Phi Fraternity (there were no sororities then). A friendly, cheerful girl, Grace had dark hair, a round face that came to a slight point, and beautifully expressive gray-green eyes. At five feet four, she was a remarkably pretty young lady.

When she graduated in 1902, "an amiable student who fell into her class work and associations very easily," Grace went from Burlington to Northampton to teach at the Clarke Institute for the Deaf. She herself learned lip reading and taught the technique to her pupils. Her three years at the Clarke Institute sparked a lifelong interest in deaf children.

The romance that developed between Grace Goodhue and Calvin Coolidge was as slow and deliberate as his speech and behavior. To mutual friends, they seemed an unlikely couple, for Grace was a "creature of spirit, fire, and dew," who loved to skim across the ice of a pond or glide across a dance floor. Calvin did neither. He totally lacked a sense of rhythm, and he was no better at skating than waltzing.

Grace's mother did not approve of Calvin; nor was Mr. Goodhue overly pleased. He did not, however, raise serious objections. The matter was settled in the summer of 1905, when Coolidge proposed to Grace with these words: "I am going to be married to you." After two years of his constant attention, Grace was not surprised, although perhaps she had hoped for a more romantic approach.

The wedding took place on October 4, 1905, in the home of Grace's parents in Burlington. There were fifteen guests, including both families. After a simple ceremony, the nervous and white-faced groom took his bride to Montreal for a two weeks' honeymoon that was cut down to one when Calvin decided they'd had enough of the sights.

For a few months after their return from Canada, they rented a small furnished house in Northampton; in 1906, they moved into half of a two-family house on Massasoit Street. They were to live in this modest dwelling for many years, even during his Presidency.

Grace had two sons, both of whom were born in Northampton—John, on September 7, 1906, and not quite two years later, Calvin, Jr., on April 13, 1908. Coolidge by then had run for a number of minor offices, winning most of them, and suffering one defeat. He lived by the slogan "Press On," which he believed "will always solve the problems of the human race." He pressed on so well, he was elected to the Massachusetts House of Representatives in 1907; in 1910 he was elected mayor of Northampton; in 1912 to the Massachusetts Senate; and in 1914, his fellow senators selected him as their president.

For Grace and Calvin, both, 1915 was a noteworthy year. Grace had always interested herself in community affairs, in spite of a busy schedule at home. Thrifty Vermonters, the Coolidges lived within his $2,000 income; they used a party telephone, and Grace did her own cooking, cleaning, and laundry. She loved music, and went to the local opera house as often as her budget would permit. She continued her work with the Pi Beta Phi, the fraternity she had joined in 1898. In the summer of 1915, she traveled to Berkeley, California, for the fraternity's annual convention; she was elected national president. While she was still in California, she received a telegram from her husband telling her he had decided to run for lieutenant-governor of Massachusetts. She took the first train back to help him in his campaign.

Coolidge's decision to enter a statewide election was stimulated and encouraged by two men who were to play decisive roles in his future career: Dwight W. Morrow, an influential lawyer and banker, and Frank W. Stearns, a wealthy Boston merchant. They steered him, successfully, to the lieutenant-governorship of Massachusetts, and then, in 1918, to the governorship itself.

At Coolidge's gubernatorial Inaugural Ball in Boston on January 2, 1919, Stearns commented that one of Coolidge's "greatest assets is Mrs. Coolidge. She will make friends wherever she goes, and she will not meddle with his conduct of the office." Stearns was correct on all counts. Grace did not interfere with her husband's political work; she was interested, but the decisions were his. She had been raised a Democrat; with her husband a dedicated Republican, she switched her allegiance and followed Calvin's lead in political matters.

Coolidge's elevation to the governorship did not alter his thrifty ways. As lieutenant-governor, he had rented a room in Boston's Adams House, where he lived during the week; on weekends he traveled back to Northampton by coach. As governor, he rented *two* rooms at the Adams House; Grace stayed with him in Boston, while the boys in Northampton were looked after by a housekeeper. (Massachusetts, at that time, had no governor's mansion.)

An event in September of 1919 suddenly catapulted the governor into national prominence. The Boston police, agitating for the right to join a union, went on strike. With no police force to maintain law and order, Boston mobs raged through the streets, destroying and looting. On the third day, Governor Coolidge ordered out the state militia and the strike was broken. To defiant labor leaders, Coolidge wired these angry words: "There is no right to strike against the public safety by anybody anytime anywhere." For a brief instant, Silent Cal had become vociferous, and a grateful public sang his praises. His status as a hero continued into 1920, when he received the Republican nomination for Vice President by acclaim.

As Frank Stearns had predicted, Grace was indeed one of her husband's greatest assets. Washington society, traditionally reserved towards newcomers, needed little urging to adopt her as one of its own. (Vice President Coolidge presented a problem—it was said that every time he opened his mouth, a moth flew out. Within a short time, his reticence assumed the proportions of a legend. Grace was fond of relating the story of a well-known Washington hostess who had invited the Coolidges to dinner. The woman said to the Vice President: "You must talk to me, Mr. Coolidge. I made a bet today that I could get more than two words out of you." Calvin answered: "You lose.")

Grace Coolidge began her years as mistress of the White House with some trepidation, but she need not have been concerned; the press was unanimous in praise of her. To some, she was a match for Dolley Madison in "charm and tact." Others found her "quick at repartee and full of fun," while her passion for baseball and her amazing knowledge of the game endeared her to men everywhere. Women admired her taste in clothes; Calvin had one extravagance—he insisted that she be beautifully gowned.

White House entertainment, under Grace's supervision, had a leisurely Coolidge quality rather than the calculated heartiness of her predecessor. Because of her fondness for music, Grace preferred musicales for her guests after state dinners. Particularly enjoyable were her afternoon teas, for they were informal and completely charming. The Coolidges held a number of official receptions; among their early guests were renowned generals of World War I, the Marshals Foch and Joffre, and the American General, John J. "Black Jack" Pershing. Royalty, too, were treated to the special brand of Grace's hospitality. Queen Marie of Rumania, her son Prince Nicholas, and her daughter, Princess Ileana, were entertained in 1926. The Queen's costume was dazzling, but one report insisted that Grace "looked as regal as her guest in a gown of heavy cream satin with a square neckline, brocaded with velvet nosegays."

The President, meanwhile, maintained his record of thriftiness. He instituted strict economy for the White House staff. As for the press, he would not permit them to interview his wife. At a luncheon for newspaperwomen, Grace was asked by one of them to make a speech. She lifted her expressive hands, and without uttering a sound, gave a five minute speech in sign language.

Eleven months after they entered the White House, Grace and Calvin Coolidge were subjected to the most personal of tragedies, the death of a son. After a game of tennis played in sneakers without socks, Calvin, Jr., sixteen, developed a blister on his right toe. He dabbed some iodine on the blister and thought no more of it; without warning, an infection spread through his foot and septicemia raced into his bloodstream. Four days later he slipped into a coma. In the words of his father, "Suddenly his body seemed to relax and he murmured, 'We surrender.'" The boy died on July 7, 1924. The following month, Grace wrote to a friend of her emotions at her son's funeral in Plymouth Notch, Vermont: "'Taps' never sounded as it did there, echoing and re-echoing from mountain to mountain. I came away filled with a 'peace which passeth understanding,' comforted and full of courage."

Coolidge's overwhelming election to a full term in November of 1924 demonstrated the affection of the voters for their impassive President and their aversion to change. They preferred to "Keep Cool with Coolidge," while they joyfully climbed aboard the booming bandwagon of prosperity. For Grace, Calvin's victory meant at least four more years as First Lady; she prepared for her responsibilities with a mixture of pride and sorrow. The tragic passing of her son was still too vivid, and she renewed her entertaining on a gradual scale.

Grace's love of the theater and music dictated the composition of many White House receptions and informal parties. Her guests ranged from Sergei Rachmaninoff, Madame Jeritza, and John McCormack, to Al Jolson, Charlotte Greenwood, and Will Rogers.

The Coolidge years moved on, uneventfully. Grace crocheted a coverlet for the famed Lincoln bed. She was painted by Howard Chandler Christy; his portrait of her in a red gown with a white collie at her side became a White House classic. In 1927, the presidential family was forced to take temporary quarters while the roof of the ancient Executive Mansion was raised, restored, refreshed, and strengthened, with a new third floor added. In that same year, Grace and Calvin honored youthful Charles Lindbergh for his daring solo flight across the Atlantic.

In August of 1927, Coolidge stunned the entire nation with a twelve-word message, "I do not choose to run for President in nineteen twenty-eight." Grace had had no advance warning; Coolidge never discussed important political matters with her.

With Herbert Hoover's Inauguration on March 4, 1929, the Coolidges were private citizens once again. They returned to their small two-family house in Northampton to pick up the threads of the quiet life they had once enjoyed. But a former President and a former First Lady do not belong exclusively to themselves; the small house was too exposed, and they moved, in 1930, to a large house on eight acres of land, surrounded by majestic old trees. They had their privacy at last.

For Calvin Coolidge, retirement was all too short. He died on January 5, 1933, of a coronary thrombosis. Death came quickly and peacefully, in his own home, at the age of sixty. He was buried in the tiny cemetery at Plymouth Notch, Vermont, next to his son Calvin.

The years that Grace lived without her husband were far from empty. Her son John had married in 1929; in 1933, ten months after Coolidge died, Grace's first grandchild was born. And Grace's abiding interest in baseball was joined by a regained passion—reading. But it was her unsparing work with the deaf that characterized her final years.

Grace never forgot the all too brief time she had spent at the Clarke Institute in Northampton. As First Lady, she helped to raise $2 million for the Clarke school, and she lived to see the institute grow to a magnificent educational establishment of seventeen buildings. Some of those who worked with her in the 1940s and 1950s were Helen Keller, Christian Herter, Leverett Saltonstall, and Spencer Tracy.

Walking was always a necessary recreation for Grace. In Washington, she had been a familiar figure striding through the streets with her white collie, Rob Roy, trotting along beside her. She often walked as much as five or six miles a day, even in her later years. But her heart began to trouble her; by 1952, when she was seventy-three, she had to stay close to home and rest as frequently as possible. For the next five years she faded. Grace died on July 8, 1957, at the age of seventy-eight. She was buried in the Plymouth Notch Cemetery, next to her husband and son.

Grace Goodhue Coolidge left a will containing exactly seventy-eight words. In it she asked that the homestead where Calvin Coolidge had been born and where he had taken the presidential oath be given to the State of Vermont. President Eisenhower spoke of her in his commemorative message:

> In setting aside this memorial Mrs. Coolidge might well have used her husband's own words: "Women seek out the birthplace and build their shrines not where a great life has its ending but where it had its beginning. . . . Life may depart, but the source of life is constant."

Lou Hoover
1875–1944

Apostles of sloganeering were in full cry during the presidential election campaign of 1928. The Republicans found a dandy to replace "Keep Cool with Coolidge." They promised the "proverbial 'chicken in every pot,' and a car in every back yard, to boot." Their solemn, moon-faced candidate, Herbert Hoover of California, assured the voters that the "poorhouse is vanishing from among us." The Democrats, countering with the Happy Warrior, Al Smith of New York, gleefully suggested at every opportunity, "Let's look at the record," their candidate's own words. But another rallying cry, an insidious hiss of intolerance, invaded the arena. "Rum and Romanism" was shouted by the drys and whispered by the Fundamentalists, for Al Smith was a man who drank and admitted it, and he was a Catholic.

Responsible Republicans and Herbert Hoover himself denounced the religious issue. But for Al Smith, the cigar-chewing, brownderbied Politician Compleat, the time was too soon. Protestant America was not ready for him. Herbert Hoover became the thirty-first President by a huge total of 21,437,227 votes to Al Smith's 15,007,698. In the electoral count, the margin was even more one-sided—444 for Hoover and 87 for Smith.

Herbert Hoover had never before held an elective office. A top-grade mining engineer who had leaped from poverty to wealth when he was still a young man, he had administered Woodrow Wilson's program of War Relief for the starving peoples of Europe; in 1927, Coolidge sent him to the flood-ravaged Midwest, where he pulled an entire section of the country out of misery and probable disaster. Hoover became, overnight, a living legend.

But the Great Engineer was better at mining than leading. The vaunted "chicken in every pot" flew away in the calamitous stock-market crash of October, 1929, and Hoover was soon guaranteeing the hungry millions that "prosperity was just around the corner." His new prophecies were no better than his old; the country and the world slipped into the worst financial depression of the modern era.

Like Al Smith, Herbert Hoover happened at the wrong time. The towering issues of the early thirties were beyond his faltering vision; he left us only his name for the Depression-born settlements of the homeless, the hungry, and poor—Hoovervilles. His First Lady has been relegated to a minor role along with him. An accomplished linguist, Lou Hoover was a highly educated, sophisticated woman who had seen much of the world. But her extensive travels gave her a surface comprehension only.

For Lou Hoover, as for her husband, it was enough to apply a poultice to the external sores and pronounce the patient cured. The Hoover inability to understand the terrifying depth of the crisis was the core of their failure.

In 1884, Charles Delano Henry, a successful banker in Water-loo, Iowa, moved his family to California. He had long been concerned about his wife; it was thought that she had consumption. With a warm, dry climate the approved therapy, he settled with her and their two daughters in the recently established Quaker town of Whittier. His wife's health improved, and it was discovered, fortunately, that she had a bronchial ailment rather than consumption. The clean, temperate air of Southern California did wonders for her.

Lou, the older of the Henry daughters, was born in Waterloo, Iowa, on March 29, 1874. She was introduced, at an early age, to outdoor living; Mr. Henry taught her to ride, hunt, and enjoy the miracles of nature. She learned how to recognize and appreciate wild creatures—animals, birds, insects, reptiles. She and her father studied wood craft together, and elementary geology.

Mrs. Henry, the former Florence Weed of Wooster, Ohio, saw to it that the gentler arts were not neglected. Sewing, music, and art were included in Lou's education. Lou attended public schools, in Waterloo and later in Whittier. She was exposed to Quaker philosophy in Whittier and often went to meetings of the Society of Friends. The Quaker belief, "There is that of God in every man," gradually became hers as well, and later motivated many of her attitudes.

When Lou was sixteen, in 1890, the family moved once again, this time a few hundred miles north to Monterey. Mr. Henry had been invited to open a bank in this ancient town settled by the Spanish almost three hundred years before. Lou finished high school in Monterey, and entered the San Jose Normal School to train for a teaching career. During the summer of 1894, she attended a lecture that altered her life.

Professor John Casper Branner, head of the Department of Geology and Mines at the newly organized Leland Stanford University, came to Pacific Grove, not far from Monterey, to speak on "The Bones of the Earth." The professor's words rekindled her interest in geology; with his help and her family's consent, she entered Stanford in the fall of 1894, and selected geology as her major. She was the only girl in the class. Aside from her academic uniqueness, fellow geologists found much about her to admire. She was a tall, lithe young lady, with clear blue eyes and a mass of brown hair that she coiled about her head "fillet fashion." Her

287

slightly irregular features gave an impression of friendly attractiveness rather than sheer beauty.

One afternoon, in Dr. Branner's laboratory, Lou and the professor were discussing the origin of a certain rock. A tall, round-faced young man walked in; Professor Branner asked him whether their specimen was carboniferous, or precarboniferous, as Miss Henry suggested. The young man, Herbert Hoover, was too shy and awkward to venture an opinion, but he did show an interest in the girl.

A sober chap of twenty, Herbert was a senior and ready to graduate. Lou, at nineteen, was only a freshman. They saw a great deal of each other during the next few months, and when he left Stanford the following June, they had reached an informal understanding.

When Lou graduated from Stanford in 1898, Bert was working in the desert interior of Australia, at Kalgoorlie. He received an offer from the young Chinese Emperor Kwang-hsü to be his mining consultant. Bert immediately cabled to Lou in Monterey. Would she marry him and live in China? The answer, which came back at once, was one word, "Yes."

After a five-week journey, Bert arrived in Monterey on January 31, 1899, and married Lou ten days later, on February 10, at the home of her parents. He was twenty-four and she was twenty-three. Since Bert was a lifelong member of the Society of Friends, Lou was determined to marry in his faith, but there was no Quaker meeting in Monterey. A suitable compromise was reached with a civil ceremony conducted by the Monterey padre, Father Ramon Mestres, who married them by taking advantage of a special dispensation. The newlyweds sailed for China the following day.

For the next nine years, Lou Hoover followed her husband to every continent except South America. They traveled on ocean liners, tramp steamers, on horses, camels, by elephant back. In Hoover's own words, "There were diverting and educational contacts with leaders of men, heads of governments . . . with snobs and crooks . . . with plain, good people [and] human boll weevils. There was good food and bad food, there were good beds, bad beds, bugs, mosquitoes, dust, sand and malaria."

Lou and Herbert Hoover arrived in China in March of 1899. They moved into the foreign settlement of Tientsin, a large seaport about fifty miles south of Peking, home of the young Emperor and site of the fabled Forbidden City and Imperial Palace. Hoover had been hired by Kwang-hsü as director of the Emperor's new Department of Mines and Railways.

Hoover's work in developing China's mineral resources took him into distant sectors of the Empire. He went to Manchuria and Mongolia, to the provinces of Chihli, Shantung, and Shansi. Lou often went with him, enduring the same hardships. An apt pupil, she learned to speak and read the complicated Chinese language.

In June of 1900, China exploded. The Boxer Rebellion, guided by the dowager Empress Tzu Hsi, an outspoken foe of Occidental influence, seized control of Peking; terrorists turned against the aliens. The foreign settlement of Tientsin, where the Hoovers lived, was put under siege; for three weeks, the settlement was subjected to heavy shelling and attack. The siege was lifted and the terrorists driven off by an Allied force composed of English, American, Japanese, German, Russian, and French troops. With the change of regime, Lou and Herbert Hoover left China and moved to England.

London became a home base for the Hoovers. Herbert was made a junior partner in the British mining firm of Bewick, Moreing & Co. On their behalf and later as a free-lance mining consultant, Hoover began a series of travels that took him back and forth and around the world many times. When she could, Lou went with him, undaunted even by the birth of two sons. On August 4, 1903, Herbert, Jr., was born in London. At the age of five weeks, he was bundled into a basket and went along with his parents and nurse to Australia. By the time he was four, he had been around the world three times. Allan Henry was born in London, July 17, 1907. Lou, thirty-two at Allan's birth, had no more children.

Lou and Bert, in their spare moments, began an English translation of Agricola's *De Re Metallica.* (Agricola was actually a

German named George Bauer who lived in Saxony in the sixteenth century.) As Hoover described it, the folio, published in Latin in 1556, was "the first important attempt to assemble systematically in print the world-knowledge on mining, metallurgy, and industrial chemistry." The translation would not have been possible without Lou's extensive knowledge of Latin and her working knowledge of French and German. The work was finally completed in 1912 and privately published in an edition of three thousand copies, printed in white vellum with illuminated pages much like the original. Many of the copies were presented to engineers and mining institutions. Stanford University honored both Hoovers for their translation.

The outbreak of World War I and subsequent blockade of Belgium by the British Navy brought near starvation to the Belgians. Hoover volunteered his services for their relief, and Lou traveled throughout the United States raising money and food for them. By this time, the Hoovers were dividing their time between London and Palo Alto, with a home in each city. (In 1919, King Albert of Belgium conferred upon Lou, with deep and humble gratitude for her efforts on behalf of his people, the Cross of Chevalier, Order of Leopold.) With the entry of the United States into the war in April of 1917, the Hoovers moved to Washington when Bert was appointed National Food Administrator. Lou campaigned actively for food conservation, and found time to join Washington's Girl Scout Troop VIII as its scout leader.

For millions, Armistice Day in November of 1918 meant a return to old ways; for Lou and Bert it meant two more years of separation and working for others. President Wilson asked Hoover to go to Europe as administrator of American relief funds. He left New York on November 17, 1918, and Lou went to Palo Alto with their two sons. In California, she began sketching and planning the new home they had waited years to build. The house, part Moroccan, part Hopi Indian, was a large stucco building with three levels of terraces. Overlooking the Stanford campus, on Palo Alto's San Juan Hill, it was to be their "permanent" home. But just at the time of completion, Lou and Bert moved again. They returned to Washington in March of 1921, when newly inaugurated President Harding asked Hoover to join his Cabinet as Secretary of Commerce.

The Hoover house on Washington's S Street was never empty; as Lou explained to a friend, "I never entertain—I just ask people to come in and see us and we enjoy each other." People did drop in, often. They came from all parts of the world, for the Hoovers had made friends wherever they had lived and visited. Lou continued her work with the Girl Scouts; in January of 1922, she was elected their national president. In April of 1923, she became vice president of the National Amateur Athletic Association. She was its only woman officer. And a month later she received an honorary Master of Arts degree from Mills College in Oakland, California.

Hoover stayed on as Secretary of Commerce at President Coolidge's request. When Coolidge stunned the country in August, 1927, with his terse announcement, "I do not choose to run," the immediate favorite for his replacement was Herbert Hoover. And Lou Hoover was looked upon as the First Lady personified. In a *Woman's Home Companion* article in April of 1928, the author said this about her:

> As a woman of the world, as an experienced observer of statesmen and statesmanship, above all as a wife, Mrs. Hoover is the ideal future mistress of what she herself describes as the most beautiful as well as the most honored home in the world.

The Inauguration of Herbert Hoover on March 4, 1929, brought more than a new President and First Lady to the White House. Many changes were instituted in the mansion itself, to the annoyance of the staff. The Hoovers did not approve of the living arrangements, nor the furniture, most of which they considered "dreary." They filled many of the rooms with their own furniture, and renovated a number of the rooms to suit their preferences. The West Sitting Room, on the second floor, became the Palm Room; Lou filled it with palms, trailing vines, other tropical plants, and many birds. In the words of one of the maids, it was a "kind of indoor-outdoor paradise."

In making these changes, the President and the First Lady were not concerned about money. If their official appropriations were not sufficient, Hoover gladly paid any excess out of his private funds. A favorite project for Lou, one that occupied her for some time, was rehabilitation of the Red Drawing Room in its original style. She had it redone exactly as it had been during the administration of James Monroe, even to the duplication of the expensive and elegant Monroe furniture (she found the description in old records). Hoover paid the entire cost of the restoration.

Under Lou's supervision, White House entertainment was informal and frequent. The household staff often grumbled at the number of unexpected guests suddenly invited to lunch. Sometimes, in a single day, the staff had to prepare a luncheon for as many as forty guests, a tea at four-thirty, a second tea at five-thirty, and a formal dinner in the evening. To quote the head usher, "This was not the exception, but the rule." Among others, the Hoovers entertained three European prime ministers, Ramsay MacDonald of Great Britain, Pierre Laval of France, and Dino Grandi of Italy; an absolute monarch and his wife, King Prajadhipok of Siam and Queen Rambai Barni; and the ruler of Hollywood, Louis B. Mayer.

Christmas of 1930 became, for the Hoovers, a memorable night. It was their first Christmas with their three grandchildren. Herbert, Jr., suffering from tuberculosis, had been sent to Asheville, North Carolina, to recuperate. His wife, Margaret, and their children, Peggy Ann, Herbert III, and Joan, came to live at the White House until he was able to rejoin them. On Christmas Eve, after a dinner for fifty people at a horseshoe table decorated with bells and candlesticks, the President and four-year-old Peggy Ann led the company through darkened parlors, with the ladies ringing the bells and the men carrying lighted candles. The procession ended on the second floor, where a surprise awaited them—a motion picture.

The onset of the Depression following the collapse of the stock market in October, 1929, found Hoover working day and night to resolve crises as they arose; he stayed at his desk until all hours, and he refused to take vacations. (From Lou's designs, Hoover had a rustic summer retreat built on the upper Rapidan River, near Cotoctin Furnace, Maryland, where he and Lou and members of his staff came for an occasional weekend and a few moments of blessed relaxation. Hoover later donated the entire encampment to the Shenandoah National Park.) Hoover's efforts to stem the onrushing tide of unemployment and nationwide financial disaster brought no results. In the election of 1932, Franklin Delano Roosevelt defeated him by a convincing margin. Lou was stunned at the enormity of her husband's loss.

Retirement from the White House meant more traveling for the peripatetic Hoovers. During the 1930s, they journeyed back and forth across the country between their home in Palo Alto and their suite in New York's Waldorf Towers. Lou kept busy with the Girl Scouts, and with various community projects. One of her home towns, Whittier, California, named the Lou Henry Hoover School in her honor.

Outbreak of World War II in September of 1939 again found both Hoovers generously giving their time, efforts, and money to victims of aggression. Lou worked closely with the Salvation Army, gathering clothes for a million war refugees. In October of 1940, she responded to a personal appeal directed to her by Queen Elizabeth of England requesting clothes for London's Generosity Warehouse. With Lou's help, schoolchildren all over the country sent clothing for the warehouse.

By the end of 1942, weariness set in, and Lou was aware, for the first time, that she too could suffer fatigue and would have to slow down. In 1943 she went back to Palo Alto to see little Lou Henry, her sixth and newest grandchild (Allan's daughter). When she returned to New York, she seemed as tired as ever, and her doctor restricted her activity. On January 7, 1944, in her suite at the Waldorf Towers, she suffered a heart attack and died within minutes. She was sixty-nine.

Two days later, a thousand people attended her funeral services at New York's St. Bartholomew's Church. Although she had embraced most of her husband's Quaker principles, she had remained an Episcopalian. The church choir sang her favorite hymn, "Nearer, My God, to Thee." Her body was taken to Palo Alto and buried there, on January 14, in the Alta Mesa Cemetery.

Herbert Hoover survived her by twenty years. He died in New York on October 20, 1964, at the age of ninety. He was buried in West Branch, Iowa, where he had been born. Lou Hoover's remains were moved from Palo Alto and reinterred in West Branch next to her husband.

A tribute to Lou Henry Hoover by an old friend, Ray Lyman Wilbur, chancellor of Stanford University, perhaps best exemplified the feelings of those who knew her:

> The place where the Hoover family lived, whether in California or China or the White House, was never a house or a mansion. It was, because of Mrs. Hoover, a home.

Eleanor Roosevelt
1884–1962

The American economy, in 1929, was a top-heavy mélange of concentrated wealth and paper profits precariously balanced over a rotting foundation of low wages and steadily decreasing farm income. Only the chronic pessimist saw danger; pundits of prosperity expansively basked in the dizzy euphoria of a spiraling stock market. A leading economist of the day announced on October 17, 1929, that the market had reached "a permanent high plateau." One week later, Black Thursday, the crash began, and stocks that had been as high as 549 plummeted to the bottom. The Great Panic was on.

By 1932, thirteen million people, 10 percent of the country's total population, were unemployed. President Hoover, with more desperation than foresight, stubbornly clung to the Republican principle of laissez faire, hands off, with one exception. "The sole function of government," he said, "is to bring about a condition of affairs favorable to the beneficial development of private enterprise." In line with this reasoning, he firmly opposed the "dole" as a socialist device.

The hungry and the poor were not to be appeased by aphorisms of the past. Revolution was in the air, and Hoover was not aware of it. The system of private enterprise he zealously supported was in danger of collapse; in 1931 alone, twenty-three hundred banks closed their doors. Factories from one end of the land to the other had shut down; breadlines and soup kitchens had replaced pay lines and lunch pails. Drastic, decisive, and bold moves were needed. As if in answer, the broadly smiling face of Democrat Franklin Delano Roosevelt was offered to the discouraged millions as an antidote to the frozen features of Herbert Hoover. The millions preferred Roosevelt; in the election of November, 1932, they made him their thirty-second President by a decisive total of 22,821,857 votes to 15,761,845 for Hoover.

FDR did not disappoint the masses who had supported him. If he did not exactly make good on the airy musical promise that "Happy Days Are Here Again," he at least averted the threat of revolution. He immediately declared a bank holiday; he created multiple initial agencies designed to give work and respectability to degraded millions of unemployed and to save the free enterprise system that Hoover almost threw away. Despite those disgruntled rich who despised his methods of saving them, Roosevelt was overwhelmingly elected three more times. He was the only man ever to be chosen for a third and fourth term.

Eleanor Roosevelt brought her own brand of greatness to the White House. She was not simply mistress of the Executive Mansion; she was the President's wife, yet far more. She gave a dimension to her role that no First Lady before her or since has equaled. She was as much a part of Roosevelt's New Deal as FDR himself. Humanitarian and reformer, she belonged not to herself but to those she served.

Nicholas, son of Martin of the Rose Field, or, as he called himself in Dutch, Claes Martenszen van Rosenvelt, arrived in the New

World in the mid-1640s. He and his bride, Jannetje, settled in Nieuw Amsterdam, and there had five children. Nieuw Amsterdam became New York, and their one surviving son, young Claes, became Nicholas Roosevelt.

Nicholas married at the age of twenty-four. Two of his sons established the principal Roosevelt families: Johannes, the Oyster Bay branch leading directly to Theodore and his niece Eleanor; and Jacobus, the Hyde Park branch leading to Franklin Delano. When Eleanor and Franklin met, they had the same last names, but their relationship was distant, indeed. They were sixth cousins, or, as certain Roosevelt biographers prefer, fifth cousins once removed. They were both born to great wealth and solid, socially entrenched families. Their lineage and credentials were impeccable.

Eleanor was twenty months younger than Franklin. She was born in New York on October 11, 1884. Her father was Elliott Roosevelt, Theodore's younger brother. Her mother, Anna Livingston Hall, she remembers as "one of the most beautiful women I have ever seen." Eleanor had two brothers, one of whom died of scarlet fever in 1893. She was never a beautiful child, much to the disappointment of her mother, who sometimes referred to her, with apparent reproval, as "Granny." But to her father, the "shy, solemn child" was an angel who could do no wrong. Between the "ugly duckling," as she called herself, and her charming, light-hearted father, there was affection and love that she never found with her mother. "Somehow," Eleanor said, "it was always he and I."

But Elliott Roosevelt had a dreadful affliction that brought anguish to his wife and puzzlement to his daughter: he was an alcoholic. He would absent himself from his family for months at a time attempting to cure himself in a sanatorium. These were painful absences for Eleanor.

Eleanor's mother died suddenly, of diphtheria, in December of 1892. Elliott was hurriedly summoned, but he arrived too late. Eleanor later wrote that she was almost untouched by her mother's death. "One fact," she said, "wiped out everything else"; her father was back. Again, however, they were to be separated. Her

297

mother's will directed that she and her brothers were to be left in the care of Grandmother Hall. Elliott returned to his sanatorium where he himself died not quite two years later, in August of 1894.

A great aunt had earlier discovered that Eleanor incredibly had reached the age of six without learning to read or sew, a must for well-bred young ladies. (With the help of a governess, Eleanor had learned to speak French before she could speak English.) Her lack of proper training was speedily rectified; she did not attend school, but was taught by a succession of tutors, who drilled her in the necessary subjects and music, ballet, social dancing, and embroidery. Plain and gawky she may have been, but Grandmother Hall saw to it that Eleanor had all the advantages of her position.

At fifteen, Eleanor received her first formal and serious education; she was sent to Allenswood, a girls' school outside of London. This school was selected because her aunt, Mrs. William Sheffield Cowles (President Theodore's sister), had studied with its headmistress, Mlle. Souvestre, at Les Ruches, prior to the Franco-Prussian War. Eleanor's three years with Mlle. Souvestre were the most important of her adolescence; Mlle. Souvestre, a deft and incisive teacher and sympathetic confidante, allowed her to exercise a measure of independence. Away from the ever-watchful domination of her grandmother, Eleanor alone decided how to spend her allowance, minimal as it was; she traveled to London, and once to Paris, without a chaperone or governess haunting her every step. And for the first time, she had friends of her own age.

In 1902, when Eleanor was eighteen, Grandmother Hall decided she had enough education, and Eleanor came back to New York for her debut, an event she faced with fear and misgiving. In her own eyes, Eleanor was still the ugly duckling, tall and ungainly, but she was not that unattractive; rather, she was willowy, and her face had an open, friendly charm.

During that same year she occasionally ran into cousin Franklin, a tall, thin student at Harvard. By the following year they were seeing each other frequently; he proposed in November.

Eleanor, no worldly wise sophisticate, was astounded. She recovered quickly enough, however, to say "Yes."

Sara Delano Roosevelt, Franklin's mother, interposed her will. A woman of firmness and determination, she thought Franklin, at twenty-one, far too young to marry. Although she had no quarrel with Eleanor's character, Mrs. Roosevelt wanted no one for her son; she preferred he remain dependent upon her, as he had always been. At the death of his father three years before, Franklin had come to lean upon her more than ever. In hopes he would change his mind about Eleanor, Mrs. Roosevelt took him on an extended cruise of the Caribbean; when they returned to New York, he immediately saw Eleanor again. By the autumn of 1904, a definite date was set for their marriage—St. Patrick's Day, March 17, 1905. Eleanor's uncle Theodore, President of the United States, would be in New York to review the St. Patrick's Day Parade. Since he was to give Eleanor away, the date was set for his convenience.

The wedding was held in twin town houses at East Seventy-Sixth Street that were owned by Eleanor's aunts. Seventy-five policemen were on hand to control the huge crowds who had come to see the President. The services were conducted by Dr. Endicott Peabody, headmaster of Groton School, which Franklin had attended. The marriage certificate was signed by Theodore Roosevelt and Edith Kermit Roosevelt as witnesses. The bride, who wore a gown of white satin trimmed with heirloom lace, was twenty and a half and the groom was twenty-three. Immediately after the ceremony, "for an awful moment . . . they were left entirely alone, while the crowd hovered around [President] Roosevelt, shaking him by the hand."

Because Franklin was still attending Columbia Law School, the newlyweds did not have a real honeymoon until that summer, when they went to Europe. After their return in the fall, they moved into a house that had been rented by Eleanor's mother-in-law, furnished by her, and staffed with her servants. This was the beginning of a clash of wills that was to last for many years; Eleanor was no match for the resolute and unswerving Sara. Too often she meekly permitted her mother-in-law to make necessary decisions and, in effect, to run her household. The rented house gave way to a new home Sara built for them on East Sixty-Fifth Street next to hers. With connecting doors for her convenience, the real mistress again was Sara Delano Roosevelt, who once more selected and paid for the furnishings, engaged and paid the staff. Franklin may have married, but Sara was still his "Dearest Mama."

Sara's influence extended to the summers as well, for the young Roosevelts spent their vacations at her comfortable Canadian cottage on Campobello Island in New Brunswick. Eleanor felt even more out of place at Campobello, since she had no taste for boating or swimming, and in fact, had never been athletic, as were most Roosevelts.

In the one area where Eleanor should have had the most to say, the raising of her family, she still allowed others to stand in for her. Her children were cared for by nursemaids, as she had been and Franklin had been. She later admitted that if she had done otherwise, her children "would have had far happier childhoods."

Eleanor had six children, one daughter and five sons. Her first four were born in New York: Anna, on May 3, 1906; James, December 23, 1907; Franklin, born on March 18, 1909, and died on November 8, that same year; and Elliott, born on September 23, 1910. The second Franklin, Jr., was born in Campobello on August 17, 1914, and the last child, John, was born in Washington, D.C., on March 13, 1916. (First marriages for the five surviving children were not successful; all were married at least twice, some three and four times.)

Franklin's political career at last gave Eleanor an opportunity for independence. In 1910 he was elected to the New York State senate. They moved to a rented house in Albany, and Eleanor found herself, at the age of twenty-six, mistress of her own home for the first time in her life. With the help of three servants, and nurses for the children, she succeeded in running an efficient household. She became what she had always "craved . . . to be an individual."

But Sara Roosevelt still exerted her subtle influence; Eleanor wrote to her almost every day, as she did whenever they were apart.

In 1913, President Wilson appointed Roosevelt Assistant Secretary of the Navy; once more Franklin and Eleanor moved, this time to Washington. For Eleanor, the move was more than physical. In Albany she had begun to take an interest in politics, for she felt "it was a wife's duty to be interested in whatever interested her husband." Everything about Washington spelled politics; it was inescapable, it was the heart and tempo of the city. Eleanor became a part of it, as she became a part of the endless social rounds and entertaining, though she often felt out of place.

Eleanor and Franklin remained in Washington through the war years. In 1920, Franklin was nominated by the Democratic national convention for Vice President to run with James M. Cox, But defeat of the Democratic ticket meant a return to New York for the Roosevelts.

In the summer of 1921, they were vacationing as usual in Campobello. One day in August, Roosevelt helped to fight a forest fire and afterward took a dip in the ice-cold Bay of Fundy. By evening he was not well; the next morning he ran a high temperature, and three days later, his legs were completely paralyzed. With the help of Louis Howe, a close friend of Franklin's and political associate, Eleanor rubbed her husband's legs constantly, and nursed him day and night until a specialist came up from Boston. The specialist, Dr. Robert W. Lovett, told her it was infantile paralysis, and the likelihood was that Franklin would never walk again.

Franklin was brought to New York. Sara Roosevelt, assuming her matriarchal stance, demanded that her son be taken to Hyde Park, where he must spend the rest of his life an invalid in a wheel chair, properly attended and properly coddled, as he deserved. Eleanor, as stubbornly, insisted that Franklin needed activity to stimulate his mind and his recovery. He would forever be locked in helplessness if he permitted his mother to make him a crippled Hyde Park squire. Eleanor wanted him to fight rather than surrender. It was a battle Eleanor could not afford to lose.

Under the combined attack of her daughter-in-law, their family physician, and Louis Howe, Sara Roosevelt backed down. For Eleanor it was the end of her fears, her shyness, her insecurities. She would never again suffer the domination of her mother-in-law. She had just begun to realize her potential as a woman and a human being.

For the next seven years Roosevelt learned to substitute crutches and then a cane and a friendly arm for his useless legs, locked in steel braces. He scored a tremendous personal triumph in 1924 when he painfully crossed the platform on crutches, alone, to place in nomination the name of Al Smith before the Democratic convention at Madison Square Garden. Four years later, he again placed in nomination the "Happy Warrior," this time in Houston. At Al Smith's insistence, Roosevelt himself ran for governor of New York in 1928. Despite a Republican sweep, which saw Al Smith decisively defeated, Democrat Roosevelt squeaked to victory with a bare margin of 25,000 votes. In January of 1929, the Roosevelts moved to the Governor's Mansion in Albany as the new First Family of the state.

Under the watchful tutelage of the gnomelike and dedicated Louis Howe, Eleanor slowly developed the ceaseless drive that was to characterize her later years in Washington. Howe trained her in public speaking; he taught her how to lose a high, nervous giggle. She addressed many groups, particularly of women, and became one of the "most authoritative and trustworthy spokesmen" of the Democratic party.

Her most important activity was the work she did for her husband. Eleanor traveled around the state, inspecting prisons, hospitals, state institutions. She recommended, and he listened. By the time they were ready to move into the White House in March of 1933, the phrase "Eleanor and I" was known over the entire country, and one embittered Roosevelt foe complained that the people were getting two Presidents, not one.

Eleanor's duties as First Lady did not slow her down; she entertained at the usual receptions, as was expected of her. With her own family, relatives, friends, and the President's associates, the White House was often overflowing with guests. As she herself once said to a group of visiting movie stars, the Roosevelts were "a noisy family."

The spectacle of Eleanor Roosevelt always on the go became a national jest. She was everywhere, watching, speaking, inspecting, writing, reporting back to the President. As in Albany, she was again the eyes and the ears for her husband, and his legs as well. She went where he could not. A famous cartoon by Robert Day in the *New Yorker* showed two miners working in a mine shaft glancing up in dismay, and one of them saying: "For gosh sakes, here comes Mrs. Roosevelt!" Eleanor did in fact visit a mine. Her mother-in-law could not resist commenting, in a letter to Franklin: "I hope Eleanor is with you this morning. . . I see she has emerged from the mine . . . that is something to be thankful for."

Eleanor's dash and style as a peregrinating First Lady did not extend to her wardrobe. Couture and high fashion meant little to her, although she did have beautiful gowns for state affairs, and she managed to look, in FDR's appraisal, "magnificent" in evening wear. She was never adept at cooking, and did not attempt it, except for huge batches of scrambled eggs made in a chafing dish, and served for Sunday night suppers.

As if there were not enough for her to do, Eleanor began writing a chatty newspaper column, which became widely known as "My Day." She broadcast regularly on the radio, and gave many lectures. Her earnings from these various activities, totaling $75,000 a year, went to charity.

White House casualness, in June of 1939, brought on a storm of protest from traditionalists and worshippers of strict protocol. King George VI of England and his Queen, Elizabeth, came to the United States on a goodwill tour. They were invited to stay at Hyde Park, in Sara Delano Roosevelt's house. Eleanor prepared a picnic for them, where American hot dogs were served. The King and Queen loved the hot dogs, but howls of anguish sounded across the country; apparently we were not presenting the proper image to Their Majesties. Even more damaging, for Sara Roosevelt, was the pitcher of Franklin's "famous Martinis" at the formal dinner that evening. Roosevelt said to the King, "My mother thinks you should have a cup of tea—she doesn't approve of cocktails." The King, never garrulous, answered after a moment, "Neither does my mother." And both men downed their cocktails with obvious gusto. To add to Sara's discomfiture, Eleanor reported the entire incident in her next column.

The World War II years found Eleanor traveling as much as she had in peacetime. But now she was going to overseas installations, to visit with the troops, to bring them a bit of cheer and encouragement, and to report back to FDR. She left at a moment's notice, with only one suitcase and a harassed general hurrying after her. She would show up unexpectedly, in as out-of-the-way a place as Espirtu Santo in the New Hebrides. GIs were ordered not to take rain-showers in the nude for fear she would suddenly appear.

On April 12, 1945, Eleanor Roosevelt was at a benefit for a Washington thrift shop when she received a phone call to return to the White House at once. She did not have to be told why; she knew "something dreadful had happened." FDR, at the age of sixty-three, had died in Warm Springs, Georgia, of a massive cerebral hemorrhage. He was buried in the rose garden family plot at Hyde Park, New York.

The seventeen years still remaining to Eleanor Roosevelt were the most remarkable for any former First Lady. Rather than retiring to a quiet eminence as a presidential widow, Eleanor more than ever devoted her life and her unflagging energies to the world she loved. She continued her concern for youth and minorities; she lectured, she wrote her columns and books. But it was her work in the United Nations that brought her the title "First Lady of the World." President Truman appointed her, in 1946, an American delegate to the UN. By acclamation, she was selected chairman of the United Nations Commission on Human Rights. It was this group, under her chairmanship, that developed the UN's covenant for human rights.

In spite of her many public commitments, she never lost touch with her family. She kept a careful record of their various sizes and birthdates, and she shopped for them wherever she happened to be. At home, she loved the large gatherings where she presided with three other generations grouped around her; to her children, who had families of their own, she was "Mummy," and to her grandchildren and great-grandchildren, she was "Grandmere."

Eleanor had known, for at least two years, that she was seriously ill, perhaps of leukemia. By the fall of 1962, she was aware that death was a matter of months or weeks. She was not afraid to die, but she was angry; she railed at the "utter nonsense" of keeping her alive. She was totally exhausted and often in pain. As Joseph P. Lash described it in his tender biography, *A Friend's Memoir,* "The last weeks were, unhappily, a time of unrelieved and intensifying horror."

She died on November 7, 1962, at the age of seventy-eight. It was found that her death was caused by a rare disease, tuberculosis of the bone marrow. She was buried next to her husband in the Hyde Park rose garden. Not far away is the grave of the infant Franklin who died in 1909 at the age of seven months. His small, flat stone bears the simple legend, "For of such is the Kingdom of Heaven."

Out of the thousands of eulogies and tributes to her, there is one compassionate and luminous phrase, by Adlai E. Stevenson, that expresses the essence of Eleanor Roosevelt.

> She would rather light candles than curse the darkness, and her glow has warmed the world.

Elizabeth (Bess) Truman
1885–

As he had in 1932, Franklin Delano Roosevelt appeared in person before the Democratic convention of 1936 to deliver his acceptance speech. Many lines in the address crackled with Roosevelt eloquence; but four short sentences toward the end spoke to the people with poetry and vision: "There is a mysterious cycle in human events. To some generations much is given. Of other generations much is expected. This generation of Americans has a rendezvous with destiny."

For the world at large and for one lone man, their rendezvous with destiny came with shattering suddenness on the afternoon of April 12, 1945, when Franklin Roosevelt sank into unconsciousness moments after complaining, "I have a terrific headache," and died at 3:35 P.M. Millions stopped whatever they were doing, to weep and to ask what would become of them now. They turned to stare at Vice President Harry S. Truman, an unimpressive and neutral man from Missouri who was just as stunned as they, but had neither the time nor the right to mourn. Without even a chance to wonder how or why this awesome thing had happened to him, he could only say later, "I felt like the moon, the stars, and all the planets had fallen on me." At exactly seven minutes past nine on the evening of April 12, Truman assumed "the most terribly responsible job a man ever had," as thirty-third President of the United States, when he took the oath of office in the White House with Bess Truman and their daughter, Margaret, looking on.

The country hoped for much from the Trumans, and expected little. Neither statesman nor orator, nor maker of eloquent phrases, Truman was no match for Roosevelt. But he confounded himself, his critics, and the world by becoming a more than capable President. Outspoken, blunt, and humble as his origins, he won his own term in 1948 by defeating Thomas E. Dewey with a vote of 24,105,695 to 21,969,170. The man on the street and the fellow next door related to this unaffected Missourian who always came out swinging and called them as he saw them.

Women responded to Bess Truman as their husbands did to Harry. The image she presented was stiff and unbending, as if she devoutly wished she were somewhere else. But the women of the country sympathized, and gave her support rather than criticism. Unlike Mrs. Roosevelt, Bess Truman was no gregarious, perambulating cosmopolitan. She chose to remain in the background, a quiet midwestern housewife without pretensions. First Lady of the land by accident, she would always remain Bess Wallace Truman of Independence by preference.

The story of Elizabeth Virginia Wallace and Harry Truman has a gaping hole. Though they had known each other for twenty-nine years, they did not marry until he was thirty-five and she was thirty-four. To inquiries about this overlong courtship, there is polite silence. Bess and Harry Truman insist her private life is her own. But the wife of a President, whether she likes it or not, is a principal performer in America's pageant. The blessed isolation of obscurity is no longer hers.

Bess Wallace's grandfather, George Porterfield Gates of Vermont, came to Missouri in 1865; he began selling Queen of the Pantry Flour, which he claimed would make "the best hot biscuits in the world." He sold enough flour to build a many-gabled, gingerbread house of seventeen rooms on North Delaware Street. The house became famous in Independence as the "Gates Victorian Mansion."

David Willock Wallace, son of the mayor of Independence, and considered "the handsomest man in town," married Madge, one of the three Gates daughters. David and Madge Wallace settled down two blocks away from the "Gates Mansion." Their first child, Bess, was born on February 13, 1885. Wallace, whose family, like the Trumans, had originally come from Kentucky, was an active young man. At the age of fourteen he worked for the Missouri state senate as an assistant docket clerk, and after that held a number of public offices. He and Madge had three more children, all sons.

Bess attended public schools in Independence. Harry saw her for the first time at the Presbyterian Sunday school, when he was six and she was five, "a beautiful little girl with golden curls." In his own words, "I was smitten at once and still am."

The studious Harry was not, in Bess Wallace's view, the *beau ideal*. Before he was eight, permanently impaired eyesight forced him to wear glasses, which eliminated him from the usual rough-and-tumble activities of the boys, and from Bess's as well. According to her contemporaries, Bess was "pretty much of a tomboy." She played mumbly-peg, baseball, and tennis, was an expert ice-skater, loved to swim, hunt, and fish (she always baited her own hook); she was a star basketball player, won a shot-put championship, and was the only girl in Independence who could whistle through her teeth.

There was never a lack of suitors at the Wallace household. Blue-eyed, golden-haired, "slim as a willow wand," Bess Wallace was easily one of the most popular girls in town, even during her school years. For someone as sober as Harry Truman to aspire to such a young lady was foolhardy, indeed. Friends later recalled that Harry was a "most unpromising prospect," while Bess was "the *crème de la crème* of aristocracy."

In 1901, Bess and Harry both graduated from Independence High School. Harry was then seventeen and Bess sixteen. He went to nearby Kansas City for a variety of minor jobs; he later moved to Grandview, a few miles south of Independence, to work on the family farm. His father had lost all his money in speculations and poor investments, and needed Harry's help.

When Bess was eighteen, in 1903, her father died. The tragedy of losing her father at a young age was particularly affecting for Bess; her mother was pregnant with a fourth child. A few months later, Bess's youngest brother, Fred, was born. Mrs. Wallace and the four children, Bess and her three brothers, moved to the "Gates Mansion."

For the next two years, Bess helped take care of her baby brother. When her mother was well enough to assume her place in the household again, Bess went back to school for a year. She commuted to Kansas City, an hour away by streetcar, to study at Miss Barstow's Finishing School for Girls.

Remarkably reticent about her personal life, Bess has nothing to say about the years after 1906. She was to see Harry only sporadically until 1914. What was she doing during all that time? According to Harry's cousin, Nellie Noland, who lived across the street from the "Gates Mansion," "Bess just stayed at home with her mother and her brothers and had herself a good time. In those days nice girls didn't work. Besides, there was always something going on in Independence."

Miss Noland may have been referring to a sensational murder case that took place in 1910 and involved a young man Bess had been seeing, Chrisman Swope. Chrisman, thirty-year-old member of a wealthy and prominent Independence family, died under highly suspicious circumstances shortly after two male relatives died without warning. Chrisman's death was attributed at first to

309

a convulsion following a "freak case of typhoid"; the diagnosis was later changed to "poisoning by strychnine and cyanide of potassium."

In all three instances, the attending physician was Chrisman's brother-in-law, Dr. Bennett Clark Hyde. Dr. Hyde was indicted for murder, but could not be found guilty after three trials, and was finally released. (The prosecution had based its case on what it presumed to be the doctor's attempt to gain control of the Swope fortune.)

It may be that Harry Truman had heard that Bess had been seeing Chrisman Swope. But in any event, Harry was in no position for resolute courtship at that time; he was far too busy on the farm, and he wasn't certain what his future was to be. In 1913 he bought a Stafford touring car "with high brass windshield and Prest-o-Lite lamps." By 1914 he was driving regularly into Independence to see Bess.

Bess was in no hurry to marry him, even after a lapse of so many years. (Daughter Margaret, in her book of memoirs, *Souvenir,* published in 1956, wrote that her parents "had several hundred dates." Harry's mother, Martha Young Truman, perhaps gave "the only proper answer" to the question of why Bess and Harry waited so long to marry. "Maybe," Martha Truman said, "Bess wouldn't have him.")

By 1917, Bess at last did decide to "have him." A formal engagement preceded service for Harry in World War I. Bess and others with fiancés or husbands overseas organized themselves into the I.W.W.s, the Independence War Widows. Harry was ultimately mustered out of the service in May of 1919.

One month later, on June 28, 1919, Bess and Harry were married in the Trinity Episcopal Church in Independence. The bride, who was thirty-four, wore a short white dress of elaborately tucked georgette and a wide-brimmed white faille hat, and carried a bouquet of rosebuds, baby's breath, and fern. The groom, thirty-five, wore a new gray checked suit. After a short honeymoon in Chicago and Detroit, Mr. and Mrs. Harry Truman returned to Independence and moved into the "Gates Victorian Mansion" on North Delaware. It was to be the only home they would ever have in Independence.

Marriage for Bess Truman simply extended the pattern of domesticity she had gradually developed after high school. She maintained her sense of humor and her quick, quiet wit, but she was no longer a lively young lady romping through a set or two of tennis. She was now a sedate housewife helping her firm-handed mother manage the affairs of the family home. On February 17, 1924, the Trumans' only child, their daughter, Margaret, was born in the "Gates Mansion" exactly four days after Bess's thirty-ninth birthday.

Truman's political career began in 1922 when Tom and Mike Pendergast, Democratic bosses of Kansas City, adopted him as a protégé. (Mike's son, Jim, had been in the Army with Harry.) Although Harry's ties to the Pendergasts lasted for a number of years, he was scrupulously honest and incorruptible. Even the Pendergasts grudgingly and admiringly admitted that he was the "contrariest cuss in Missouri" and could not be budged from his consistent position of rectitude.

In 1934, with the help of the Pendergast machine, Truman was elected junior United States senator from the State of Missouri. Truman, Bess, Margaret, and Bess's mother moved to Washington in January of 1935, where they lived in a five-room apartment in Tilden Gardens. Bess found their modest quarters confining and tiny after her spacious house in Independence, and Washington at first disturbed her. She feared "the coldness of an Eastern city," but she was pleased to find that other Senate women were as anxious as she to talk of "household matters and family questions."

One problem plagued the Trumans—a shortage of money. His senatorial salary of $10,000 could not cover their needs. Bess was placed on Truman's payroll as a secretary at a salary of $4,500 a year. News of the appointment raised a minor storm, but both Trumans stoutly defended it with the assertion that she earned her pay and deserved it. She had always helped him with his speeches, his correspondence, and all the small, irritating items that plague a senator. The Trumans decided, in their forthright fashion, that she ought to be paid for all that work. (Truman later admitted that "the Missus" helped him with his decisions as well, even as President; he constantly consulted her on major issues and often coordinated her views with his. Some of his decisions were monumental: the atom bomb, the Truman Doctrine, the Marshall Plan, NATO, the Korean War.)

Truman's reelection as senator in 1940, and his chairmanship of the Senate Investigating Committee (to examine expenditures in the National Defense Program) were the prime factors that brought him to the attention of the Democratic hierarchy in 1944 and led to his election as Vice President. Bess had refused, during his senatorial years, to be grist for the gossip mills. She saw no reason to change now that her husband had been elevated to the second highest position in the land. She and her family continued to live in the same five-room apartment in the Tilden Gardens; she removed herself, as before, from the glare of publicity. To the disappointment of the press, she was "poor copy," but that was her intent.

When her husband became President in April, 1945, Bess Truman was sixty, one of the oldest First Ladies ever to enter the White House. She faced the enormity of her new position with misgiving, for she knew she was being watched and measured by the entire country. She refused to hold press conferences, as had Eleanor Roosevelt; capital reporters and columnists were incensed. Many on the distaff side vented their displeasure in writing, but Bess would not relent.

There were other difficulties facing her. Her Independence cook, Vietta Garr, had taken a job at a soda fountain, and she had some doubts about returning to work for the Trumans. "I'm fountain manager now," she said, "and you don't give up that kind of a job without thinking it over." (Bess finally persuaded her to come back.) Another source of concern was Adam Clayton Powell, New York congressman, who undoubtedly echoed the sentiments of many when he acidly referred to Bess as "the Last Lady of the land." But Bess went about her responsibilities with a quiet, unruffled resolution. Publicly, she often seemed rigid and uncomfortable; in private, away from the relentless presidential spotlight, she was a warm, friendly wife and mother who was not above chiding the President for speaking his mind too freely.

During their first years in the White House, the Trumans had a number of illustrious guests: President-elect and Señora Mariano Ospina-Perez of Colombia; President Miguel Aleman of Mexico; and Grandma Moses.

Bess's favorite guests were The Girls, her Tuesday Bridge Club from Independence (the former I.W.W.s of World War I). Whenever the Trumans returned to Independence, Bess played bridge with The Girls. Her friends came to the White House in 1946 for a highly publicized weekend that has to be the major event of their lives. (Their deference to Bess as First Lady annoyed her; one afternoon in Independence they greeted her by rising in a body, stiffly bowing, and chanting in unison: "Welcome home, Madam President!" Her answer was a testy, "Oh sit down! Sit down! You all make me so mad!")

In 1948, a White House ceiling caved in under the weight of Margaret's piano (encouraged by her parents, she was studying for a concert career as a singer). Hastily summoned architects discovered that the ancient Executive Mansion was on the point of collapse. The Trumans moved to Blair House across the way, and the White House was completely rebuilt, except for the outer walls and a controversial balcony Truman had added to the South Portico for $10,000. (The restoration took three years and cost a total of $5,761,000. The original "President's Palace" had been built for less than $500,000.)

The presidential election of 1948 must be ranked the upset of the century. To counter the polls, which had Truman's Republican opponent, Thomas E. Dewey, winning easily, Truman con-

313

ducted an intensive campaign. With Bess and Margaret accompanying him, he traveled thirty thousand miles, made 351 speeches, met thousands of people, and introduced Bess everywhere as "The Boss." On election night, the *Chicago Tribune* printed a jubilant headline: "Dewey Defeats Truman." (A copy of that paper is now on display at the Truman Library.) The voters, however, had other ideas. They wanted "the family next door," not "the little man on the wedding cake." Final returns gave Truman a plurality of 2,000,000 votes.

Entertainment, on a reduced scale, continued while the Trumans lived at Blair House. Because of limited facilities, Bess gave a series of teas rather than the huge receptions she had hosted at the White House. In 1951, the Trumans entertained Princess Elizabeth of England and her husband, Philip, the Duke of Edinburgh. On March 27, 1952, the Trumans returned to the magnificent new White House; it was at last a "Palace" fit for a President, with 132 rooms and 20 baths.

After a long illness, Mrs. Madge Gates Wallace, Bess's mother, died in the White House on December 5, 1952. Her passing, at an advanced age, must have been for Bess like the turning of a last page, for she and her mother had always lived together. The following month, after eighteen years in Washington, Bess and Harry and Margaret left the White House to make way for the new occupants, President and Mrs. Eisenhower. Bess, who had never really cared for the capital city, was relieved at last to return to her home town and the "Gates Mansion"; but it was no longer the "Gates Mansion." It was now the "Truman House," and had been since his Presidency.

There were five thousand people jamming the Washington terminal to bid them Godspeed, and thousands more in Independence to shout a neighborly welcome. It was to be like that for some time. Bess and Harry Truman in their home on North Delaware Street were a prime tourist attraction. They once managed to cross the street to visit his cousins, but a huge crowd in the meantime had gathered in front of their own house, and they had to wait until everyone had left before daring to go back. Bess later reported the incident to her daughter: "We had to spend most of the evening on the front porch all by ourselves because our cousins weren't home."

In time, the Truman excitement slackened enough for Bess and Harry to enjoy a relative privacy. Bess picked up the routine of her old life; she did her own shopping at the supermarket, as she always had, and she rejoined her Tuesday Bridge Club. Harry supervised the building of his Indiana limestone Harry S. Truman Library. (Built through the efforts of friends and neighbors at a cost of $2 million, the library was dedicated in 1957. It houses three and a half million documents, all of Truman's personal papers and those of political associates. Independence officials estimate that 300,000 people a year visit the Truman Library, his home, and his birthplace.)

On April 21, 1956, in the same Trinity Episcopal Church where Bess and Harry were married thirty-seven years before, Margaret was married to Clifton Daniel of Zebulon, North Carolina. (Daniel is associate editor of *The New York Times*. He and Margaret have four sons.)

When former President Harry S. Truman and former First Lady Bess Wallace Truman observed their fiftieth wedding anniversary on June 28, 1969, they had a quiet celebration, with only a few close friends dropping in. As reported by *The New York Times,* "It was the way the Trumans wanted it."

Seven and a half months later, on February 13, 1970, Bess celebrated her eighty-fifth birthday. This, too, was a quiet day, for she devoted most of her time to her husband, who was not as energetic as he had once been. She had given up, some time before, joining The Girls at the Tuesday Bridge Club, although she spoke to them frequently. "She's a great telephone visitor," one of them said, "and we keep in touch."

The Trumans have settled into a pattern of pleasant domesticity.

They both get up early and retire early. Bess has her reading and her flowers. She receives floral gifts from all over the country; her favorites are yellow roses, red tulips, and azaleas in any color. But above all, according to friends, "Bess and Harry Truman need no close companionship except each other."

Mamie Eisenhower
1896–

War creates its own mythology. Victorious commanders assume heroic proportions; overnight, a leader of men becomes a leader of nations. The American people believed this of Zachary Taylor in 1848, though he had never held political office, did not know his party affiliation, and in fact had never voted; 104 years later, they believed the same of Dwight David Eisenhower. He, too, had never voted and did not know, until early 1952, whether he was a Democrat, a Republican, or neither.

Pressed by frantic Republican functionaries to declare for their party (they sorely needed his immense popularity), he at last made up his mind, and chose what he believed to be "the more enlightened principles of the Republicans," although he felt he "could have been a conservative Democrat." He permitted the Republican convention, meeting in Chicago in July of 1952, to nominate

317

him for President on the first ballot, with Richard M. Nixon of California to run for Vice President.

In the words of Clare Boothe Luce, General Ike Eisenhower, Supreme Commander of Allied Forces in World War II, was to everyone "a combination of father, husband and son." His friendly grin, his open, appealing manner, his undisputed status as a folk-hero, easily elected him thirty-fourth President of the United States with a total of 33,936,234 votes to 27,314,992 for Democrat Adlai E. Stevenson, intellectual idol of the "eggheads."

Whether intentional or not, Eisenhower was all things to all men; he appealed to the moderates, and sought the support of right-wing conservatives. His political innocence was an asset rather than a liability. In the election of 1956, again with Nixon as his running mate and Stevenson his opponent, his margin was even more impressive—35,590,472 to 26,022,752, and 86 percent of the electoral count to a mere 14 percent for Stevenson.

It may perhaps be too soon to make a proper evaluation of Eisenhower's two terms. But one fact emerges from the conflicting appraisals: to the average American, "I Like Ike" is not a slogan, it is a living testimonial to one of the most popular men of the twentieth century.

Mamie Geneva Doud Eisenhower was almost as widely admired as her husband. Basically as shy as Bess Truman, she nevertheless projected a far different image. She seemed more outgoing, more sure of herself. But she, too, had little to say in public. A long-time Army wife with one major purpose, "Looking after Ike," she deferred to her husband. Thoroughly feminine in her attitudes and appearance, Mamie Eisenhower changed the no-nonsense, efficiently midwestern character of Bess Truman's White House to a pink and fluffy dwelling.

The last First Lady to be born in the nineteenth century and the first to have Scandinavian grandparents, Mamie Geneva Doud spent more time in the White House than in any of the Army posts or villas she occupied as Mrs. Eisenhower. She and Ike moved twenty-seven times in thirty-seven years—one year they moved six times. Not until they bought a farm in Gettysburg, Pennsylvania, in 1950 did they ever have a permanent home. (Mamie once declared, rather plaintively, "I'd like to be a homebody, but I'm really just a movebody.")

The second of four daughters, Mamie was born in Boone, Iowa, on November 14, 1896. Her father, John Sheldon Doud, was a successful meat packer who retired at the age of thirty-six. Mamie's mother, the former Elivera Carlson, was also born in Boone. Her parents, Carl and Johanna Carlson, had come from Sweden in 1869 to settle in Iowa. Elivera married John Doud when she was sixteen and he was twenty-three.

John and Elivera Doud moved to Cedar Rapids, Iowa, when Mamie was seven months old. Mamie began school just before her sixth birthday, but remained only for a brief time. Her mother was not well, and at a doctor's suggestion for a change of climate the family moved to Colorado and settled in Colorado Springs.

Colorado proved to be exactly what Mrs. Doud needed, but the high thin atmosphere of Colorado Springs seven thousand feet above sea level was too much for the frail heart of the oldest daughter, Eleanor; the family moved once again, in 1905, this time to Denver, two thousand feet lower. They settled in the new residential section of the city, in a solid, substantial house on Lafayette Street.

In the fall of 1906, when Mamie was not quite ten, she enrolled at the Corona School, one of the best in the city, and the only school she attended for more than a year. Mamie was never a top student; she applied herself to her studies just enough to satisfy minimal requirements of scholarship, but she was popular both with her classmates and her teachers.

By 1910, when the fragile Eleanor was fifteen, the Douds decided to spend a winter in the sunny climate of San Antonio, Texas. They liked San Antonio and bought a house there; they planned to make it a second home. The Texas climate did not improve Eleanor's health and she died in 1912.

Mamie graduated from Corona in June of 1912; her education after that was irregular. She attended a high school in Denver for a short time and one in San Antonio; her final schooling occurred in 1914–15, when she was eighteen, at Denver's most fashionable "finishing school," Miss Wolcott's. Here too, Mamie was accomplished neither in her studies nor athletics. She was a bright young lady, but lacked both the drive and interest to be a scholar.

In the late summer of 1915, when Mamie was eighteen, the family motored once again to San Antonio to spend the winter. On the first Sunday in October, Mamie, against her wishes, joined her family and some friends in a drive to Fort Sam Houston, just outside of San Antonio. She had a date that evening, and was anxious to get back to town. She changed her mind when she met a newly arrived lieutenant, Dwight David Eisenhower, a tall, erect, and friendly young man with the measured shine of West Point still evident.

As it happened, Ike was Officer of the Day. He was making his rounds when he passed Mamie and her group, and was introduced. The one who caught his eye, as he later wrote, was "a vivacious and attractive girl, smaller than average, saucy in the look about her face and in her whole attitude." Mamie thought he was "the spiffiest looking man she'd ever talked to in her whole life." Ike asked her to join him on his rounds. That was the beginning for them. They were soon seeing each other on a more or less regular basis. Ike's pay of $141.67 a month precluded lavish evenings. For dinner, they normally went to a Mexican restaurant called The Original. In Ike's words, "The menu was unchanging: chili, tamales, enchiladas. There we could have dinner for two for about $1.00 or $1.25 including tip." By Christmas, Mamie's other beaux had given up, leaving the field clear for Ike. They were engaged on Valentine's Day of 1916; Ike gave her a gold and amethyst replica of his class ring.

Their marriage took place on July 1, 1916, in the Douds' Lafayette Street home in Denver. Mamie, blue-eyed, dark-haired, and petite, wore a gown of white Chantilly lace with a pink cummerbund. The twenty-five-year-old Ike, newly promoted to first lieutenant, wore a tropical white uniform, starched and spotless. The only guests were family and close friends. For a wedding gift, Ike gave his bride a pair of seed-pearl earrings (now in the Eisenhower museum in Abilene). When Ike and Mamie left for a weekend honeymoon, a matronly neighbor sighed, "She could have married *anybody* in Denver."

After two days in the mountainous Eldorado Springs just west of Denver, the newlywed Eisenhowers traveled to Abilene, Kansas, to meet his family, and from there went back to Fort Sam Houston to set up their first housekeeping. For the nineteen-year-old bride, who had always known comfort and luxury, the two small, bare rooms and bath that Ike had been assigned were dreadful. But she assiduously set about the task of settling herself and her husband into their new quarters. Ike gave her his pay, raised to $161.67 a month, and she managed the budget. They bought furniture as they could afford to pay for it (she refused to go into debt, and would not consider installment buying). They set up an icebox in the bathroom, which had the only available space.

Ike was away at another military installation when Doud Dwight Eisenhower (later nicknamed "Icky") was born in the post hospital at Fort Sam Houston on September 24, 1917. Mamie was not alone, however; her mother had come from Denver to be present at the birth of her first grandchild, and Mr. Doud followed within a short time.

Mamie's long journeys as an Army wife began in March of 1918 when she moved from Fort Sam Houston to join Ike at Camp Colt, Gettysburg, Pennsylvania. From there they went to Camp Meade, Maryland. Their closest friends at Meade were Colonel and Mrs. George Patton.

Christmas week of 1920 should have been a festive time for the Eisenhowers, but Mamie and Icky were ill. Mamie had a bad cold; three-year-old Icky was hot and feverish. The camp doctor reported grim news to the worried parents—Icky had scarlet fever, caught from a local girl Ike had hired as a maid. Without modern wonder drugs, scarlet fever was frequently fatal, as it proved for Icky. He died on January 2, 1921. Ike wrote, "We were completely crushed. For Mamie, the loss was heartbreaking, and her grief in turn would have broken the hardest heart."

As with so many other Army posts, Camp Meade was no more than a way station for Mamie. Mamie once said, "I've lived in everything from shacks with cracks to palaces." From 1922 to 1924 she and Ike were in Panama, at Camp Gaillard. Mamie had more than her usual discomforts at Panama. She had to fight the crawling and flying inhabitants of the nearby jungle, including a creature she particularly detested—bats.

In the late spring of 1922 Mamie returned to Denver; on August 3, 1922, her second son, and last child, John Sheldon Doud Eisenhower, was born. Her two years of silent grief for Icky were relieved at last by the birth of her new baby, who closely resembled her first son.

Reassignment to Fort Meade brought the Eisenhowers back to the United States in 1924. In the next seventeen years, they moved to various parts of the world—Washington, Paris, the Philippines, to Fort Lewis in the State of Washington, and finally, in 1941, to Fort Sam Houston, where they had begun their married life twenty-five years before.

Mamie's health, never too robust, had deteriorated alarmingly in the spring of 1937; a mysterious stomach ailment failed to respond to medical treatment. A severe hemorrhage left her in a coma and she was on the point of death. After her recovery, she restricted her activity for at least two years. Because her older sister had died of a heart ailment, Mamie was always concerned about her own heart, and participated in few physical activities. She developed an inner-ear disorder known as Ménière's Disease, which disturbs the sense of balance. She was often dizzy, and needed a steadying hand to help her on stairs and out of cars.

Eisenhower's promotions during World War II came with a

rush. In 1941, he was a brigadier-general; two years later he was a full general, and appointed, at the end of 1943, Supreme Commander of the Allied Expeditionary Force. After the invasion of Normandy on D-Day, June 6, 1944, the name of Ike Eisenhower was known in every corner of the world.

Mamie would have preferred to remain in the background, but her husband's fame inevitably forced her into the limelight. The shy, slender figure with the typically Mamie bangs became a familiar sight in newsreels and newspapers.

In February of 1948, Ike retired from the Army, after two years as Chief of Staff. The following June, he was appointed president of Columbia University; he and Mamie moved to New York's Morningside Heights, adjoining the campus. But this, too, was to be only a temporary home. In December of 1950, President Truman asked him to assume command of the NATO Forces (North Atlantic Treaty Organization). In 1951 Mamie and Ike were living in the Villa St. Pierre, ten miles west of Paris.

General and Mrs. Eisenhower had indeed come far from their tiny Fort Sam Houston quarters in 1916. When they married, Ike's monthly pay was $161.67; he now had over a half million tax-free dollars realized from his book, *Crusade in Europe*. Ike and Mamie were financially solvent; he was perhaps the most famous military man of the decade. But there were greater honors ahead for both Eisenhowers. In January of 1953 they made their most important move, to the White House. Ike was sixty-two, and Mamie was fifty-six.

Their longest term of residence began for the Eisenhowers with Ike's Inauguration as thirty-fourth President on January 20, 1953. That evening, the new President and his First Lady attended two Inaugural Balls. Because of the unprecedented demand for tickets, two sites were chosen, the National Guard Armory and Georgetown University's McDonough Hall. Mamie wore her favorite color—a peau-de-soie ball gown in Renoir pink, with two thousand rhinestones. The color scheme was carried over to the

Inaugural decorations that night. As reported by a leading newspaper the next day, "Sunsets have had no more shades of rose than last night's two parties." (For the 1957 Inaugural, which had four separate balls, Mamie wore "a change of pace"—a gown of shimmering citron-yellow lace embroidered in tiny pearls.)

Eisenhower receptions and state dinners ranged over a broad spectrum of guests, from royalty to heads of government. The royalty included King Paul and Queen Frederika of Greece, Emperor Haile Selassie of Ethiopia, the bachelor King Baudouin of Belgium and his fiancée, Princess Fabiola of Spain, King Frederick and Queen Ingrid of Denmark, a return visit for Elizabeth, now Queen of England, and Prince Philip, and the King and Queen of Thailand. Among the chiefs of state were DeGaulle of France, Gronchi of Italy, Frondisi of Argentina, and perhaps the most controversial visitor the Executive Mansion had ever seen—Nikita Khrushchev of the Soviet Union. Fidel Castro of Cuba visited Washington in 1960, but the Eisenhowers did not invite him to the White House.

During Eisenhower's second term, in 1959, Alaska and Hawaii were admitted to the Union. There were now fifty United States.

Mamie made no attempt to influence her husband; it was not her place, she believed, to participate in the affairs of the government. Neither would she grant interviews, nor hold press conferences. She gave no speeches, and expressed no political opinions. She considered "hospitality" and the supervision of the mansion's domestic details her primary functions. Mamie Eisenhower's frilly style was evident in the White House, with pink the dominant color (yellow and green were Mamie's secondary choices).

Despite her preference for privacy, Mamie was a gracious hostess at her large receptions. But the evenings she enjoyed most were those she spent with her husband or friends, playing Scrabble or canasta, watching television, reading mysteries, or giving an impromptu concert on the electric organ she had received from her mother as a birthday gift. And she found particular pleasure in her four grandchildren. (John, who graduated from West Point and was now a major in the infantry, married "Army brat" Barbara Jean Thompson on June 10, 1947.)

For their weekends and their various vacations, Mamie and Ike had four favorite retreats—the Doud Lafayette Street home in Denver; Maryland's Camp David (named for their grandson); Palm Springs, California; and "Mamie's Cabin" on the Augusta National Golf Course in Augusta, Georgia. (The "Cabin," built for the Eisenhowers by the members of the club, was actually a white brick, split-level house.)

By 1955, health became a serious concern for the Eisenhowers. Mamie fatigued easily; she had not been entirely well for some years, and the White House pace proved wearing. In September of 1955, when Mamie and Ike were in Denver, Ike suffered a coronary occlusion; he was ill for four months. Mamie was with him constantly. In Ike's own words, "She took on a task which amazed me. . . . Thousands of letters of sympathy and encouragement flowed in . . . she answered every one individually." In 1956, Ike had an ileitis operation.

In spite of two severe attacks upon his constitution in less than a year, Ike was more concerned for Mamie's health. Mrs. Doud feared that "Mamie can't stand another four years in the White House." But a careful watch on her physical resources, together with a reduction in official and formal social activities, permitted Mamie to complete her second four years as First Lady without complications.

When the Eisenhowers retired from Washington in January of 1961, Mamie at least was grateful the long ordeal was over. She had "kept house in everything but an igloo," but now, at the age of sixty-four, she at last had the peace and comfort of living in her own permanent home, a large farmhouse in Gettysburg. The original structure, built almost two hundred years before, had been extensively renovated and rebuilt.

The press allowed Mamie the full pleasure of retirement; she was mentioned only occasionally. (As she recently said, through her personal secretary, "The years after the White House were very happy ones in her own home with her beloved husband.")

But Mamie returned to the limelight tragically in May of 1968 when General Eisenhower entered the Army's Walter Reed Hospital after suffering his fourth heart attack in thirteen years. He had another heart attack in June, and two more in August. He was, at times, near death, but pulled through to a partial recovery. Mamie was given a nearby room in the hospital and stayed with him for almost eleven months. At one point, at the age of seventy-two, she went without sleep for thirty hours.

On March 28, 1969, despite constant attention and the best medical efforts, Ike's severely damaged heart at last stopped beating. He was seventy-eight. Mamie was at his bedside.

Throughout the three days of official mourning for her husband, Mamie maintained her composure. But at the state funeral in the Washington Cathedral, she faltered when she attempted to sing "A Mighty Fortress Is Our God"; she stood silently, her eyes brimming with tears, while the final hymn, "Onward Christian Soldiers," was sung. She wept openly, for a brief moment, during President Nixon's eulogy when he repeated the general's last words: "I've always loved my wife, I've always loved my children; I've always loved my grandchildren. And I've always loved my country."

General Eisenhower was buried in Abilene, Kansas, in a crypt on the grounds of the Eisenhower Center, next to Icky, as he and Mamie had planned. Although Ike had been born in Denison, Texas, he spent his boyhood in Abilene, and to him it was home. At the services in Abilene, the Reverend Dean Miller said this of Mamie: "I would speak also of a companion soldier, Mamie Doud Eisenhower. Mrs. Eisenhower graciously shared her husband with the world but he belonged uniquely to her. . . . [She] stands as a symbol of the beauty and holiness of marriage."

After a trip to Europe in the summer of 1969 to see her son and his family in Belgium, where John was serving as U.S. ambassador, and a visit to her husband's grave in September, Mamie

Eisenhower once again returned to her peaceful farmland in Gettysburg.

In the 1969 Gallup Poll to determine the most admired woman in the world, Mrs. Dwight D. Eisenhower headed the list for the first time.

Jacqueline Kennedy
1929–

Presidential elections have seen many changes since John Adams first declared that "the office seeks the man." In 1960, a bright, witty, and determined young campaigner openly sought the Presidency. A different breed of politician had arrived. And an old word was given a fresh application. John F. Kennedy dazzled the voters with his "charisma." But he was fighting against odds; he was a Roman Catholic, and it was no secret that his enormously rich father had poured millions into his campaign. Fortunately for the country, religious intolerance did not succeed, nor did his father's immense fortune discredit him.

In one of the closest elections on record, in November of 1960, Democrat John F. Kennedy barely defeated his Republican opponent, Richard M. Nixon, 34,227,096 to 34,107,646. He received 56.43 percent of the electoral count to become the thirty-fifth President of the United States.

At forty-three the youngest man ever to be elected President, John Fitzgerald Kennedy of Massachusetts brought exhilaration and youth to the White House. One phrase in his Inaugural speech on January 20, 1961, revealed the substance of the thousand days that he was to serve: "The torch has been passed to a new generation of Americans—born in this century, tempered by war, disciplined by a hard and bitter peace, proud of our ancient heritage—and unwilling to witness or permit the slow undoing of those human rights to which this nation has always been committed." The New Frontier was exactly that, a refreshing breeze of enthusiasm and intelligence.

The country had never seen a President like John F. Kennedy or a First Lady like Jacqueline Bouvier Kennedy. They were the handsomest presidential couple ever to serve in the White House. Jacqueline Kennedy, thirty-one, the first First Lady born in the twentieth century, was a woman of style and chic in everything she did. Attractive, elegant, accomplished, she was the pride of those who could never be her peers and the envy of some who thought they were.

At the age of two, Jacqueline Bouvier of New York City and Easthampton, Long Island, was already being mentioned in a number of society columns. Her birthday party was dutifully reported, as was her entry in a dog show with her first pet, "a wee Scotch terrier of about her own size." Coverage by the press began early for Jackie and has never stopped.

Jackie had the multiple advantages of position, wealth, intelligence, and beauty. Her mother, Janet Lee, was a leading New York debutante; at twenty-one Janet married swarthy and dashing John Vernou Bouvier III, a man of thirty-seven. The Bouviers were a handsome and fortunate couple. Their first daughter, Jacqueline, was born in Southampton, New York, on July 28, 1929. Their second daughter, Caroline Lee, was born in 1933. (Caroline Lee achieved fame in her own right as the Princess Lee Radziwill.)

Dogs were not the only Bouvier pets. Horses played a far more important role for all the feminine Bouviers. Janet Bouvier was considered one of the best horsewomen of the time; at five, Jackie herself was appearing in horse shows. Jackie was a chubby, round-faced youngster with huge brown eyes, a wide, generous mouth, and cheeks that seemed to square a bit as they reached her chin. She rode with an easy confidence and competence, even as a child. She won a number of prizes, including a rare double championship at the age of eleven.

It was apparent from the beginning that Jacqueline Bouvier was a gifted young lady. She had a quick, inquiring mind that absorbed information with little effort. Though she probably did not understand it completely, she read a book of Chekhov short stories when she was six, with reported enjoyment, except for puzzlement over the word "midwife."

Never difficult or obstreperous, Jackie adapted discipline to her own convictions. At The Chapin School, one of the most exclusive in the New York area, her streak of independence sometimes found her in conflict with the stern headmistress, Miss Ethel Stringfellow. Miss Stringfellow eventually persuaded Jacqueline to adjust to necessary regulations.

Scholastically, Jacqueline did well at Chapin. When she was fifteen, she enrolled at Miss Porter's School in Farmington, Connecticut, where she was permitted to have a horse. (Grampy Jack, her Bouvier grandfather, and her favorite male next to her father, paid the horse's keep of $25 per month.)

Like the Roosevelts and the Kennedys, the Bouviers were a numerous, wealthy, and lively clan. Jackie's summers were spent at Easthampton, in a huge stucco mansion called "Lasata" (an Indian word meaning "Place of Peace"). Jackie and her father had a secure and devoted relationship; he was a handsome, demonstrative man who adored and indulged his daughters.

Financial reverses during the Depression impaired the Bouvier fortune; the marriage between Jack and Janet Bouvier, slowly crumbling, came to an end with a divorce in 1940. For Jackie, the security of the happy home she had once known was broken, but she at least had weekends with her father. In June of 1942, her mother married Hugh Auchincloss of Virginia and Rhode Island. (Though the Bouviers were Catholic, Janet Lee Bouvier was not, nor was Hugh Auchincloss, who had himself been married and divorced twice before.)

Hugh Auchincloss, far wealthier than the Bouviers, owned two magnificent estates, forty-six-acre "Merrywood" in McLean, Virginia, and "Hammersmith Farm" in Newport, Rhode Island. A new life began for Jacqueline and her sister, Lee. Winters were spent in "Merrywood," on the Virginia shore near Washington, and summers at "Hammersmith Farm."

It was a small step for Jacqueline from the New York–Easthampton circuit to the Virginia–Newport social colony; her Bouvier ancestry guaranteed position, and wealth was simply a matter of degree. She had grown into a slender and beautiful young lady. A facile, articulate scholar, she mastered Latin, French, and Spanish; she had a flair for acting, painting, and writing. Her class yearbook recorded that she was "Most Known For" *Wit,* and added, under "Ambition," *Not to be a housewife.*

Jacqueline Bouvier scored a singular triumph in 1947, at the age of eighteen. Igor Cassini, more widely known as Cholly Knickerbocker, doyen of the Hearst society columnists, bestowed a supreme honor upon her. "Queen Deb of the Year is Jacqueline Bouvier," he wrote, "a regal brunette, who has classic features and the daintiness of Dresden porcelain."

She began two years at Vassar in the fall of 1947. She dated frequently, although at least one of her escorts dissented with the prevailing opinion that she was "a fairytale princess [who] doesn't know the meaning of the word snob." The young man stated that "she was rather aloof and reserved," and he expressed astonishment that "she seemed to talk an awful lot about animals."

After Vassar, she spent a year at the Sorbonne in Paris, and then returned to Washington. Through the intervention of the distinguished journalist, Arthur Krock of *The New York Times,* a family friend, Jacqueline landed a job with the Washington *Times-*

Herald as "Inquiring Camera Girl." Her starting salary, in 1951, was $42.50 a week. A number of small raises brought her pay to $56.75.

During her stay on the *Times-Herald,* she interviewed two senators, Richard M. Nixon of California and John F. Kennedy of Massachusett. She had met Kennedy on a more formal basis, in May of 1951, at a small dinner party arranged by friends who thought Jacqueline and Jack ought to get together. (Kennedy later said about that first meeting: "I leaned across the asparagus and asked her for a date.") Jacqueline at first considered him "quixotic," because he had the temerity to state he "intended to become President."

The romance their friends had hopefully arranged was slow in developing. They saw each other occasionally; Jack escorted her to President Eisenhower's Inaugural Ball in January of 1953. He went off to Bermuda, and sent her a single postcard that said, "Wish you were here, Jack." He sent her no other communications and no love letters. In June of 1953, they were formally engaged. Public announcement had to be withheld because the lead article in the next issue of the *Saturday Evening Post* bore the title: "Jack Kennedy—The Senate's Gay Young Bachelor."

The Gay Young Bachelor and the Queen Deb of 1947 were married on September 12, 1953, in Newport, Rhode Island. Kennedy was thirty-six and Jacqueline was twenty-four. The ceremony, before six hundreds guests, took place in Newport's St. Mary's Church, with Archbishop Richard Cushing of Boston officiating. Jacqueline had expected her father to give her away, but 1953 was a low point in the life of John Vernou Bouvier III; he could not participate. So it was that Jacqueline's stepfather, Hugh Auchincloss, walked down the aisle with her. After the church services, an outdoor reception was held at "Hammersmith Farm." Music was provided by Meyer Davis, who had played at the wedding of Jacqueline's parents, twenty-five years before.

Superficially, Jacqueline's life with the Kennedys was much like her years with the Bouviers and the Auchinclosses. Instead of Easthampton, McLean, or Newport, she lived in Palm Beach, Hickory Hill in Virginia, and the Kennedy Compound in Hyannis Port, Cape Cod. She had her horses, and the Kennedy sailboats and yacht. But there was a subtle difference. The Bouviers and the Auchinclosses were "Old Guard"; the Kennedys were part of the new aristocracy. The Kennedy children had all been born into wealth, but it was their father who had earned it. (His fortune was once estimated at $250 million.) All the Kennedys, father, mother, brothers, sisters, were filled with a fiercely competitive spirit and dedication to the elder Kennedy's dream—a son in the White House.

Competition for Jacqueline had been confined to horse shows, where she excelled because of her natural grace and skill. The Kennedys' passion for politics perplexed her at first; it puzzled her that her husband actually wanted to be President and had carefully made his plans years before. (Her mother-in-law once told a group of reporters, "My son was rocked to political lullabies.")

A major operation in 1954 threatened the Kennedy timetable. Surgery was performed in October of that year to correct a painful back injury Jack had suffered during World War II. The operation did not succeed, and it was thought for a few despairing hours that he would not live; six weeks later, he had a second and successful operation. During his long period of convalescence, he wrote his Pulitzer Prize book, *Profiles in Courage.*

For Jacqueline Kennedy, who did everything easily and well, it was tragically ironic that the most important function for a woman, the bearing of children, should have been dangerously difficult. In 1955, she lost one child through a miscarriage; the following year, her second child, a baby girl, was stillborn. On November 27, 1957, Jacqueline gave birth to Caroline; three years later, on November 25, 1960, John, Jr. (John-John), was born. On August 7, 1963, Jacqueline bore her last child, Patrick Bouvier Kennedy. He lived for only two days. He was buried in the Kennedy family plot in Brookline, Massachusetts, and was later reburied in Arlington National Cemetery near his father. (All of Jacqueline's children were delivered by Caesarian operation.)

John F. Kennedy's march to the White House was interrupted by his defeat for the vice-presidential nomination at the Democratic convention of 1956. But a smashing victory in the Massachusetts senatorial election of 1958, which he won with a margin of 875,000 votes, and a string of unbroken wins in the 1960 presidential primaries, including a decisive triumph in Protestant West Virginia, easily assured him the Democratic nomination on the first ballot in 1960. In November, his Republican opponent, Richard M. Nixon would not concede until eleven o'clock on the morning after the election.

The new First Lady was almost universally hailed for her beauty and elegance. One Washington hostess referred to her as a "beatnik"; to old friend Arthur Krock, however, Jacqueline Kennedy was "a Beaux Arts type of girl, merry, arch, satirical, terribly democratic, and yes, brilliant." Jacqueline had an immediate impact upon American womanhood; the "Jackie Look" swept the country. Women copied her hairdo and her clothes. Jackie-type mannequins appeared in department store windows. Jacqueline Kennedy was the new star of the young sixties. In the words of her social secretary, "She is a woman who has everything, including the President of the United States."

There were five Inaugural Balls on the evening of January 20, 1961. Jacqueline wore a gown of white peau d'ange, with a bodice embroidered in silver and a white chiffon overblouse for a misty effect. All of the clothes she wore during her three years as First Lady had a dramatic influence upon the country. As a fashion editor recently declared, "The brunette queen of the New Frontier became the Pied Piper of fashion."

The arts, too, benefited from her interest. She invited many prominent musicians and writers to the White House; Pablo Casals, Isaac Stern, and the American Shakespeare Festival of Stratford, Connecticut, gave White House performances, as did opera stars Roberta Peters and Jerome Hines.

Perhaps the most memorable Kennedy reception was the dinner in April of 1962 for all living recipients of the Nobel Prize in the Western Hemisphere. Frederic March read excerpts from the works of Ernest Hemingway, George Marshall, and Sinclair Lewis. (As John Steinbeck put it, "Syntax no longer is subversive at the White House.")

The Jacqueline Kennedy charm and appeal were not restricted to the United States. An official visit to Canada with the President in 1961 elicited this comment in a New York newspaper: "Jacqueline Kennedy captured the Canadian capital today without firing a shot." She did even better in a visit that same year to France, where she enchanted the entire French population, including General Charles de Gaulle, with her perfect command of their language. President Kennedy afterward referred to himself as "the man who accompanied Jacqueline Kennedy to Paris." On a joint visit with Nikita Khrushchev and Madame Nina Khrushchev to Vienna's historic Schönbrunn Palace, the matronly Mrs. Khrushchev and the trim Jacqueline clasped hands while a huge crowd enthusiastically shouted their names. In 1962, Jacqueline made a semiofficial tour of India and Pakistan, where thousands greeted her as "Queen of America!"

Jacqueline's favorite project, during her first year in the Executive Mansion, was restoration of the interior of the White House with authentic furnishings and art reflecting the various periods in the history of the country and the White House itself. In February of 1962, she conducted a one-hour television tour of the restored mansion for an estimated forty-eight million viewers who were enthralled by her work and by her low, breathless voice.

With all of her travels and her work on the restoration, Jacqueline insisted upon making time for her children and her husband. President Kennedy considered this her "primary responsibility [and] her real job as a woman."

Jacqueline Kennedy's remarkable control through four days of agony in November, 1963, united the country in admiration. John F. Kennedy's assassination in Dallas, Texas, on November 22, subjected her to an ordeal shared by the world. While millions wept, she found a source of dignity that sustained her through the harrowing hours. Archibald MacLeish wrote that she "made the darkest days the American people have known in a hundred years the deepest revelation of their inward strength." Leaders from every major country and from many smaller ones came to pay their homage and respect to a dead President and his beautiful First Lady who submerged her private grief in a grace and calm that few others could command.

Not quite a year later, she wrote this about her husband:

> Now I think that I should have known that he was magic all along. I did know it—but I should have guessed that it would be too much to ask to grow old with him and see our children grow up together. . . . So now he is a legend when he would have preferred to be a man.

Jacqueline Kennedy herself had become a legend, but idolatry demands perfection. Jacqueline was not permitted the solace of sorrow. Tourists by the thousands came to gape at the house she had bought in Georgetown, an exclusive Washington suburb where she had hoped to raise her children. She sold the house and fled to New York. Because she attempted to restore a sense of normalcy to her life, recent worshippers gave voice to criticism. Photographers and reporters followed her everywhere. Other former First Ladies were not disturbed, but Jacqueline Kennedy was hounded by a stream of never-ending publicity.

Her marriage to the fabulously wealthy Aristotle Onassis on the Greek Island of Skorpios in October of 1968 released a flood of disbelief. She was thirty-eight and he was sixty-three. Her brother-in-law, Robert Kennedy, the one person who had been her principal support after the death of her husband, was himself assassinated a few months before she married Onassis. The public demanded from Jacqueline Kennedy eternal grief; she should not have married so soon. The press churned with continuous stories about her; onetime members of her personal staff took advantage of the publicity to write White House memoirs in violation of their loyalty to the former First Lady.

The haunting memories of Jacqueline Kennedy as she was on those four shattering days in November of 1963 were apparently forgotten. But the searing photographs remain for those who care to remember: a distraught First Lady climbing on the back of an open car searching for she knew not what; a First Lady still wearing a suit and stockings stained with the President's blood—watching, in the stark and somber floodlight at Andrews Air Force Base, his body being removed from the presidential jet, Air Force One; a little boy saluting his father's flag-draped coffin.

In April of 1841, an obscure poet named N. P. Willis commemorated the sudden passing of President William Henry Harrison with a frankly eulogistic poem. Two lines in that poem might well have been written for John Fitzgerald Kennedy:

> For the stars in our banner grown suddenly dim
> Let us weep, in our darkness—but weep not for him.

Claudia (Lady Bird) Johnson
1912–

In a December, 1969, interview, Lyndon B. Johnson asserted he had never wanted to be President and ran in 1964 only at the urging of his wife, Lady Bird. It is astonishing for a man generally conceded to be one of the most powerful politicians of his time to admit that so momentous a decision was not his own.

Most Johnson biographers give another picture. In the spring of 1960, he actively worked for the presidential nomination, and had no doubt that the Democrats, to meet in July, would select him as their standard bearer. When the convention turned instead to John Kennedy, Johnson accepted the vice-presidential spot.

It was clear why Kennedy had named Lyndon Baines Johnson as his running mate; he needed Johnson to help carry the Protestant South. But why did a man with vast power in the Senate agree to a secondary role? A fellow senator offered a partial answer: "Lyndon was living on borrowed time as a strong majority leader. Those guys would have pinned his hide to the wall."

Whatever the motives that prompted Johnson, he made the right decision, as events were so fatefully to prove three and a half years later. Despite the dismissal of him as "Uncle Cornpone" by many of the Kennedy people, Lyndon Baines Johnson, when he assumed the Presidency in November of 1963, gave every effort to continuity of the Kennedy program; he completed the vital legislation that Kennedy had proposed but never achieved.

The election of November, 1964, saw Johnson running, for the first time, as his own man, in his own image. His 1969 disclaimer notwithstanding, he wanted to win his own term and to win it decisively. As he suggested and hoped, the voters went "All the way with LBJ," to give him the most stunning presidential victory ever recorded, 43,129,484 to 27,178,188 for the Republican candidate, ultra conservative Senator Barry Goldwater of Arizona. But Johnson stumbled on "an ugly little war that consumed him"; by 1968, his immense popularity had dribbled away.

Lady Bird Johnson, faced with the continuing Kennedy mystique, had her own problems. In 1965, despite her eminence as First Lady, she placed second to Jacqueline Kennedy in a Gallup Poll to select the woman most admired by Americans. Lady Bird had no need for apologies, then or later. She succeeded admirably in overcoming any deficiency in public opinion; in her own way, she left more of an impact on the nation than had Mrs. Kennedy.

The only First Lady from the State of Texas, Lady Bird Johnson was born Claudia Alta Taylor; on her mother's side her ancestry was Spanish and Scotch, on her father's, English. The date of her birth, in the uninspiring Texas hamlet of Karnack, on the Louisiana border a few miles west of Shreveport, was December 22, 1912. She had two older brothers.

Claudia's father, Thomas Jefferson Taylor, was the local "Dealer in Everything." He had married Minnie Lee Pattillo of Alabama against the express wishes of her well-to-do father, who had no use for a poor dirt-farmer. With the help of Minnie Lee's income, Taylor went into business in Karnack, prospered, and bought the largest house in town. Built in the 1840s by slaves, the ancient mansion, known as "Brick House," was the only home Claudia was to know until she met Lyndon Johnson.

A bright, brown-eyed little baby, Claudia was raised mostly by nursemaids. One of them exclaimed about her: "She's purty as a ladybird," and from then on, Claudia Alta was known as Lady Bird. (The ladybird is a brightly colored beetle.)

By the time she bore her third child and only daughter, Minnie Lee Taylor was in no condition to care for an infant. She suffered racking headaches, had more than one nervous breakdown, and alternated between moods of overwhelming depression and giddiness. She hated the stupefying boredom of Karnack, and longed to escape. She finally did, in September of 1918, at the age of forty-four, when she tripped over the family collie and fell down a circular flight of stairs. A miscarriage and blood-poisoning led to her death.

The two boys were sent off to boarding schools, but Lady Bird, not yet six, was kept at home. Mr. Taylor sometimes took her to his general store, where he had her sleep upstairs when he found himself working at night. This arrangement, he knew, could not continue; he sent for his sister-in-law, thirty-nine-year-old Effie Pattillo, an ethereal spinster with little practical knowledge in the rearing of children but willing to devote time and love to her motherless niece.

Aunt Effie proved to be an important influence for Lady Bird. Lady Bird remembers her as "the most other worldly human in the world . . . delicate and airy and very gentle, and she gave me many fine values which I wouldn't trade for the world." From Aunt Effie, and from a library of classics her mother had collected, Lady Bird acquired a love of literature and art.

Schooling for Lady Bird began in a one-room schoolhouse; most of the students were children of tenant farmers working the nearby fields. Sometimes, if a large family moved away, enrollment at the school dropped to one, Lady Bird Taylor.

High school meant traveling fourteen miles to Marshall, the county seat. When Lady Bird was thirteen, her father taught her to drive, gave her a car, and had her make the trip every day on her own, over a winding dirt road. She graduated from Marshall High School two years later with a 94 average.

After a short stay at St. Mary's Episcopal School for Girls, Lady Bird entered the University of Texas in Austin, where she earned a Bachelor of Arts Degree and finished in the top ten of her class. Because she had nothing better to do, she stayed for one more year to study journalism. She joined the staff of the campus newspaper, and became secretary of Theta Sigma Phi, the honorary journalism fraternity for women. As a graduation present, in the summer of 1934, her father gave her a trip to Washington, D.C.

A friend suggested she drop in on a young man in Washington, Lyndon Johnson. Lady Bird accepted his name on a slip of paper, but did nothing about it. She had no intention of calling on a complete stranger.

Some weeks later, back in Austin, she visited her friend's office. The young man she had been asked to see, Lyndon Johnson, walked in. Recalling her first impression of him, she said that he was "excessively thin but very, very good-looking with lots of hair, quite black and wavy." She thought him "the most outspoken, straight-forward, determined young man I had ever met."

Her fellow students at the University of Texas remember her as a shy girl and "unstylish" in her clothing. Her nose was too long, and she was addicted to "muley" browns and grays. But Lyndon Johnson saw something in her he liked; she was a slender, dark-haired girl with an appealing smile. He immediately made plans to see her again. Lady Bird wasn't so sure. She had a "queer moth-in-the flame feeling about this remarkable young man."

The very next day he asked her to marry him; she of course said no, as she said no to his second proposal at the end of a week. After his return to Washington, where he worked as secretary to Congressman Kleberg, owner of the famous King Ranch in Texas, Lyndon sent her his photograph. "For Bird," he had inscribed, "a lovely girl with ideals, principles, intelligence and refinement, from her sincere admirer, Lyndon."

With characteristic Johnson tenacity and single-minded industry, he pursued his courtship of the wavering Lady Bird. In November, only two months after their first meeting, he somehow persuaded her to drive with him to San Antonio, four hundred miles away, to be married that same day. She still hadn't said yes, but she was afraid to lose him, as she later admitted. She finally agreed to be his wife as they were walking up the steps of the St. Mark's Episcopal Church in San Antonio that evening. Before twelve people, most of whom were strangers, Lady Bird Taylor married Lyndon Baines Johnson on November 17, 1934. The bride, twenty-one, used a $2.50 Sears and Roebuck wedding ring bought at the last minute by the best man, San Antonio postmaster Dan Quill, friend of the twenty-six-year-old groom. The service was conducted by the Reverend Arthur E. McKinstry, who called after them as they were leaving, "I hope this marriage lasts."

The Johnson campaign for the mutual advancement of husband and wife began early. Lyndon persuaded Lady Bird to concentrate on "style"; the drab tones she once preferred gave way to bright colors, and low, comfortable shoes to high heels. She tried to interest him in reading; she often marked passages for him, and followed him around their apartment reading aloud.

Their two rooms in Washington saw many guests. Lyndon cultivated the right people, and expected his bride to entertain them, though she had never before been involved in housekeeping of any kind.

Lady Bird and Lyndon had one trait in common—thrift. Out of each month's salary of $267, they managed to buy a government bond for $18.75, which they set aside for the family they hoped to raise.

With the help of friends, Johnson received an appointment from President Roosevelt as Texas director of the National Youth Administration. Lady Bird and Lyndon moved back to Austin, where they lived for eighteen months. In 1937 Lyndon won a special election against nine other candidates for a seat in the U.S. House of Representatives, to replace a Texas congressman who had died suddenly. Lyndon's campaign was financed by a $10,000 advance from his father-in-law against Lady Bird's ultimate inheritance (from her mother's share of the Patillo estate in Alabama and community property in Texas).

Lyndon's twelve years as a congressman meant a full schedule for Lady Bird. In addition to constant entertainment, she shepherded Lyndon's constituents all over Washington. She devoted herself to her husband's career with the same total intensity he gave it. She began to advise him, and he listened. (He said of Lady Bird that she was "one of the wisest and certainly the most trusted counselor I've had.")

By 1942, Lady Bird decided she needed other interests. She invested more of her inheritance (which now totaled some $64,000) in a small 250-watt radio station in Austin, Texas. Five months after she plunged into the task of straightening out the tangled affairs of the tiny station, as well as wielding a mop and broom to clean the premises, the balance sheet showed a profit of $18. The wattage was increased to 1,000; under her aggressive management and sales policy, the station grew and brought fortune to the Johnsons. By 1962, KTBC, the hub of a Texas communications empire, was worth at least $7 million.

After ten years of marriage and four miscarriages, Lady Bird at last had her first child, Lynda Bird, on March 19, 1944, in Washington. Lucy Baines, her second and last child, was born three years later, on July 2, 1947, also in Washington.

In a run-off Democratic primary between Johnson and Texas politician Coke Stevenson in 1948, Johnson won a contest that has to rank as the closest in senatorial elections. Out of a million-vote total, Johnson was the victor by 87 votes. (As the Democratic candidate, he easily won the election that fall.) But it was his impossibly narrow win in the primary that haunted him when he took his seat as junior senator from Texas in January of 1949. His fellow Senators referred to him as "Landslide Lyndon."

Johnson's rise in the Senate was meteoric; within two years he was the Democratic whip, and two years after that, at the age of

343

forty-four, he became the majority leader, a position he held until his election as Vice President in 1960. By universal agreement, he was the most powerful and persuasive majority leader in decades. His principal instruments were pressure, influence, and the telephone.

His selection as Kennedy's vice-presidential candidate brought Lady Bird for the first time into the national arena as an active campaigner. Shy by nature, she had trained herself to face crowds; as she explained it, "Lyndon expects a lot of me, so I have learned not to be afraid any more." She traveled 35,000 miles in seventy-one days, and spoke at hundreds of breakfasts, luncheons, and tea parties. Her cheerful Texas sign-off, "So glad all y'all came," charmed thousands of potential Kennedy–Johnson supporters.

Her two and a half years as Second Lady saw no letup in her activity as a hostess. She and Lyndon did more entertaining, both at their Washington home, "The Elms," and at the LBJ Ranch in Texas, than any other vice-presidential couple. Their guests ranged from Ayub Khan, President of Pakistan, to Bashir Ahmed, a Pakistani camel driver Johnson had impulsively invited to the United States during a 1961 journey to Asia.

Lady Bird Johnson stood at the right side of her husband while Jacqueline Kennedy, widow of the slain President Kennedy, stood at his left as Lyndon Baines Johnson took the oath of office in the presidential jet, Air Force One, on the afternoon of November 22, 1963. Some four hours later, in Washington, Lady Bird was again at his side when he made a brief statement to the country and ended with these words: "I will do my best. That is all I can do. I ask for your help—and God's."

When the Johnsons moved into the White House, Lady Bird confided to a close friend: "I feel as if I am suddenly on stage for a part I never rehearsed." She was far too modest. Barring only Eleanor Roosevelt, she was the best prepared First Lady of the past fifty years. The general public knew little about her; to most of the country the wife of the Vice President is normally a shadowy figure. Lady Bird was no exception, in spite of her campaign activity in 1960 and her presence on her husband's trips abroad. But her long years of executive experience in her various commercial enterprises, her meetings with many foreign dignitaries, her extensive entertaining in Washington and Texas, all combined to give her a superb background for her new role.

As First Lady, members of the press found her cooperative and quotable. She hired a newspaperwoman, Liz Carpenter, as her staff director and press secretary, and made herself far more available to reporters than any of her immediate predecessors. She proved a delightful and willing source of copy. Her colloquialisms, expressed in complete sincerity, displayed her lack of pretension, while her statements for the record demonstrated a spirited intelligence. She once admitted, "Of all the talents I wish I had, the one I admire most is the ability to make words march and sing and cannonade." She did make them sing, in her own idiomatic way, when she exclaimed that she was "busy as a man killin' rattlesnakes," or "I'll see you Saturday if the Lord be willin' and the creek don't rise."

Not quite fifty-one, Lady Bird became an active and hardworking First Lady. She visited the depressed areas of Appalachia to promote her husband's War on Poverty; she began the first of forty trips across the country on behalf of her own brand of "flower power." Part conservation of our natural resources and part de-uglification of our man-made eyesores, Lady Bird's "Beautification" program took her from one end of the continent to the other. She eventually covered over 200,000 miles, much of it by "rubber raft, bus, ski lift, surrey, orchard wagon, rail and foot" (in the words of her press secretary).

Johnson's campaign for reelection in 1964, which he later insisted was urged on him by Lady Bird, featured the "Lady Bird Special," a train of nineteen cars and three hundred people, including members of the press, and Lady Bird. They started from Alexandria, Virginia, and visited eight states in five days. They made forty-five stops, sometimes in remote hamlets where a passenger train hadn't been seen for years. Lady Bird gave forty-five speeches and shook countless hands. As she had in 1960, she helped to carry the South for her husband. (He had initially thought he would not run in 1964, but changed his mind when Lady Bird sent him a memo with these words: "Beloved—To step out now would be wrong for your country and I can see nothing but a lonely wasteland for your future.")

President Johnson and Lady Bird continued the custom, originated by the Kennedys, of inviting prominent writers, artists, and musicians to the Executive Mansion. Their "White House Festival of the Arts" in 1965 was attended by almost one hundred writers and artists. For the public, however, the oustanding social events of the Johnson administration were the weddings of the two Johnson daughters. Luci (she changed the spelling) married Patrick Nugent on August 6, 1966, in the National Shrine of the Immaculate Conception; Lynda married Marine captain Charles S. Robb in the White House on December 9, 1967. It was the first White House wedding since Alice Roosevelt's, sixty-one years before. (Happy and adoring parents, Lady Bird and Lyndon Johnson became equally happy and adoring grandparents.)

When President Johnson announced, during a nationally televised speech in March of 1968 that he would not seek reelection, it was thought by most people that the unpopularity of the Vietnam War had forced him into retirement. He has since divulged that he and Lady Bird had agreed in 1964 he would not run again four years later, and his announcement would be made no later than March 31, 1968.

President and Mrs. Johnson, since they left the White House in January of 1969, have spent most of their time on their LBJ Ranch near Johnson City, Texas. They have offices in Austin, where they supervised completion of the Lyndon Baines Johnson Library and School of Public Affairs at the University of Texas. The largest of the presidential libraries, the Johnson complex was built at a cost of $11.8 million.

Although she has not been hounded by the press as has been Jacqueline Kennedy, Lady Bird Johnson has not been forgotten. In May of 1969, the 190-acre Lady Bird Johnson Municipal

Park was dedicated by the people of Fredericksburg, Texas, with Lady Bird and the former President making their first public appearance since his retirement. On August 27, 1969, Johnson's sixty-first birthday, President Nixon, with the entire Johnson family as his guests, dedicated the Lady Bird Johnson Grove, in California's Redwood National Park. President Nixon said that Lady Bird had done "more for beautification than any other First Lady."

Lyndon B. Johnson would agree. And he would most certainly second the words of the late Sam Rayburn, his Texas colleague, associate, and close friend. Speaking one time of Johnson and Lady Bird, Rayburn said, "The smartest thing Lyndon ever did was to marry her."

Thelma (Pat) Nixon
1912–

He lost the Presidency by 118,000 votes; two years later, he ran for governor of California and lost by a wider margin. It was a disastrous defeat for Richard Milhous Nixon; in his bitter disappointment he berated the press for their prejudicial reporting of his campaign. He ended his denunciation by telling the startled reporters: "You won't have Nixon to kick around any more, because, gentlemen, this is my last press conference." The year was 1962; Richard Nixon had dramatically and capably removed himself from the political scene.

But he achieved the impossible; he did what no man had ever done before. Eight years after losing the Presidency, he returned in 1968 to a triumphant first-ballot nomination by the Republican convention, and went on to a narrow election victory. Out of 73,211,562 votes, he received a minority total of 43.4 percent— 31,770,237 to 31,270,533 for his Democratic opponent Hubert

Humphrey and 9,906,141 for Alabama's George Wallace. In the electoral count, he had the necessary majority, 56.2 per cent, to become the thirty-seventh President of the United States.

The experts had said it could never happen. But Richard M. Nixon's determination, planning, and patience proved them wrong. He was helped by a mood of uncertainty and unrest in the country. The people were weary of the Vietnam War, and desperate to be out of it. He assured them he had a plan to end it, although he did not divulge what he had in mind. He had suggestions too for the violence and agitation of the cities, for the inflation that showed no signs of slowing, for the mounting taxes that threatened to bring on a tax-payers' revolt.

As in any presidential election, the voters of 1968 chose Richard M. Nixon for a variety of reasons, both simple and complex; one reason certainly must be his incredible success as a politician and Wall Street lawyer after the humblest of beginnings on a farm in Yorba Linda, California. In the finest American tradition, a poor boy had made it all the way to the top.

His wife, Pat Ryan Nixon, had a childhood even more difficult. The only First Lady of the twentieth century who had to work for a living, Pat Nixon is a controlled, even-tempered woman who does not mind admitting, "I've never had time to dream about being someone else. I had to work." As a girl, she knew many hardships; she has since found ample reward in her husband's success and in her own.

When Thelma Catherine Ryan was born in Ely, Nevada, a small mining town, on March 16, 1912, her father, William Ryan, was working in the copper mines. He did not hear of the birth of his only daughter until he returned home after midnight. To the joyous Ryan, the date of her birth had to be March 17, not March 16, and he called her "St. Patrick's Babe in the Morn," shortened to Pat. Family and friends picked up the name, and Pat herself celebrated her birthday on March 17, St. Patrick's Day.

Pat had two older brothers. Her mother, Kate Halberstadt Bender, from Hessen County, Germany, not far from Frankfurt,

349

was a widow when she married William Ryan. By 1914, mine work had become impossible for Ryan; there were far too many accidents and the copper mines endangered his health. The family moved from the barren mountains of eastern Nevada to Artesia, California, eighteen miles southeast of Los Angeles, where they settled on a ten-acre truck farm.

With the entire family pitching in, the small farm supported the Ryans. They raised potatoes, peppers, cauliflower, and tomatoes. Pat toddled along after her father and brothers until she was old enough to do her share; she learned to drive the team of horses, and sometimes rode them.

Pat's first school was a mile away. She and her brothers walked both ways. She later attended Excelsior High School in Norwalk, five miles from Artesia.

Mrs. Ryan died in 1925, when Pat was thirteen. Care of the house was left entirely to Pat; she had to do the cooking, help in the fields, perform her household chores, and attend school. Two years after her mother's death, she had the additional responsibility of nursing her father through a long and lingering illness (he had developed silicosis in the Ely copper mines).

It was a painful and demanding time for a young girl; as Pat later remembered, "Life was sort of sad, so I tried to cheer everybody up. I learned to be that kind of person." Her father was ill for two years; he died in 1929.

Seventeen at her father's death, Pat finished high school, worked in a local bank, and then in 1930, drove to New York with an elderly couple. Though the Depression was beginning, Pat found a job at New York's Seton Hospital, where she stayed for two years, as a secretary and later as an X-ray technician. She returned to Los Angeles with enough savings to enter the University of Southern California.

A good student, Pat majored in merchandising. A constant need for money, however, made it necessary for her to take odd jobs during her holidays and vacations and spare time; she graded papers, worked at a Wilshire Boulevard department store, and appeared in a number of movies as an extra. An attractive redhead, she had been casually interested in acting; as an extra she earned $7 a day. She said about those appearances, "You would have to hunt real hard to find me, but I made quite a bit of money." In *Becky Sharp*, she was promoted to a walk-on part with one speaking line that was cut from the final version; it was her most important role and her biggest Hollywood paycheck—$25.

She graduated from the university with honors, and intended making her career in merchandising, but an offer of a teaching job in Whittier for $190 a month (as she said, "fabulous for 1937") intervened. Whittier had been established as a Quaker settlement in 1887; fifty years later, when Pat moved there, it was no longer completely Quaker in character, although it was a quiet town of 25,000 that tolerated "no establishments that may be an invitation to hoodlumism."

Pat soon became part of the community life; teachers were expected to participate in the local events, and Pat was encouraged to try her hand at the Little Theater, a thriving enterprise. A young lawyer, Richard Nixon, heard about the "glamorous new schoolteacher" who was to be in a play, *The Dark Tower*. He came down to have a look, and ended up trying out for the part of a district attorney. He got the role, second romantic lead opposite her, and that very night, after the first rehearsal, he proposed.

For a young man as reserved as he seemed to be, it was a most surprising declaration. Pat was momentarily too astonished to respond. "I guess I just looked at him," she said. She was not ready to settle down, particularly not with a man she had only just met; she had visions of a far more exciting life than she had known. She put him off, and continued to go out with most of the town's other eligible bachelors. Nixon waited patiently, and saw her as often as he could. By the spring of 1940, two years after they met, she finally said yes. They were married in a Quaker ceremony, on June 21, 1940, at the Mission Inn, Riverside, California. According to Pat, "It was a fine wedding." She was twenty-eight, and he was twenty-seven (he had been born on January 9, 1913).

They drove to Mexico in a car bought with her money, a 1939 Oldsmobile, and enjoyed a two-week honeymoon financed by their joint savings. (During the 1968 presidential campaign, Nixon spoke nostalgically about that 1940 trip. "Sometimes we drove all night to save the cost of a hotel, and I think we saw every temple, every church in old Mexico and it all cost us only $178.")

Mr. and Mrs. Richard Nixon moved into a rented apartment over a garage. Nixon, not yet interested in politics, had no intention of remaining a small-town lawyer in Whittier, although he was doing fairly well, and he seemed a natural leader on a community level. Pat and Dick became part of the young marrieds of Whittier, none of whom had too much money. Ice-skating and dancing, both of which Pat enjoyed, were the favorite recreations, with an occasional excursion to Los Angeles for a performance of the civic opera company.

While Pat continued with her teaching, Dick cast about for other prospects. With the entry of the United States into World War II in December of 1941, Nixon took a position with the Office of Price Administration. Pat followed him to Washington, and later to Ottumwa, Iowa, when he joined the Navy as a lieutenant, junior grade. She worked in an Ottumwa bank during his training period. After his transfer to active duty in the South Pacific, she returned to the OPA, for assignment to the San Francisco office, where she stayed until Dick came back to California at the end of 1944.

The birth of the Nixons' first child came shortly before Dick's debut as an active politician. Patricia (now known to the world as Tricia) was born in Whittier on February 21, 1946. One month later, on March 19, 1946, Richard M. Nixon entered his name as a candidate to oppose incumbent Congressman Jerry Voorhis. In a careful and skillfully plotted campaign, Nixon defeated the veteran congressman by a total of 65,586 to 49,994 (Voorhis was first elected as U.S. representative in 1936). Nixon carried his own home town of Whittier by a better than 2 to 1 margin, 5,727 to 2,678. Nixon's extraordinary career had begun auspiciously.

The Nixons moved to Washington in January of 1947. Their second daughter, Julie, was born in the capital city on July 5, 1948.

Nixon catapulted into national prominence with his tenacious prosecution of the Alger Hiss–Whittaker Chambers case as a member of the House Un-American Activities Committee. By 1950, he was running for the United States Senate; he defeated Congresswoman Helen Gahagan Douglas by a 680,000 vote margin. The stage was set for the Vice-Presidency.

Public life, for Pat Nixon, had a double edge of gratification and despair. Her husband's nomination by the Republican convention, in July of 1952, to run as Vice President on General Eisenhower's ticket, was the first of many triumphant moments she was to know in the coming years. On their way to California to begin their campaign, the Nixons stopped in Ely, Nevada, where Pat had been born forty years before. The predominantly Democratic town turned out en masse for a rousing welcome to its most famous daughter, despite her marriage to a leading Republican.

But Dick Nixon's prominence brought her disquiet and anguish as well. Newspaper revelations in September of 1952 of a "secret Nixon fund," supplied by supporters and allegedly used for living purposes, led to a nationwide disclosure on television of the Nixon family finances. Pat was terribly upset at this blatant invasion of their privacy; she could see no reason why Nixon had "to tell people how little we have and how much we owe." Nixon and the Republican hierarchy believed the telecast to be an absolute must; the vice-presidential candidate had to rescue his career and pull the Republican ticket from the brink of possible disaster.

In a widely heralded and celebrated address watched by an estimated sixty million viewers, Richard Nixon assured his audience that the secret fund had been used for electioneering purposes only, not for living expenses, and he and Pat in fact owed more than they owned. "Pat," he said, "doesn't have a mink coat. But she does have a respectable Republican cloth coat, and I always tell her that she would look good in anything." He also made reference to Checkers, their black and white spotted cocker spaniel, a gift to his daughters from a Texan.

The speech elicited unabashed tears, from many listeners, from his wife, and from the candidate himself. Nixon's public cleansing of his political soul paid huge dividends; at the age of thirty-nine, he joined General Eisenhower in an easy victory over the Democrats. (For Pat, there was at least one unlooked-for result—she had to wait a number of years for her first fur coat. She now owns a pale mink.)

Richard Nixon's eight vice-presidential years were years of work and travel for Pat. She spent more and more time as a hostess and governmental wife, and less as a mother and mistress of her household. Daytime responsibilities required her to visit hospitals and schools; at night she dined with heads of state. Accompanying her husband, she traveled to fifty-three countries and covered 150,000 miles. By 1960, she estimated that she was giving less than 10 percent of her time to her house and children.

Forbearance was another virtue Pat had to develop. In April and May of 1958, she joined her husband on a highly publicized swing through South America. They were well received in most of the countries they visited, but open hostility greeted them in Caracas, Venezuela. A large crowd of shouting, jeering, and spitting anti-American demonstrators gathered at Maiquetia Airport to await their arrival. As the Nixons came down the steps from the plane and walked rigidly toward the doors of the terminal building, obscenities and insults were shrieked at them. Behind a barricade, Pat saw a young lady whose face was distorted with hatred. Pat reached over the barricade, and gently, without a word, took the girl's hand. The girl's eyes filled with tears; overcome with shame and remorse, she turned away.

Election night, Tuesday, November 8, 1960, was a long evening of agony for Pat and the two Nixon daughters (Tricia was fourteen, and Julie twelve). Unbelievably, Richard Nixon lost to John F. Kennedy by one of the narrowest margins ever recorded in a presidential election—49.71 percent for Kennedy and 49.55 percent for Nixon. Pat knew she could no longer endure the pain of defeat; she asked Nixon to sign a pledge that he would never run for office again. He gave her his word.

The Nixons sold their Washington home and moved to Los

Angeles, where Nixon joined a prestigious law firm. Nine months later, at a small dinner party, he announced his candidacy for the governorship of California. Pat made it a rule never to lose her composure in public. Nixon's announcement disappointed and distressed her; he had violated his pledge. "The squabble that ensued," according to one report, "reverberated in Republican circles for weeks."

But the Nixon girls wanted their father to run; Pat gave in, reluctantly. And once again it was up to her to console her heartsick husband and daughters when he lost the governorship to his Democratic opponent. November, 1962, marked a low point for all of them.

The summer of 1963 saw a new life begin for the Nixon family. Nixon joined a prominent New York law firm specializing in work for Wall Street. They bought a twelve-room cooperative on Fifth Avenue, in the same building where Governor Nelson Rockefeller lived. Nixon's earnings, as a senior partner in his firm, averaged $200,000 a year. It was a far cry from the copper mines of Ely, Nevada, and the truck farm of Artesia, California. Pat Nixon, who had once been happy to earn $7 a day as a movie extra and $190 a month as a high school teacher, now had a live-in couple taking care of her apartment. She had money to spend on clothes and style, without regard for expense. Her brownish hair (red in her early years) became ash blonde; but her clothes changed only in price—they were still simple, comfortable, and lacking in dash.

Her five years in New York were far less busy than those she had known in Washington. Her life was orderly, as was her apartment. Her daughters, making their formal debuts, were introduced to society, and sent to the Northeast's most exclusive schools, Chapin and Finch in New York and Smith College in Massachusetts.

Pat Nixon was neither surprised nor enthusiastic when she realized her husband meant to run for the Presidency again in 1968. She deferred to his wishes, as she had in the past. "Once he makes his decision," she said, "I'm a good sport."

When Richard Milhous Nixon defeated Hubert Humphrey and

George Wallace in November of 1968 to become the thirty-seventh President, he gave Pat a diamond and pearl pin, with earrings to match. And seven weeks later, Julie Nixon, twenty, daughter of the President-elect, married Dwight David Eisenhower II, twenty, grandson of the former President. The wedding, one of the most publicized of the year, was solemnized at New York's First Marble Collegiate Church, with Dr. Norman Vincent Peale officiating.

On January 20, 1969, there were six Inaugural Balls to welcome the new President and the new First Lady. Pat wore a mimosa-yellow silk satin gown, glittery and jewel studded. *The New York Times* reported that she was "properly radiant."

The Nixons have entertained many heads of state, including Pierre Trudeau of Canada, Eisaku Sato and Madame Sato of Japan, New Zealand Prime Minister and Madame Holyoake, Golda Meir of Israel, British Prime Minister Harold Wilson, and French President Georges Pompidou and Madame Pompidou. But the Nixon social influence was slow in extending beyond the boundaries of the Executive Mansion. In early 1970 the President and the First Lady began a series of monthly "Evenings at the White House." The best publicized was the presentation, on Washington's Birthday, of the hit Broadway musical, *1776*, on a specially constructed stage in the East Room. Another highlighted event was the one-man show of Andrew Wyeth paintings in the White House; it was the first time any artist had been so honored by a President and his wife.

Pat Nixon's imprint was slow in developing as well. During the early months of her husband's administration, she presented a stiff, uncomfortable image. It was not until July of 1969, when she made a junket to Portland, Oregon, and Los Angeles, California, on behalf of a "volunteerism" project, did she begin to display herself as a warm, feeling, friendly, and humanly dedicated person. The newswomen who accompanied her were thoroughly charmed by the new Pat Nixon. They had expected her to remain wrapped in "an icy cocoon of literal anonymity." Instead, she emerged as an attractive, fashionable woman who spoke with complete sincerity of her program.

"If millions would get involved," she said, "if everyone would give just twenty minutes a day being neighborly and kind and lending a helping hand, the quality of life would be enriched." To lend weight to her own role, Pat Nixon embarked in March, 1970, on a tour of five college campuses to witness the results of her "volunteerism." At a Michigan Center for Blind and Deaf Children, where student volunteers were working without pay, she met a four-year-old who could neither hear nor see. Pat Nixon said this about the child: "But she knows what love is. She can feel. That's the difference."

Bibliography

Previously published material about the First Ladies is surprisingly sparse; except for a handful of individual biographies and a few collective biographies, sketchily written and incomplete, there is almost nothing. In contrast, a vast amount of information about our Presidents has been compiled and published, including biographies, diaries, and first-hand observations. Here, too, there is the barest mention of the First Ladies, or none at all. In the preparation of this project, I consulted, read, and researched many hundreds of volumes, periodicals, newspapers, diaries, and letters. Unfortunately, much of this material is either out of print and not readily available or is accessible only to scholars and historians. In deference to the casual reader, therefore, I have decided to give simply a partial listing of a few representative titles. The serious student of American history will know where to find the works and sources that interest him.

General

Armbruster, Maxim E. *The Presidents of the United States,* New York, Horizon Press, 1966.

Buchanan, Lamont. *Ballot for Americans,* New York, E. P. Dutton and Company, 1956.

Butterfield, Roger. *The American Past,* New York, Simon and Schuster, 1947.

Carpenter, Frank. *Carp's Washington,* Frances Carpenter, ed., New York, McGraw-Hill Book Company, 1960.

Colman, Edna M. *White House Gossip,* Garden City, Doubleday, Page & Company, 1927.

Crook, Colonel W. H. *Memories of the White House,* Boston, Little, Brown and Company, 1911.

Furman, Bess. *White House Profile,* Indianapolis, The Bobbs-Merrill Company, 1951.

Hess, Stephen. *America's Political Dynasties,* Garden City, Doubleday & Company, 1966.

Holloway, Laura C. *Ladies of the White House,* Philadelphia, Bradley and Company, 1881.

Hoover, Irwin Hood (Ike). *Forty-two Years in the White House,* Boston, Houghton, Mifflin Company, 1934.

Jeffries, Ona Griffin. *In and Out of the White House,* New York, Wilfred Funk, Inc., 1960.

Kane, Joseph Nathan. *Facts About the Presidents,* Bronx, N.Y., H. W. Wilson Company, 1968.

Kohlsaat, H. H. *From McKinley to Harding,* New York, Charles Scribner's Sons, 1923.

Lorant, Stefan. *The Glorious Burden,* New York, Harper & Row, 1968.

Morison, Samuel Eliot. *The Oxford History of the American People,* New York, Oxford University Press, 1965.

Parks, Lillain Rogers (with Frances Spatz Leighton). *My Thirty Years Backstairs at the White House,* New York, Fleet Publishing Corporation, 1961.

Poore, Ben:Perley. *Perley's Reminiscences of Sixty Years in the National Metropolis,* (2 vols.), Philadelphia, Hubbard Brothers, 1886.

BIBLIOGRAPHY

Sadler, Christine. *Children in the White House,* New York, G. P. Putnam's Sons, 1967.

Schachner, Nathan. *Founding Fathers,* New York, G. P. Putnam's Sons, 1954.

Smith, Margaret Bayard. *The First Forty Years of Washington Society,* New York, Charles Scribner's Sons, 1906.

Smith, Marie, and Durbin, Louise. *White House Brides,* Washington, D.C., Acropolis Books, 1966.

Steinberg, Alfred. *The First Ten,* Garden City, Doubleday & Company, 1954.

Wellman, Paul I. *The House Divides,* Garden City, Doubleday & Company, 1966.

Specific Sources

Adams, Abigail. *Letters of Mrs. Adams,* (2 vols.), Boston, Charles C. Little and James Brown, 1840.

Alexander, Holmes. *The American Talleyrand,* New York, Harper & Brothers, 1935.

Balch, William Ralston. *Life of James A. Garfield,* Philadelphia, Hubbard Bros., 1881.

Bassett, John Spencer. *The Life of Andrew Jackson* (3 vols.), Garden City, Doubleday, Page & Company, 1911.

Bemis, Samuel Flagg. *John Quincy Adams* (2 vols.), New York, Alfred A. Knopf, 1949.

Bergquist, Laura. *A Very Special President,* New York, McGraw-Hill Book Company, 1965.

Bobbé, Dorothie. *Mr. and Mrs. John Quincy Adams, An Adventure in Patriotism,* New York, Minton, Balch & Company, 1930.

Bowen, Catherine Drinker. *John Adams and the American Revolution,* Boston, Little, Brown and Company, 1954.

Brandon, Dorothy. *Mamie Doud Eisenhower,* New York, Charles Scribner's Sons, 1954.

Brant, Irving. *James Madison* (4 vols.), Indianapolis, The Bobbs-Merrill Company, 1953–61.

Buell, Augustus C. *History of Andrew Jackson* (2 vols.), New York, Charles Scribner's Sons, 1904.

Carpenter, Liz. *Ruffles and Flourishes,* Garden City, Doubleday & Company, 1970.

Churchill, Allen. *The Roosevelts, American Aristocrats,* New York, Harper & Row, 1965.

Cleaves, Freeman. *Old Tippecanoe,* New York, Charles Scribner's Sons, 1939.

Coolidge, Calvin. *Autobiography,* New York, Cosmopolitan Book Corporation, 1929.

Croy, Homer. *The Trial of Mrs. Abraham Lincoln,* New York, Duell, Sloan & Pierce, 1962.

Daniels, Jonathan. *The Man of Independence,* Philadelphia, J. P. Lippincott Company, 1950.

Davis, John H. *The Bouviers,* New York, Farrar, Straus & Giroux, 1969.

Desmond, Alice Curtis. *Martha Washington, Our First Lady,* New York, Dodd, Mead & Company, 1953.

DeToledano, Ralph. *One Man Alone,* New York, Funk & Wagnalls, 1969.

Dos Passos, John. *The Shackles of Power,* Garden City, Doubleday & Company, 1966.

Eisenhower, Dwight D. *At Ease: Stories I Tell to Friends,* Garden City, Doubleday & Company, 1967.

360

BIBLIOGRAPHY

Ekenrode, H. J. *Rutherford B. Hayes, Statesman of Reunion,* New York, Dodd, Mead & Company, 1930.

Freeman, Douglas Southall. *George Washington* (7 vols.), New York, Charles Scribner's Sons, 1948–57.

Grant, Ulysses S. *Personal Memoirs,* E. B. Long, ed., Cleveland, The World Publishing Company, 1952.

Hagedorn, Hermann. *The Roosevelt Family of Sagamore Hill,* New York, The Macmillan Company, 1954.

Hall, Gordon Langley. *Mr. Jefferson's Ladies,* Boston, Beacon Press, 1966.

———, and Pinchot, Ann. *Jacqueline Kennedy,* New York, Frederick Fell, Inc., 1964.

Hamilton, Holman. *Zachary Taylor* (2 vols.), Indianapolis, The Bobbs-Merrill Company, 1941, 1951.

Hatch, Alden. *Edith Bolling Wilson, First Lady Extraordinary,* New York, Dodd, Mead & Company, 1961.

———. *Red Carpet for Mamie,* New York, Henry Holt and Company, 1954.

Hickok, Lorena A. *Reluctant First Lady,* New York, Dodd, Mead & Company, 1962.

Hoover, Herbert. *Memoirs* (3 vols.), New York, The Macmillan Company, 1951, 1952.

Howard, Oliver Otis. *General Taylor,* New York, D. Appleton and Company, 1892.

Howe, George Frederick. *Chester A. Arthur,* New York, Frederick Ungar Publishing Company, 1957.

Hoyt, Edwin P. *James A. Garfield,* Chicago, Reilly & Lee Company, 1964.

Hughes, Rupert. *George Washington* (3 vols.), New York, William Morrow & Company, 1926.

Irwin, William Henry. *Herbert Hoover, A Reminiscent Biography,* New York, The Century Company, 1928.

James, Marquis. *Andrew Jackson, Portrait of a President,* New York, Grosset & Dunlap, 1937.

Jenkins, John Stilwell. *James Knox Polk and a History of His Administration,* Buffalo, John E. Beardsley, 1850.

Johnson, Sam Houston. *My Brother Lyndon,* New York, Cowles Book Company, 1970.

Keckley, Elizabeth Hobbs. *Behind the Scenes,* New York, G. W. Carleton & Company, 1868.

Lash, Joseph P. *Eleanor Roosevelt, A Friend's Memoir,* Garden City, Doubleday & Company, 1964.

Leech, Margaret. *In the Days of McKinley,* New York, Harper & Brothers, 1959.

Lynch, Denis Tilden, *Grover Cleveland,* New York, Horace Liveright, Inc., 1932.

Malone, Dumas. *Jefferson, The Virginian,* Vol. I, Boston, Little, Brown and Company, 1948.

Manchester, William. *The Death of a President,* New York, Harper & Row, 1967.

Mazo, Earl, and Hess, Stephen. *Nixon,* New York, Harper & Row, 1968.

McAdoo, Eleanor Wilson, ed. *The Priceless Gift,* New York, McGraw-Hill Book Company, 1962.

Minnigerode, Meade. *Some American Ladies,* New York, G. P. Putnam's Sons, 1926.

Mitchell, Stewart, ed. *New Letters of Abigail Adams, 1788–1801,* Boston, Houghton, Mifflin Company, 1947.

Monroe, James. *Autobiography,* Stuart Gerry Brown, ed., Syracuse, N.Y., Syracuse University Press, 1959.

361

BIBLIOGRAPHY

Montgomery, H. *The Life of Major-General William H. Harrison,* Cleveland, Tooker & Gatchell, 1853.

Montgomery, Ruth. *Mrs. LBJ,* New York, Holt, Rinehart and Winston, 1964.

Nevins, Allan, ed. *The Diary of John Quincy Adams, 1794–1845,* New York, Charles Scribner's Sons, 1951.

———, ed. *Polk, The Diary of a President, 1845–1849,* New York, Longmans, Green and Company, 1929.

———. *Grover Cleveland,* New York, Dodd, Mead & Company, 1932.

Nichols, Roy Franklin. *Franklin Pierce,* Philadelphia, University of Pennsylvania Press, 1958.

Nixon, Richard M. *Six Crises,* Garden City, Doubleday & Company, 1962.

Padover, Saul K. *A Jefferson Profile,* New York, The John Day Company, 1956.

Parton, James. *Life of Andrew Jackson,* New York, Mason Brothers, 1860.

Pryor, Helen B., M.D. *Lou Henry Hoover, Gallant First Lady,* New York, Dodd, Mead & Company, 1969.

Randall, Ruth Painter. *Mary Lincoln, Biography of a Marriage,* Boston, Little, Brown and Company, 1953.

Rayback, Robert J. *Millard Fillmore, Biography of a President,* Henry Stewart, Inc. for Buffalo Historical Society, 1959.

Roosevelt, Eleanor. *Autobiography,* New York, Harper & Brothers, 1937 to 1961.

Roosevelt, Mrs. Theodore (and others). *Cleared for Strange Ports,* New York, Charles Scribner's Sons, 1927.

Ross, Ishbel. *An American Family, The Tafts, 1678–1964,* Cleveland, The World Publishing Company, 1959.

———. *The General's Wife, The Life of Mrs. Ulysses S. Grant,* New York, Dodd, Mead & Company, 1959.

———. *Grace Coolidge and Her Era,* New York, Dodd, Mead & Company, 1962.

Russell, Francis. *The Shadow of Blooming Grove,* New York, McGraw-Hill Book Company, 1968.

Sandburg, Carl. *Abraham Lincoln,* New York, Harcourt, Brace and Company, 1954.

Seager, Robert, II. *And Tyler Too,* New York, McGraw-Hill Book Company, 1963.

Shepard, Edward M. *Biography of Martin Van Buren,* Boston, Houghton, Mifflin and Company, 1888.

Sievers, Harry J., S.J. *Benjamin Harrison* (3 vols.), Chicago, Harry Regnery Company, 1952; New York, University Publishers, 1959; Indianapolis, The Bobbs-Merrill Company, 1968.

Sinclair, Andrew. *The Available Man, Warren Gamaliel Harding,* New York, The Macmillan Company, 1965.

Smith, Marie. *The President's Lady,* New York, Random House, 1964.

Smith, Page. *John Adams* (2 vols.), Garden City, Doubleday & Company, 1962.

Steinberg, Alfred. *The Man From Missouri,* New York, G. P. Putnam's Sons, 1962.

———. *Mrs. R: The Life of Eleanor Roosevelt,* New York, G. P. Putnam's Sons, 1958.

———. *Sam Johnson's Boy,* New York, The Macmillan Company, 1968.

Stryker, Lloyd Paul. *Andrew Johnson,* New York, The Macmillan Company, 1929.

Styron, Arthur. *The Last of the Cocked Hats,* Norman, University of Oklahoma Press, 1955.

Syrett, Harold C. *Andrew Jackson,* Indianapolis, The Bobbs-Merrill Company, 1953.

BIBLIOGRAPHY

Taft, Mrs. William Howard. *Recollections of Full Years,* New York, Mead & Company, 1914.

Thane, Elswyth. *Washington's Lady,* New York, Dodd, Mead & Company, 1954.

Thayer, Mary Van Rensselaer. *Jacqueline Bouvier Kennedy,* Garden City, Doubleday & Company, 1961.

Thomas, Lately. *The First President Johnson,* New York, William Morrow & Company, 1968.

Townsend, William H. *Lincoln and His Wife's Home Town,* Indianapolis, The Bobbs-Merrill Company, 1929.

Truman, Harry S. *Mr. Citizen,* New York, Bernard Geis Associates, 1953.

Truman, Margaret (Daniel). *Souvenir,* New York, McGraw-Hill Book Company, 1956.

Walworth, Arthur. *Woodrow Wilson* (2 vols.), New York, Longmans, Green & Company, 1958.

White, Theodore H. *The Making of the President, 1964,* New York, Atheneum Publishers, 1965.

————. *The Making of the President, 1968,* New York, Atheneum Publishers, 1969.

White, William Allen. *A Puritan in Babylon,* New York, The Macmillan Company, 1958.

Williams, Charles Richard. *The Life of Rutherford Birchard Hayes* (2 vols.), Boston, Houghton, Mifflin Company, 1914.

Wilson, Edith Bolling. *My Memoir,* Indianapolis, The Bobbs-Merrill Company, 1939.

★ *Index* ★

INDEX

INDEX

INDEX

369